AFRIKAANS

SELF-TAUGHT

BY THE NATURAL METHOD WITH
PHONETIC PRONUNCIATION
(THIMM'S SYSTEM)

LEONARD W. VAN OS.

GYAN

Published by

GYAN

Gyan Publishing House
5, Ansari Road
Daryaganj, New Delhi-110002
Phone: 011-47034999, 9811692060
E-mail: books@gyanbooks.com

Distribution Network
gyanbooks.com
India, USA, Canada, UK, Australia, France

ISBN : 978-81-212-4241-7 (PB)
First Published, London, 1927

2nd Impression 2020

Printed at: Gyan Press, Delhi.

Afrikaans Self-Taught
Author: Leonard W. Van Os.

AFRIKAANS

SELF-TAUGHT

CONTENTS

Vocabularies—(*continued*).

Vocabularies—(*continued*).

Conversational Phrases and Sentences—(*continued*).

PREFACE

AFRIKAANS, one of the two official languages of South Africa, is a dialect of Nederlands (Dutch), and may rightly be said to be debilitated because it has lost most of the inflexions of Nederlands: It has likewise lost a large number of consonants at the end and in the middle of words. Its vowels differ distinctly from those of Nederlands, and some of its consonants too.

Afrikaans is a dialect of Nederlands in the same sense as English is of Anglo-Saxon. Both languages are greatly deflected and consequently on the same level.

Jesperson, *Progress in Language*, has it that loss of flexion most often argues a high standard of development in language.

It is unnecessary here to expound on the history of the language. The purport of this Manual is to assist students and those whose business or pleasure renders a practical acquaintance with the language a necessity, or at any rate a *desideratum*.

Merchants, professional and commercial men visiting South Africa, and travellers, officials, and settlers in South Africa, will find it of great service and value. Afrikaans as spoken in South Africa[1] has been adhered to, as it is the tongue that is being taught side by side with the English language in the Government Schools throughout South Africa. The very full outline of Grammar that forms a special and important feature of the work will prove most helpful to the student and all who desire to master the language.

The phonetic or third column will be found to give, at a glance, the pronunciation of the Afrikaans words in the second column, as they are spoken by the Afrikanders in South Africa.

[1] With the exception of the Malay mode of pronunciation indulged in in the Cape Peninsula, i.e. the too frequent use of the diminutive termination -tjie in almost every word uttered, and the very unbecoming and jarring pronunciation of the j in jy, jou, julle, joune, etc.

This is accomplished by means of

MARLBOROUGH'S SYSTEM OF PHONETICS,

as employed throughout their Series of "Self-Taught" Manuals. The system is so simple that those previously unacquainted with either Dutch or Afrikaans can, with its aid, make themselves readily understood.

In conclusion I may emphasise that this work makes no pretence to originality. Although the translations are mine, and are given in the simplest form that Afrikaans will admit of being written and spoken, for the section "Elementary Grammar" I have relied mainly on what body of knowledge was to be found in various works on the subject; and notably the excellent works on Afrikaans by Professors M. C. Botha, M.A., J. F. Burger, M.A., both of the University of Cape Town; M. S. B. Kritzinger, M.A., Transvaal University College, Pretoria; H. A. Steyn, M.A., *Gimnasium Hoërskool*, Potchefstroom; Dr. P. C. Schooness, M.A., Pietermaritzburg; U. J. Cronjé, M.A., Graaff Reinet; Messrs. de Waal, Malherbe, van Ryn, Elffers, Dingeman and van Braam's *Idiomen* and P. J. Hoogenhout and J. J. A. Schoeman's *Afrikaans Idiome*, which I herewith gratefully acknowledge.

It is hoped that by facilitating the study and acquisition of the language, this Manual may help to strengthen the commercial and social ties between the Afrikanders and their British fellow-subjects in South Africa, and so prove another link in binding two great nations together.

LEONARD W. VAN OS.

Kensington, Johannesburg,
South Africa, 1927.

It was my privilege to collect and arrange the MSS. of the *Afrikaans Self-Taught* which was commenced by my late father.

Owing to his untimely death on July 11th, 1927, I had to complete the sections on Greetings and Polite Expressions; Idiomatic Expressions and Phrases; Wireless and Electrical Terms; and Money, Weights and Measures, etc.

I was also responsible for the reading of the "Proofs," and shall therefore esteem it a great favour if any errors, that might have crept in, will be pointed out to me.

Any suggestions and constructive criticisms from my colleagues and others interested in the little work, will be much appreciated.

H. J. L. v. O.

Kensington. *April 12th*, 1930.

AFRIKAANS SELF-TAUGHT

INTRODUCTORY REMARKS

THE PHONETIC SYSTEM.—The aim of Marlborough's Phonetic System is to make use of such signs that anyone who speaks English, by reading them naturally, will correctly pronounce the Afrikaans. To prevent confusion arising from the various ways in which many sounds are represented in English, the principle has been laid down that each sound in the new language shall be separately represented. Each phonetic sign must be pronounced in the same manner throughout the book. In many instances, where this has been departed from, the reason, usually obvious, is to facilitate ready and correct pronunciation, as in the alternative use of *g* and ch, both hard as in the Scotch word Loch.

PRONUNCIATION.—The phonetics in the third column should be pronounced lightly, not in a laboured manner, or dwelt upon. Frequent practice in speaking will prove of the greatest assistance, and no opportunity should be lost of perfecting one's accent by hearing the language spoken by an Afrikander.

HYPHENS.—The division of the words in the third column by means of hyphens is made merely to facilitate correct pronunciation, and does not necessarily show the proper division of the Afrikaans words into syllables.

DOUBLE CONSONANTS are pronounced as one, as in English :
Akkomodásie, accommodation.

THE APOSTROPHE is frequently used to indicate where a vowel is practically silent, like the e in novel (nov'l).

AFRIKAANS EQUIVALENTS.—It should be noted that many of the Afrikaans phrases in the latter part of the book are not literal translations of the English, but the Afrikaans equivalents, i.e. what an Afrikander would say in similar circumstances.

THE ALPHABET WITH PHONETIC PRONUNCIATION

Most modern languages, of which Afrikaans is one, have adopted the Latin alphabet ; but this alphabet does not accurately express all sounds of the different languages. This fact must here particularly be kept in view, because it explains the following material points in Afrikaans orthography.

For this reason, then, all the twenty-six (26) letters of the Latin alphabet are, strictly speaking, *not* used in Afrikaans, since Latin had sounds which are not used in Afrikaans. Thus the following letters are only used in foreign names and words ;

but in Afrikaans they are replaced by corresponding letters, better adapted to the relative sounds:

C is replaced by k, as in kabinet (cabinet), kabel (cable), kapittel (chapter), kandidaat (candidate), etc., and sometimes by s as, sement (cement), sensus (census), sertifikaat (certificate).

Q or qu (which are inseparable) is replaced by kw, as in: kwaksalwer (quack), kwartaal (quarter), kwartel (quail), kwaliteit (quality), kwantiteit (quantity), kweper (quince), kwessie (question), kweek (quick—couch-grass).

x is replaced by ks, as: eksketeur (executor).

z is replaced by s, as in sink (zink).

On the other hand there are insufficient letters in the Latin alphabet to express all sounds in Afrikaans—or, shall we say, we have sounds in the Afrikaans language for which the Latin alphabet has no letters. To meet this deficiency provision is made in the following three ways:

(*a*) by doubling letters, as in sal (shall, will), saal (plural, sale), hall;

(*b*) by placing signs over letters, as in wêreld (world), gésel (scourge, to beat), hê (to have), hè? (heigh? what's it?), êe (to harrow), Hoërskool (High School), dèl (take! here you are!), nè? (is it not? yes?), dêl (now! see!).

(*c*) by using *two* or *three* vowels to express one sound as: baie (many, much, very), mooi (pretty).

PRONUNCIATION

The signs (¨), (^), (`), found over the vowels e, i, o, u, are placed there to "modify" (i.e. somewhat alter) the sound of the vowel. We have some examples of this modification in English: man, men; mouse, mice; cow, kine; and just as we learn these as irregular plurals in English, we may note them as grammatical changes in Afrikaans.

The Afrikaans alphabet consists of twenty-two letters: a, b, d, e, f, g, h, i, j, k, l, m, n, o, p, r, s, t, u, v, w, y, to which must be added the modified vowels.

The vowels are employed as Simple Vowels, and also to form Diphthongs.

The Simple Vowels are Single and Double, viz., a, aa ; **e, ee** ; (-), eu ; i, ie ; o, oo ; u, uu ; also (-), oe.

The Diphthongs are ai, aai, au ; ei, eu, eeu ; ie ; **oe, oei,** oi, ooi, ou ; ui.

The Consonants are, like the vowels, single and **double** : b, d, dj, f, g, gh, ghw, h, j, k, l, m, n, ng, p, r, s, sj, t, tj, v, w (c, ch, sch, x, z).

The following is a complete list showing how the Afrikander expresses his sounds in letters :

Character's Name.		English Pronunciation.	Phonetics Used.
A, a	(ah)	(i) in a *closed syllable*, that is to say, a syllable ending in a consonant, pronounce like the Northern English dialect a in sat, or the a in French pas : man (man), kan (can), brand (bra(h)nt) (fire) ..	**a(h)**
aa		(ii) in an *open syllable*, that is to say, a syllable ending in a vowel or diphthong (in a closed syllable represented by aa), pronounce like the a in English farthing : nader (near), vader (father), maan (moon)	**ah**
ai		pronounce like i in English might : baie (bah'i), many, much, very ; fraiing (frah'ing), fringe	**ah'i**
aai		a lengthened y in English "why" would approximate this : saai (sah'i), to sow ; maai (mah'i), to reap	**ah'i**
au		is the same as ou pronounced like the o in English hoe. This au is preserved only in proper names : Rautenbach	**o(h)**
B, b	(bee)	when final, is like p, ab, ap, otherwise it has the same sound value of its English equivalent..	**p, b**
C,		This High Dutch c is in Afrikaans replaced by k, but is occasionally met with only in proper names : Cloete (kléuh'te(r))	**k**
(ch)		has no corresponding sound in English. It is a guttural aspirate resembling the ch in the Scotch word Loch, but is much sharper. It is found, as an alternative to	

Character's Name.	English Pronunciation.	Phonetics Used.
	k, only in the word Christus (Christ) = Kristus, its compounds and derivatives. Its sound is that of the Afrikaans g, hard, hence the phonetic sign	ch
D, d (dee)	has the sound value of its English equivalent. When preceded by l, n, or r, it is assimilated to the preceding consonant in speech, but kept in writing: helder =heller (clear); kinders=kinners (children); perde=perre (horses). At the end of a word d is like t, as land=lant (land, country, field); pad=pat (path) (pa(h)t)	t
dj	is pronounced like tj: mandjie=mantjie (basket)	tj
E, e (ee)	(i) in a *closed accented syllable*, pronounce like e in English get, but slightly broadened, somewhat approximating the a sound in English bat: vet (fat) ..	e
ee	(ii) in an *open accented syllable* (in closed syllables and at the end of words represented by ee) this sound approximates the ée in French fée, nearly the e in English merely: lepel (spoon) (ley'ple); tee (tea) (tey')	ey
	(iii) in *unaccented syllables* this sound is equivalent to the e in English manner, or the first a in ajar: lepel (spoon); te (to, at, on, in)	e(r)[2]
ê	pronounce like ai in English air: wêreld (world); hê (have); dê! (now! see!) ..	ai(r)[2]
ei	pronounce like the ey in English whey: lei (slate); eis (demand); meid (maid)	ey
eu	pronounce like eu in French lieu, and ew in English lewd: deur (door); geur (fragrance); neus (nose) [nu(r)ss]	u(r)

[2] The ai(r) represents the sound of e in manner, the e(r) that of e in term and the u(r) that of eu in lieu; the (r) is added (where necessary) in the phonetics, merely in order to give the a, e and u, respectively, this sound—Not to Lengthen them—*and must itself remain unheard.*

Character's Name.	English Pronunciation.	Phonetics Used.
eeu	pronounce like the ew in English pew: eeu (century), leeu (lion)	ee'w
F f (ef)	has the sound value of its English equivalent	f
	N.B.—In inflected forms this f changes to w: stof (dust), sto*wwe*; stoof (stove), sto*we* (stoves).	
G g (gee)	has no corresponding sound in English; it is a heavy guttural sound like ch in the Scotch word Loch, and at the end of a word is pronounced like this ch, as mag (power, might, strength); but where it is preceded by r (and sometimes by l) and followed by a semi-accented e, it has the sound value of g in English go: berge (mountains); gevolge (consequences). This is also the case with g in nege. Some Afrikanders prefer this g between an accented vowel or diphthong and mute e: dage for dae (days); hoger for hoër (higher). It is equivalent to sj in argipel (archipelago), argitek (architect), energie (energy), geneer (to feel embarrassed, be shy), genie (genius), girag (giraffe), girurg (surgeon), kollege (College), korrigeer (to correct), prestigie (prestige), priwilege (privilege), religie (religion), their compounds and derivatives ..	ch
gh	has the sound value of g in English go: ghoeroe (a native musical instrument), ghoo'roo	g, gh
ghw	is equivalent to gu in English guano: ghwano (guano)	ghw
H h (hah)	at the beginning of a word or syllable is always aspirated, as: hah'e(r)l, hael (hail)	h
I, i (ee)	(i) when short, that is, in an *accented syllable*, pronounce like i in English wit, milk, pin: pit (kernel, wick)	i
	(ii) when *long*, that is, in an *unaccented syl-*	

Character's Name.	English Pronunciation.	Phonetics Used.
	lable, pronounce like ee in deep, as: ivoor (ivory), likwideer (liquidate), indiwidu (individual)	ee
î	a long open i used in the plural of a word like wig (wedge), i.e. wîe (ver'heh) (wedges)	î,ee
ie	this is ea in English speak, or ie in field but much shorter: r*ie*t (reed), b*ie*tj*ie* (a little, some, please). The ee sound in Dund*ee* and diep (deep) is perhaps more correct	ee
J, j (yee)	has the sound value of its English equivalent, like y in yet (***never that of English j***): jaar (year) (yahr); ja (yes) (yah) .. (But see under "T".)	y
K, k (kah)	has the sound value of its English equivalent and ***always sounded*** before n, as knie (k-nee) (knee)	k
L, l (ell)	as in English.	l
M, m (em)	as in English	m
N, n (en)	as in English	n
ng	is a soft, ***one-consonant***, nasal sound, pronounced like ***ng*** in thing. It should never be divided into ***two sounds***, as finger, hunger, etc.; e.g. vinger [fing'e(r)r] ..	ng
O, o (oh)	(i) when *short*, that is, in a *closed syllable*, pronounce like o in English pot, not, as: los (loose, free), (lo(h)ss)	o
	(ii) when *long*, that is, in an *open syllable* (in a closed syllable represented by oo), is the first element in oo in English moor: spore (tracks), verloor (to lose), doring (thorn)	oh
oo	like oo in moor, as vroom (frohm) (pious)	oh
ô	pronounce like aw in English law: môre (morning, morrow)	aw
oe	pronounce like oo in English foot; when followed by r, like u in English ruler:	

Character's Name.	English Pronunciation.	Phonetics Used.
	moenie (don't); Boer (Dutch South African) (a farmer, peasant)	u
oei	pronounce like oui in French Louis: koei (cow), roei (to row), moeite (trouble) (moo'i-te(r))	oo'i
oi	this is like oy in English toy: toilings (rags, tatters); goiing (canvas); goiing-sak (canvas bag)	oy
ôi	this is a lengthened oi: nôi (mistress, girl, sweetheart, young lady)	ôi, oy
ooi	say the English word Moorish without sounding the r at all; ooi approximates this oo-i: mooi (pretty), sooi (sod), ooi (ewe)	oh'i
ou	pronounce like o in English go: gou (quick), stout (naughty), sout (salt), ou (old, aged, chap, fellow; die "ou"= the "old chap")	o, ou
P, p (pee)	as in English	p
R, r (err)	is pronounced with greater vibration than in English, and is *never silent*: er in very is the correct sound	r, rr
S, s (ess)	is a sharp sibilant, like ss in loss, as: mes (knife), *never like z*, as in lose ..	ss, s
(sch)	is preserved in proper names only; it has the sound value sk, unless when at the end of a word, in which case it is not pronounced: Schoeman (skoh'man), Stellenbosch, pronounce stell'n-boss. The adjective is Stellenbosse	sk
T, t (tee)	as in English	t
tj	t and y sounded as one, the y retaining its sound as in yet	ty
U, u (êû) (i)	in an open syllable (in a closed syllable represented by uu) is the ü in German über, or like the French u in mur. Pronounce by forming the lips into a circle (as for whistling) and sounding "êû" as one sound; or produce the sound ie with well protruded lips: bure (neigh-	

Character's Name.	English Pronunciation.	Phonetics Used.
	bours), muur (wall), natuur (nahtêûr) (nature)	êû ie
(ii)	when between two consonants, that is, in a closed syllable, it is like u in mud, as nut (use, benefit, profit) ; juk (yoke) ..	u
û	pronounced like the u in English pug, mug : brûe (bridges), rûens (hills), being the plurals of rug (ridge), and brug (bridge)	û
	N.B.—Care must be taken not to pronounce the g in " brug " and " rug " as in English rug (a piece of carpet), but as ch in the Scotch word Loch : bruch, ruch. Some Afrikanders, however, use a short u and say : brugge, rugge, pronouncing the g's as in English go.	
ui	The a in English lady pronounced with well protruded lips or the rounded vowel-sound of ei or y, would approximate this sound : muis (mouse), huis (house), lui (lazy), vuil (dirty), ruik (smell), ui (onion)	ui
V, v (fey)	is like a soft f, as vergaan (fe(r)rchahn')	f
W, w (vee)	sounds like v in English very, ***never like*** the *English* w. The upper teeth should touch the lower lip in pronouncing it : water (water), wed (to wager), wil (will), wol (wool), woud (forest), wyn (wine), wyf (a mean woman, a wench), twak (tobacco)	v
Y[3] **y** (a) (ei)	this is equivalent to ei (English a) : ly (to suffer), ys (ice), phonetically represented by ey, as ley and eys	ey
(x, z)	are only met with in proper names : Ale*x*ander, *C*oet*z*ee (Koot'see)	

[3] The ai(r) represents the sound of e in manner,
the e(r) that of the e in term,
the o(r) that of o in orchestra, and
the u(r) that of eu in lieu.

The (r) is added (where necessary) in the phonetics, merely in order to give the a, e, o, and u these sounds—NOT TO LENGTHEN them—***and must itself remain unheard.***

PRELIMINARY NOTES

PRONUNCIATION.—The student is recommended to familiarise himself at the outset with the few points in connection with the pronunciation of Afrikaans which present any difficulty, viz., the guttural g, the diphthongs and the double and treble vowels, etc. The phonetic sign g conveys no adequate idea of the guttural, which should, if possible, be learned from a Dutch South African. The same plan would be advantageous as regards the diphthongs and the double and treble vowels, although their pronunciation is much simpler.

It is best to learn the VOCABULARIES and CONVERSATIONS by heart, by *repeating them aloud*, following the pronunciation in the third column. Thus the tongue becomes expert in forming the words and the ear familiar with the sounds.

ACCENT (AKSENT).—1. In words of more than one syllable the stress is laid mostly on the *root syllable*, as in érgste (worst); wóedend (wild); beléwe (experience); onthóof (behead); but in long or compound words the accent is thrown on the first part of the word: dénneboom (fir-tree); wáterslang (water-snake); wónderlik (wonderful).

N.B.—In words of non-Teutonic origin the accent generally falls on the last syllable: studént (student); hospitaál (hospital); uniwerseél (universal).

2. PREFIXES are accented, as in Aartsbiskop (ahrts'bisskop), *antwoord* (a(h)nt'wohrt), *ondank* (on'da(h)nk).

Exceptions.—Be, ge, er, her, ont, ver; as in: behául (obtain); gewérk (worked); erkén (acknowledge); herínner (remind); ontwíkkel (develop); verbied (forbid).

3. SUFFIXES are NOT accented; as in *bedelaar* [bee'de(r)lahr] (beggar); *lomperd* (lom'pe(r)rt) (clumsy person); *kinderlik* (kin'de(r)rlik) (childlike), etc.

N.B.—The accented syllable is marked in the phonetics by the apostrophe ('), as above. In many Afrikaans words the accentuation follows the English or falls naturally, and the mark is omitted.

LONG AND SHORT VOWELS.—(1) Double Vowels are always long, as *paar* (pahr); *stroom* (strohm).

(2) Single Vowels are long or short, viz.:

(*a*) Long at the end of a syllable, as olifant [oh-lee-fa(h)nt], except at the end of a word, as *stille* [stille(r)], *kraai* (krah'i), *viooltjie* [fee-ohlt'ye(r)].

(*b*) Short:

(1) between two consonants in the same syllable, as *kos* (koss), (food);

(2) in prefixes and suffixes, as *gesang* [ge(r)-sa(h)ng];

(3) before g, as lug, lig.

Note.—A single consonant *commences* a syllable, as papegaai [pah-pe(r)-gah'i], seeboesem [see-boo-se(r)m]. Where two consonants occur in the middle of a word, the syllables are divided *between* them, as donder [don'de(r)r], except when the preceding syllable is merely a prefix ending in a vowel, as *geblaf* [ge(r)-bla(h)f'].

Rules of Spelling.—(1) The vowels a, e, o, u are written single at the end of a syllable, when accented, as va'der, ste'de, lo'we, mu're; except in a number of words which have ee, and others which have oo, etc.

(2) The double vowels ee, ie, ei, are written:

(*a*) At the end of words of one syllable; as see (sea), vee (cattle), drie (three), knie (knee), klei (mud), Mei (May).

(*b*) In suffixes; as Europees, werkloos, massief, graniet.

(3) In open syllables or at the end of a word the lengthened forms of short e (ê) and of short o (ô) get the sign (^). In closed syllables ending in an r, e sometimes gets the ^, but not if the r is followed by another consonant: sê, lê, wêreld, kêrel, môre, sôre, perd, bord, stert, etc.

(4) The dieresis (¨) is used in Afrikaans to mark the division of syllables where two vowels come together which would be pronounced as one sound if there were no mark of division: breë, knieë, vroeër, hoër, seë (broad, knees, earlier, higher, seas).

If there is no danger of the two syllables being taken and pronounced as one, the dieresis need not be used: dae, koeie, luie, goue,[1] etc. In these words there can be no doubt as to the number or division of syllables.

[1] days, cows, lazy, golden.

GENDER (GESLAG).—There is no "grammatical" gender in Afrikaans. Just as in English, the only distinction in gender is a distinction in sex. Thus only living beings are classified as to masculine, feminine, or common gender; inanimate objects have no gender—they are neuter.

ARTICLES (LIDWOORDE).—Afrikaans ARTICLES are of two kinds:

(*a*) Definite (Bepaalde): die (the);
(*b*) Indefinite (Onbepaalde): 'n (a, an).

These articles are NOT subject to inflexion.

g and ch.—The sound of g is what one would hear in the throat sound made by an angry ostrich, very much like the clearing of the human throat, i.e. the sound of the final two letters—ch—in the Scotch word Lo*ch*.

-tj.—As some diminutives in Afrikaans end in -tjie (pronounced -tyee, the y retaining the sound as in English yet), as moertjie (moort'yee), an iron nut, it follows that tj must (in phonetics) be represented by ty; hence, tj, the combination heard in: tjek (tye(r)k), cheque; tjilp (tyilp), chirp; tjiekorie (tyee-kohree), chicory; tjingel (tyinge(r)l), jingle; tjoekie (tyookee), prison; tjoepstill (tyoopstill), quiet, still; tjokvol (tyo(r)kfo(r)l), choke-full; tjop (tjo(r)p), chop; tjou-tjou (tyou-tyou), chutney; tjap (tya(h)p), to stamp, frank a letter; tjank (tya(h)nk), howl, yell; tjalie (tya(h)lee), shawl.

N.B.—Care must be taken not to bring out the English j sound in the above examples.

(See Preliminary Notes.)

METHOD OF STUDY

The METHOD adopted here is that which is natural to every child learning to speak his mother-tongue, who, long before he is taught the rules of grammar, acquires one by one a number of words and everyday sentences which enable him to take his part in the talk of the home: and here, to meet the requirements of men and women in daily life, vocabularies, phrases, and conversations have been most carefully selected, that students, instead of learning a vast number of comparatively useless words, may find every word and expression given of such frequent service as to afford facilities of conversation far beyond what might be expected from a book of this size.

The student is recommended to learn the words in the following Vocabularies by heart, repeating them *aloud* with the aid of the phonetic spelling in the third column. Then, closing the book, he should write out the Afrikaans words in their proper spelling from memory, carefully comparing with and correcting by the Afrikaans column afterwards. In this way a very large number of Afrikaans words will be acquired, the ear being familiarised with their sound, the tongue with their utterance, and the eye with their appearance. The same plan may then be followed with the Conversational Phrases and Sentences, and imaginary conversations can be worked out by the substitution of other nouns, adjectives, adverbs, etc., which have already been learnt from the vocabularies.

VOCABULARIES

THE WORLD AND ITS ELEMENTS

(Die Wêreld en sy Elemente)

English.	Afrikaans.	Pronunciation.
Air	lug	luch
climate	klimaat	kleemaht
cloud	wolk	vol'k, vo(r)l'k
cold	koue	koue(r) (ou like o in go)
Creator	Skepper	skep-pe(r)r
darkness	duisterniss	duiste(r)rniss
dew	dou	dou (ou like in go)
dust	stof	sto(r)f
earth	aarde	ahrde(r)
East	Oos, die Ooste	ohs, die Ohste(r)
eclipse	verduistering	ferduiste(r)ring
fire	vuur, brand	fêur, bra(h)nt
fog	mis	miss
frost	ryp	reyp (like English rape)
God	God	chot
hail	hael	hahe(r)l
heat	hitte	hitte(r)
ice	ys	eyss
Heaven	hemel	heyme(r)l
Hell	hel	he(r)l
light	lig	lich
lightning	weerlig, blits	veyrlich, blits
moon	maan	mahn
—, full	volmaan	fo(r)lmahn
—, new	nuwe maan	nêuve(r) mahn
moonlight	maanlig	mahnlich
nature	natuur	na(h)têur
North	noord, die Noorde	nohrt, dee Nohrde(r)

English.	Afrikaans.	Pronunciation.
rain	reën	reye(r)n
rainbow	reënboog	reye(r)nbohch
shade, shadow	skaduwee	skahdeûvey
sky	lug	luch
snow	sneeu	snew
sun	son	so(r)n
star	ster	ste(r)r
thunder	donder	donde(r)r
thaw	dooi (sneeu)	doh'i
weather	weer	veyr
West	wes, die Weste	vess, dee veste(r)
wind	wind	vinnt
world	wêreld	vai(r)r'lt

Land and Water (Land en Water)

Bay	baai	bah'i
bank	bank	ba(h)nk
beach	strand	stra(h)nt
calm	kalm	ka(h)lm
cliff	klip, krans	klip, kra(h)ns
canal	kanaal	ka(h)nahl
coast	kus	ku(r)ss
cape	kaap	kahp
current	stroom	strohm
dale	dal	da(h)l
ebb	eb	ep
flow (rising tide)	vloed	floo't
foam	skuim	skui'm
hill	heuwel	hu(r)ve(r)l
ice	ys	eyss
island	eiland	eyla(h)nt
lake	meer	meyr
mainland	vasteland	fa(h)ste(r)la(h)nt
marsh	moeras	moora(h)s
mud	modder	mo(r)'de(r)r
mountain	berg	berch
ocean	oseaan	ohseeahn
rain	reën	reye(r)n
river	rivier	re(r)feer
sand	sand	sa(h)nt

English.	Afrikaans.	Pronunciation.
rock	rots	ro(r)ts
sand-bank	sandbank	sa(h)ntba(h)nk
sea-shore	lae seekus	lahe(r) seyku(r)s
shingle	ruigte	ruichte(r)
shore	strand	stra(h)nt
snow	sneeu	snew
star	ster	ste(r)r
storm (on land)	storm op land)	sto(r)rm (o(r)p la(h)nt)
stream	stroom	strohm
thunderstorm	donderstorm	donde(r)rsto(h)r'm
thaw	dooi	doh'i
tide	gety	che(r)tey
high tide	hoogwater	hohchvahte(r)r
low tide	laagwater	lahchvahte(r)r
valley	vlakte, laagte	fla(h)kte(r), lahchte(r)
water, fresh	vars water	fa(h)rs vahter
—, salt	sout water	sout vahter
waterfall	waterval	vahterfa(h)l
wave	golf	cho(r)l'f
well	put, bron	put (u as in pup), bro(r)n

Minerals and Metals (Minerale en Metale)

English.	Afrikaans.	Pronunciation.
Aluminium	alumienium	a(h)leumeenium
agate	agaatsteen	a(h)chahtsteyn
alum	aluin	a(h)luin
amber	amber	a(h)mbe(r)r
brass	geel koper	cheyl kohpe(r)r
bronze	brons	bro(r)ns
carbuncle	karbonkel	ka(h)rbo(r)nke(r)l
cement	sement	se(r)ment
chalk	kryt	kreyt
clay	klei	kley
coal	kool	kohl
copper	koper	kohper
coral	koraal	korahl
crystal	kristal	krista(h)l
diamond	diamant	deeahma(h)nt

English.	Afrikaans.	Pronunciation.
emerald	smarag	sma(h)ra(h)ch
glass	glas	chla(h)s
gold	goud	chout
granite	graniet	chra(h)neet
gravel	gruis	chruis
iron	yster	eyster
—, cast	gegote yster	che(r)chohte(r) eyster
—, wrought	gesmede yster	che(r)smeyde(r) eyster
lead	lood	loht
lime	kalk	ka(h)lk
marble	marmer	ma(h)rme(r)r
mercury	kwiksilwer	kviksilve(r)r
metals	metale	me(r)tahle(r)
mine	myn	meyn
mortar	mortier, kalk	morteer, ka(h)lk
nickel	nikkel	nikke(r)l
ore	erts	e(r)rts
pearl	pêrel	pai(r)r'l (or, pai(r)e(r)l)
quartz	kwarts	kva(h)rts
ruby	robyn	rohbeyn
sapphire	saffier	sa(h)feer
steel	staal	stahl
slate	lei	ley
soda	soda	sohda(h)
tin	tin, blik	tin, blik
zink	sink	sink

Animals, Birds, and Fishes (Diere, Voëls en Visse)

English.	Afrikaans.	Pronunciation.
Animal	dier	deer
antelope	anteloop, hartbees	a(h)nteelohp, ha(r)rtbe's
barking	geblaf	ge(r)bla(h)f
bear	beer	béer, beyre
bird	voël	foh'e(r)l
blackbird	merel	may(ere(r)l)
bleating	geblêr	ge(r)blai(r)r
braying	gebalk	ge(r)ba(h)lk

English.	Afrikaans.	Pronunciation.
bull	bul, stier	bul (like but), steer
calf	kalf	ka(h)lf
carp	kurper	ku(r)rpe(r)r
cat	kat	ka(h)t
cattle	vee	fey
chicken	kuiken	kuike(r)n
claw	klou	klou
cock	haan	hahn
cod	kabeljou	ka(h)be(r)lyou
colt	vulletjie	ful'le(r)t-yee
cow	koei	koei
crab	krap	kra(h)p
cries	gille	gil'le(r)
crow	kraai	krah'i
crowing	gekraai	ge(r)krah'i
cuckoo	koekoek	koo'kook
deer	wild	vilt (i as in bill)
dog	hond	hont
donkey	esel	eyse(r)l
dove	duif	duif
duck	eend	eynt
eagle	arend	ahre(r)nt
eel	paling	pahling
elephant	olifant	oh'leefa(h)nt
feather	veer	fey'e(r)r
fins	vinne	fin'ne(r)
fish	vis	fiss
fox	vos	foss
fur	bont	bont
gills	kieue	kee'we(r)
goat	bok	bok
goose	gans	ga(h)nss
grouse	korhaan	korr'hahn
growling, grunting	geknor	ge(r)knor
gull	seemeeu	see'meeu
haddock	skelvis	skel'fiss
hair	hare	hahre(r)
hare	haas	hahss
hawk	valk	fahlk
hen	hen	hen

English.	Afrikaans.	Pronunciation.
herd	kudde	kud'de(r)
herring	haring	hahring
hoof	hoef	hoof
horn	horing	hohring
horse	perd	pehrt
howling	gehuil	ge(r)huil
lamb	lam	la(h)m
lark	lewerkie	ley've(r)rkey
lion	leeu	leeu
lobster	seekreef	see'kreef
mackerel	makriel	ma(h)kreel
magpie	ekster	ekste(r)r
mane	mane (pl.)	mah'ne(r)
mewing	gemeeu	ge(r)meeu
monkey	aap	ahp
mouse	muis	mayss
mule	muilesel	mayl'eyse(r)l
neighing	gehinnik, -runnik	ge(r)hin'nik, -run'nik
nightingale	nagtegaal	na(h)gte(r)gahl
ostrich	volstruis	fohl-struiss
owl	uil	uil
ox	os	oss
oysters	oesters (pl.)	ooste(r)rss
parrot	papegaai	pahpe(r)gah'i
partridge	patrys	pahtreyss'
paw	poot	poht
peacock	pou	po
pheasant	fisant	feesa(h)nt'
pig	vark	fa(h)r'k
pigeon	duif	duif
pike	snoek	snook
quail	kwartel	kwa(h)rte(r)l
rabbit	konyn	kuhneyn
rat	rot	ro(h)t
raven	raaf	rahf
rook	kraai	kraai
salmon	salm	sa(h)l'm
salt fish	soutvis	soatfiss
scales	skobbe	skobbe(r)

English.	Afrikaans.	Pronunciation.
sheep	skaap	skabp
shell-fish	skulpdier	skulpdeer
snipe	snip	snip
sole	tong (vis)	tong
sparrow	mossie	moss'ee
swallow	swaeltjie	svah'lyee
swan	swaan	shvahn
tail	stert	stehrt
thrush	lyster	leyste(r)r
tiger	tier	teer
trout	forel (vis)	forell, fohre(r)l'
turbot	tarbot (vis)	ta(h)rbot
turkey	kalkoen	ka(h)lkoon
turtle	water-seeskilpad	wahte(r)r-see'skil-pa(h)t
whale	walvis	vahl'fiss
whiting	wyting	vey'ting
wing	vlerk, vleuel	fle(r)rk, fleū'e(r)l
wolf	wolf	vollf
woodpecker	houtkapper	howtkappe(r)r
wood-pigeon	bosduif	bossduif
wool	wol	wol

Reptiles and Insects (Kruipende gedierte en Insekte)

English.	Afrikaans.	Pronunciation.
Ant	mier	meer
bee	(heuning) by	(heūning) bey
beetle	tor, kever	tor, keyfe(r)r
butterfly	skoenlapper, vlinder	skoonlahppe(r)r, flin'de(r)r
caterpillar	rispe	rispe(r)
flea	vlooi	flohi
fly	vlieg	fleeg
frog	padda	pahd'da(h)
gnat	muggie	mug'gee
grasshopper (locust)	sprinkaan	sprin'khahn
insect	insek, gogga	insek', gaw'ga
moth	mot	mot
serpent	slang	sla(h)ng
silkworm	sywurm	seyve(r)rm
snail	slak	sla(h)k

English.	Afrikaans.	Pronunciation.
snake	slang	sla(h)ng
spider	spinnekop	spinne(r)kop
sting	angel	a(h)ng'e(r)l
toad	padda	pa(h)da
viper	adder	a(h)d'de(r)r
wasp	perdeby (pêrreby)	pairde(r)bey, pair're(r)bey
worm	wurm	vu(r)rm

Fruits, Trees, Flowers, and Vegetables

(Vrugte, Bome, Blomme en Groente)

Apple	appel	a(h)p'pe(r)l
almond	amandel	amahnd'l
artichoke	artisjok	a(h)rtisyok
apricot	appelkoos	ahp'pe(r)lkohss
ash (tree)	es (boom)	ess (bohm)
asparagus	aspersie	a(h)sspersee
beans	boontjies	bohnt'yees
beech-tree	beukeboom	bu(r)'ke(r)bohm
beetroot	beet	beet
birch	berk	berrk
blackberry	braambessie	brahm'bessee
bouquet	ruiker	rui'ke(r)r
branch	tak	ta(h)k
bunch (grapes)	tros (druiwe)	tross (dravve(r))
buttercup	botterblom	bott'err-blomm
cabbage	kool	kohl
carrot	wortel	vorrtel
cauliflower	blomkool	blomm'kohl
celery	seldery	sel'de(r)rey
cherry	kersie	ke(r)rs'see
chestnut	kastaiing	kahstai'ing
cinnamon	kaneel	kahnneyl'
crocus	krokus	krohkus
cucumber	komkommer	komkom'me(r)r
currant, black	swart korent	swa(h)rt kor'rent
daffodil	môresterretjie	mawre(r)-sterre(r)-[yee
daisy	madeliefie, gansblommetjie	made(r)leefee, gahns-blomm-e(r)-[yee
fagot, faggot	takbos	ta(h)kboss

English.	Afrikaans.	Pronunciation.
dates	dadels	dahtt'ls
elm	olm	ol'm
evergreen (shrub)	altyd loofgroen	ahlteyt loafgruhnn
fern	varing	fahr'ing
fig-tree	vyeboom	feye(r)'bohm
filbert	haselneut	hase(r)lnewt
fir-tree	denneboom	denn'e(r)-bohm
flower	blom	blomm
forest	bos	boss
fruit-tre	vrugteboom	freûgte(r)bohm
garlic	knoflok	k-noflok
ging	gemmer	gem'me(r)r
gooseberry	appelliefie	a(h)p'pe(r)l-lee-fee
grapes (bunch of)	tros druiwe	tross, drayve(r)
holly	steekpalm	steek'pahl-m
ivy	klimop	klimop
kernel	pit	pit
leaf	blad, blaar	bla(h)t, bla(h)rr
lemon	suurlemoen	seûrr-le(r)-moon
lettuce	slaai	sly
lily	lelie	ley'lee
mace	foelie	foo'lee
melon	waterlemoen, spanspek	vahte(r)r-le(r)-moon spanns'speck
mulberry	moerbei	moor'bey
myrtle	mirt	mir't
nettle	brandnekel	brahnt-née-ke(r)l
nut	neut	newt
oak-tree	eikeboom	eyke(r)'bohm
onion	ui	a(y)
orange	lemoen	le(r)'moon
parsley	piterselie	peete(r)r-see'lee
pear	peer	pier
parsnip	witwortel	vihtvort'l
peas (green)	groen ertjies	groone(r)rt'yees
pine (tree)	pynboom, denneboom	peynbohm, den'ne(r)bohm
pine-apple	pynappel	peyna(h)p'pe(r)l
pink	grasangelier	grahss-a(h)nyeleer
plant	plant	plahn't

English.	Afrikaans.	Pronunciation.
plum	pruim	pra(h)m
potato	ertappel	ert-a(h)p'pe(r)l
radishes	radyse	rahdey'se(r)
raisins	rosyne	rhoseyne(r)
raspberry	framboos	fra(h)m'bohss
root	wortel	vor'te(r)l
rose	roos	rohss
spinach	spinasie	spinahsee
stalk (of a plant)	steel, stengel	steyl, shteng'l
strawberry	aarbei	ahr'bey
stump (of a tree)	stam	stahm
tree	boom	bohm
tulip	tulp	tulp
turnip	raap	rahp
vine	wingerdstok	vinger'd-stalk
violet	viooltjie	fee-ohlt'yee
walnut	okkerneut	okke(r)r'newt
watercress	bronkors	brohnkohrss
wax	was .	va(h)ss
willow	wilgerboom	vilgerbohm

Colours (Kleure). (*N.B.*—**g**=ch in loch)

Black	swart	sva(h)rt
blue	blou	blow (as in BLOW the trumpet)
brown	bruin	breyn
crimson	karmosyn	karmohseyn'
dark	donker	don'ke(r)r
green	groen	ggroon
grey	grys	greyss
light	lig	lig
lilac	liela, pers	leelah, pê(r)rs
orange	oranje	ohra(h)n'ye(r)
pink	ligrooi rooskleur	ligrohy rohss'klew(r)r
purple	purper	purpe(r)r
red	rood	roht
scarlet	skarlaken	ska(h)rlahken
violet	violet, pers	feeohlett', pairs
white	wit	vit
yellow	geel	geel

Times and Seasons (Tye en Jaargetye-Seisoene)

English.	Afrikaans.	Pronunciation.
Afternoon	namiddag	nahmid'da(h)g (g=ch)
birthday	verjaarsdag	fe(h)ryahrsda(h)g
Christmas	Kersmis, Kersfees	Kerrsmiss
— eve	Kersaand	Kerrsahnt
dawn	dagbreek	da(h)gbreek
day	dag	da(h)g
— after to-morrow	oormôre	ohrmawr're(r)
— before yesterday	eergister	eargiste(r)r
day, to-	vandag	fahnda(h)g
days of the week	dae van die week	da(h)e(r)-fahn dee ve(r)k
Sunday	Sondag	son'da(h)g
Monday	Maandag	mahn'da(h)g
Tuesday	Dinsdag	dinss'da(h)g
Wednesday	Woensdag	voonss'da(h)g
Thursday	Donderdag	don'de(r)rda(h)g
Friday	Vrydag	frey'da(h)g
Saturday	Saterdag	sah'terda(h)g
Easter	Pase, Paasfees	pah'se(r), pahs'fees
evening, eve	aand	ah'nt
fortnight	veertien dae	feerteen dahe(r)
Good Friday	Goeie Vrydag	gooye(r) frayda(h)g
holidays, vacation	vakansie	fah'kahn-see
hour	uur	êûr
—, half an	'n halfuur	'n ha(h)lfêûr
last night	gister aand	giss'te(r)r-aunt
Lent	vastetyd	fa(h)ste(r)teyt
Michaelmas	Sint-Michiel	Sint me(r)geel
midday	middag	mid'da(h)g
midnight	middernag	mid'de(r)r-na(h)g
Midsummer	midsomer (in die hartjie van die somer)	midsohme(r) (in dee ha(r)rt-yeé fahn dee sohme(r)r)
minute	minuut	meenêût'
month	maand	mahnt
months, the	die maande	dee mahnde(r)

English.	Afrikaans.	Pronunciation.
January	Januarie	yahneûah'ree
February	Februarie	feebreûah'ree
March	Maart	mahrt
April	April	ahpril'
May	Mei	mey
June	Junie	yeeû'nee
July	Julie	yeû'lee
August	Augustus	owguss'tuss
September	September	septem'be(r)r
October	Oktober	oktoh'be(r)r
November	November	nohfem'be(r)r
December	Desember	dey-sem'be(r)r
morning	oggend	aw'gent
morrow, to-	môre	maw're(r)
New Year's Eve	Oujaarsdag	ohyahrsda(h)g
night	nag	na(h)g
noon	middag	mid'da(h)g
quarter (3 months)	kwartaal	kwa(h)rtahl
— of an hour	'n kwartier	kwa(h)rteer
seasons, the	jaargetye	yahrge(r)teye(r)
Spring	Lente	lente(r)
Summer	Somer	sohme(r)r
Autumn	Herfs	herrfs
Winter	Winter	vin'te(r)r
second	sekonde	se(r)konde(r)
sunrise	sonsopgang	sonsop'ga(h)ng
sunset	sonsondergang	sonson'de(r)r-ga(h)ng
time	tyd	teyt
twilight	skemering	skeeme(r)ring
week	week	veek
week-day	werkdag	verrkda(h)g
weekly	weekliks	veekliks
Whitsuntide	Pinksterdae	pinkste(r)rda(h)e(r)
year	jaar	yahr
—, a	'n jaar	en jahr
—, the	die jaar	dee jahr
yesterday	gister	giste(r)r
— morning	gisteroggend	giste(r)r-aw'gent
— evening	gisteraand	giste(r)r-ah'nt

Holidays in South Africa (Vakansiedae)

(*a*) THE UNION

English.	Afrikaans.	Pronunciation.
New Year's Day	Nuwejaarsdag	ne͡uve(r)yahrss-da(h)g
Good Friday	Goeie Vrydag	gooye(r) freyda(h)g
Easter Monday	Paasmaandag	pahss'mahnda(h)g
Ascension Day	Hemelvaartsdag	heem'l-fahrtss da(h)g
Victoria Day	Victoriadag	fiktooriada(h)g
Union Day	Uniedag	e͡uneeda(h)g
Whit Monday	Pinkstermaandag	pinkste(r)rmahn-da(h)g
First Monday in August	Eerste Maandag in Augustus	aye(r)rste(r) mahnda(h)g in owguss'tuss
First Monday in October	Eerste Maandag in Oktober	aye(r)rste(r) mahnda(h)g in Oktoh'be(r)r
Dingan's Day	Dingaansdag	Dingahnssda(h)g
Christmas Day	Kersdag	kerrsda(h)g
Boxing Day	Boksdag	boxda(h)g

(*b*) RHODESIA

The following additional holidays are observed in Rhodesia only: Die volgende additionele vakansiedae word net in Rhodesia alleen gevier:

Occupation Day Mashonaland	Okkupasiedag Masjonaland	oke͡upasseeda(h)g massyonnala(h)nt
Occupation Day Matabeleland	Okkupasiedag Matabeleland	oke͡upasseeda(h)g mahtahbeelee-la(h)nt
Shangan Day	Shanganidag	shang'gahneeda(h)g

Town and Country (Dorp en Buitedistrikte)

Bank	oewer	oo've(r)r
barley	gars	garrss
barn	skuur	ske͡ur

English.	Afrikaans.	Pronunciation.
bridge	brug	brûg
brook	spruitjie	spruityee
building (edifice)	gebou	ge(r)bou'
bush	bos	boss
castle	kasteel	kahsteel
cathedral	domkerk, katedraal	dom'kerrk, kateedraal
cattle	vee	fee
club (association)	klub	kl'up
corn	koring	koo(r)ring
cottage	'n klein huisie	en kleynn huis'see
crop	oes	ohs
country	platteland	plaht'te(r)la(h)nt
courtyard	binneplaas	binne(r)plahss
custom-house	doeanekantoor	dooahne(r)ka(h)n-tohr
dale	dal	da(h)l
dining-room	eetkamer	eetkahme(r)r
ditch	sloot, voor	sloht, fohr
environs	omstreke	om'streyke(r)
exchange	beurs	beû(r)rss
factory	fabriek	fahbreek
farm	boerplaas	boo(r)rplahss
farmer	boer	boo(r)r
fence	heining	heyn'ning
field	veld	felt
fisherman	visser	fisse(r)r
flock	trop, kudde	trop, kud'de(r)
footpath	voetpad	foo'tpa(h)t
forest	bos	boss
garden	tuin	tui'n
gate	hek	hek
grass	gras	gra(h)ss
harvest	oes	ohs
hay	hooi	hoh'i
hedge	laning	lahn'ing
high road	grootpad, transportpad	groht'pa(h)t, tra(h)nsporrt'-pa(h)t
hospital	hospitaal	hoss'peetahl

English.	Afrikaans.	Pronunciation.
huntsman	jagter	yahg'te(r)r
hut	hut	hut
inn (public-house)	herberg	herr'be(r)rg
labourer	werksman	verrksma(h)n
lamp, street	straatlamp	strahtla(h)mp
library	biblioteek	bibliohteehk
market	mark	ma(h)rk
market-place	markplaas	marhrk'plahss
meadow	weiveld	vey'felt
mile	myl	meyl
mill	meul	mew'l
monument	gedenkteken	ge(r)denk'teeken
palace	paleis	pahleyss
mud	modder	mod'de(r)r
oats	hawer	hahverr
path	pad	paht
peasant	boer	boo'rr
pier	hawehoof	hahve(r)hohf
place, spot	plek	plekk'
plough	ploeg	ploo'g
police-station	poliesiekantoor	poh-lee'see-kahn-tohr
prison	gevangenis	ge(r)fa(h)ng'e(r)niss
river	rivier	reefeer
railway	spoorweg	spohrrveg
road	pad, weg	paht, veg
rye	rog	rawg
school	skool	skohl
seed	saad	saht
shepherd	veewagter, herder	feevahgterr, herr'de(r)r
shop	winkel	vin'kel
soil	grond	gront
square	plein	pleyn
stable	stal	stahl
street	straat	straht
strand	strand	strahnt
timber	hout	houht
tower	toring	tohr'ing
town	stad	sta(h)t

English.	Afrikaans.	Pronunciation.
town-hall	stadhuis	sta(h)t'huiss
university	uniwersiteit	e͡uneeverseeteyt'
tramway line	tremspoor	tremspohrr
valley	vlei	fley
village	dorp	dorp
vineyard	wyngaard	veyngahrrt
wall	muur	muhrr
well	put	putt (u as in putty)
wheat	koring	koh(r)ring
windmill	windmeul	vint'me͡ul
waterfall	waterval	vahte(r)r'a(h)l
wood (trees, etc.)	woud	vout

Mankind : Relations (Menslike Geslag : Familiebetrekkinge)

English	Afrikaans	Pronunciation
Aunt	tante	ta(h)n'te(r)
bachelor	vrygesel	freyche(r)sell
boy	jongetjie	yo(h)nge(r)tyee
bride	bruid	bruit
bridegroom	bruidegom	bruide(r)chom
brother	broer	brurr
brother-in-law	swaer	svahrr
child	kind	kinnt
cousin	neef (m.), niggie (f.)	neyff, nich'chee
—, second	kleinneef, klein-niggie	kleyn-neyff, klein-nich'chee
daughter, -in-law	dogter, skoon-	dochte(r)r, skohnn-
family	famielie, gesin	fahmeel'eeh
father	vader	fah'de(r)r
father-in-law	skoonvader	skohn'fahde(r)r
gentleman, sir	jentelman, seur	yentelma(h)n, su(r)r
gentlewoman	edelvrou	eydelfro
girl	meisie	meyssee
granddaughter	kleindogter	kleyn'dochte(r)r
grandfather	grootvader	chroh'fahde(r)r
grandmother	grootmoeder	chroht'moode(r)r
grandson	kleinsoon	kleyn'sohn
guardian	voog	fohch
heir	erfgenaam	erf'chenahm
husband	man, eggenoot	ma(h)n, ech'che(r)-noht

English.	Afrikaans.	Pronunciation.
lady	dame, vrou	dahme(r), fro
man	mens, man	menss, ma(h)n
marriage	huwelik	hu(r)ve(r)lik
mother	moeder	moode(r)r
mother-in-law	skoonmoeder	skohn'moode(r)r
nephew	neef	neyf
niece	niggie	nichee'
orphan	weeskind	veeskint
parents	ouers (m. & f., pl.)	ohe(r)rs
relatives	familie	fahmeel'eeh
sister	suster	susste(r)r
sister-in-law	skoonsuster	skohn'susste(r)r
son	seun	seun
son-in-law	skoonseun	skohn'seun
uncle	oom	ohm
widow	weduwee, wedevrou	vey'deûvee, vey-de(r)fro
widower	wewenaar	veeve(r)nahr
wife	vrou, eggenote	fro, ech'che(r)-nohte(r)
woman	vrou	fro

The Human Body (Die Menslike Liggaam)

Ankle	enkel	en'kel
arm	arm	a(h)rm
back	rug	ruch
beard	baard	bahrt
blood	bloed	bloo't
body	liggaam	lichahm
bones	bene	bey'ne(r)
bowels	ingewande	inche(r)va(h)nde(r)
brain	harsings	hahr'sings
cheek	wang	va(h)ng
chest	bors	borss
chin	kin	kin
complexion	gelaatskleur	che(r)lahtsklu(r)r
ears	ore	ohre
elbow	elmboog	elmbohch
eye	oog	ohch
eyes, the	oë	ohe(r)

English.	Afrikaans.	Pronunciation.
face	gesig	ge(r)sich
fingers	vingers	fing'e(r)rss
foot	voet	foo't
forehead	voorhoof, voorkop	fohr'hohf, fohr'kop
hair	haar	hahr
hand	hand	ha(h)nt
head	hoof, kop	hohf, kop
heart	hart	hah(r)t
kidneys	niere	nee're(r)
knee	knie	k-nee
leg	been	beyn
limb	lit	lit
lips	lippe	lip'pe(r)
liver	lewer	leyve(r)r
lungs	longe	long'e(r)
moustache	snorbaard	snorr'bahrrt
mouth	mond	mont
nails	naels	nah'e(r)lss
neck	nek	nek
nose	neus	nu(r)ss
pulse	pols	polss
shoulders	skouers	skou'e(r)rss
side	sy	sey (same as say)
skin	vel	fel
spine	ruggraat	ruch'chraht
stomach	maag	mahch
throat	keel	keyl
thumb	duim	duim
toe	toon	tohn (like tone)
tongue	tong	tong
tooth	tand	ta(h)nt
teeth	tande	ta(h)n'de(r)
whiskers	bokbaard	bohk'bahrrt
wrist	handgewrig, pols	hahnt'ge(r)vrich, pohls

Health (Gesondheid)

Accident	ongeluk	o(h)nche(r)luk
ambulance	ambulans	a(h)mbeula(h)ns
apoplexy	beroerte	beroorte(r)

English.	Afrikaans.	Pronunciation.
appetite	eetlus, appeteit	eetluss, a(h)pe(r)-teyt
bandage	verband	fe(r)rba(h)nt'
biliousness	galagtigheid	chahla(h)ch'te(r)-cheyt
blister	blaar	blahr
bruise	kneusplek	k-nu(r)splek
burn	brandplek	bra(h)nt'plek
catch a disease, to	'n siekte kry	'n seekte(r) krey
contagious	besmettelik	be(r)smetlik
contagion	besmetting	be(r)smetting
chemist's shop	apteek	ahpteyk'
chill	koue	koue(r)
catch a chill, cold, to	koue vat	koue(r) faht
chilblains	winterblare, -hande, -voete	winte(r)r blahrre(r) -hahnde(r), -foot'te(r)
cough	hoes	hoos
corn	liddoring	litdohring
cramp	kramp	kra(h)mp
cure	genesing	che(r)neysing
deaf	doof	dohf
dentist	tandedokter, tandarts	ta(h)nde(r)dok-te(r), ta(h)nt'-a(h)rts
diarrhœa	diarree, blood-	deeahrey, bloht-persee
diet	dieet	dee-eyt'
disease, illness	siekte	seekte(r)
doctor	dokter, arts	dokte(r)r, a(h)rtss
draught	geneesmiddel, drankie	che(r)neyss'mid-de(r)l, dra(h)nk'ee
dysentery	bloedpersie	blohtpersee
dumb	stom	stom
exercise	liggaamsoefening	lichahmsoo'fening
exhausted, to be	gedaan, uitgeput	che(r)dahn,uitge(r)-put
exhaustion	uitputting	uit'putting (as *nut*)
faint, to	flou val	flow fa(h)l
fainting, -fit	floute	flowte(r)

English.	Afrikaans.	Pronunciation.
fatigued	vermoeid	fe(r)rmoo'it
fever	koors	kohrass
fit	toeval, aanval	too'fa(h)l, ahn'fa(h)l
fracture	beenbreuk	beynbru(r)k
gout	jig, pootjie	yich, pohtyee
headache	hoofpyn	hohf'peyn
hoarse	hees	heyss
hospital	hospitaal	hosspeetahl
ill	siek	seek
illness	siekte	seekte(r)
indigestion	slegte spysvertering	slechte(r) speyss'-fe(r)rteyring
indisposed, to be	siek, ongesteld wees	seek, on-ch̤e(r)-stelt'vees
indisposition	ongesteldheid	on-che(r)stelt'-heyt
inflammation	ontsteking, imflam-masie	ontsteyking, in-fle(r)mahsee
lame	mank, kruppel	ma(h)nk, kru(r)pel
medicine	medisyne, genees-middel	me(r)de(r)seyne(r), ge(r)neyss'middel
nurse	erpleegster	ferpleechster
ointment	salf	sa(h)lf
pain	pyn	peyn
paralysis	verlamming, be-roerte	ferla(h)mming, be(r)roorte(r)
pill	pil	pil
poison	gif, vergif	chif, fe(r)rchif
poultice	pap	pa(h)p
prescription	reseppie, voorskrif	re(r)sep'pee, fohr-skriff
quinine	kiena	keenah
remedy	middel	mid'del
rest, repose	rus	russ
scald	brandwond, -seer	bra(h)nt'vont, -seyrr
scratch	krap, skraap	kra(h)p, skrahp.
sea-sickness	seesiekte	sey'seekte(r)
sick	mislik	misslik
sore throat	seer keel	seyrr keyl
sprain	verstuiting	fe(r)rstui'ting

English.	Afrikaans.	Pronunciation.
sting	steek	steyk
surgeon	snydokter	sneydokterr
symptom	simptoom, teeken	simtohn, teyke(r)n
tonic	versterkmiddel	ferste(r)rk'middel
temperature	temperatuur	tempehrahtêûr'
thermometer, clinical	termometer, klienies	teyrrmohmeh'terr, kleenees
clinic-thermometer	koorstermometer	kohrssteyrrmohmeh'terr
wart	vratjie	fra(h)tyee
wound	wond	vonnt

Dress (Klere)

bath	bad	baht
blouse (lady's)	bloes	blooss
bonnet	kappie	kahpee
boots	skoene	skohne(r)
boot laces	skoenveter, -riem	skohnreem
bracelet	armband	a(h)rm'ba(h)nt
braces	kruisbande	kruisba(h)nde(r)
brooch	borsspeld	bawrsspelt
brush	borsel	borse(r)l
buttons	knope	k-nohpe(r)
button-hook	knoophakie	k-nohphahkee
calico	katoen	kahtohn
drawers	onderbroek	on'de(r)rbroo-k
dress	klere	kleyre(r)
—, evening (ladies)	balkostuum	bahlkostêûm
—, — (gentlemen)	galatenu	chahlahtenu(r)
—, fancy	maskeradekostuum	masskerahde(r)-kostêûm
flannel	flennie	flen'nee
fur	pels	pels
gaiters	kamaste	kamahste(r)
garters	kousbande	kousba(h)nde(r)
gloves	handskoene	ha(h)nt'skohne(r)
hair-pins	haarnaald	hahr-nahlt
handkerchief	sakdoek	sa(h)k'dook
hat	hoed	hoot
jewellery	juwele	yêûvele(r)

English.	Afrikaans.	Pronunciation.
lace	kant	ka(h)nt
linen	linne	linne(r)
lining	voering	fooring
looking-glass, mirror	spieël	spey'l
mackintosh	reënjas	reynja(h)s
muffler	serp	se(r)rp
muslin	neteldoek, moeslien	neetel-dohk, moos-leyn
necklace	halskettinkie	ha(h)lskettinkee
necktie	das(sie)	da(h)s(see)
needle	naald	nahlt
overcoat	jas, warmjas	ya(h)ss, vahrr'm-ya(h)ss
parasol	sambreel	sa(h)mbreyl
petticoat	onderrok	onderrock (as in rock)
pins	spelde	spelde(r)
—, safety	veiligheidspelde	feylichheytspelde(r)
pocket	sak	sa(h)k
— book	sakboek	sa(h)kbook
purse	beurs	bu(r)rss
razor	skeermes	ske(h)rrmess
ribbon	lint	lint
ring	ring	ring
scissors	skêr	skai'(r)r
sewing-cotton	naaigare	nah'ichahre(r)
sewing-silk	naaisy	nah'i-sey
shawl	tjalie	tjahlee
shirt	hemp	hemp
shoehorn	skoenhoring	skoonhohrring
shoe	skoen	skoon
silk	sy	sey
sleeve	mou	mo
skirt	rok	rock
slipper	slipper	slip'perr
soap	seep	seep
spectacles	bril	brril
sponge	spons	spawns
stud	hempsknoopie	hempsknohpee

English.	Afrikaans.	Pronunciation.
suit	pak klere	pa(h)k kleyre(r)
stays	borsrok	bawrsro(r)k
stockings	kouse	kouse(r)
tape	band	ba(h)nt
thread	draad	draht
tie	das	da(h)ss
trousers	broek	broo'k
thimble	vingerhoed	fingerhohtt
tooth-brush	tandeborsel	ta(h)nde(r)bawrsel
umbrella	sambreel	sa(h)mbre(h)l
veil	sluier	slui'e(r)r
waistcoat	onderbaadjie	onderbahdyee
watch	oorlosie	ohrlohsee
walking-stick	loopstok	lohpsto(h)k
waterproof-coat	reënjas	reynjahs

Food and Drink (Voedsel en Drank)

Bill-of-fare	spyslys	speys-leys
bacon	spek	spek
beef	beesvleis	beesfleys
beef-steak	biefstuk	beef'stuk
beer	bier	beer
bread	brood	broht
—, brown	growwe brood	chraw-ve(r)-broht
—, white	wit brood	vit-broht
—, stale	vermufte brood	fermuffte(r) broht
—, new	vars brood	fa(h)rs broht
breakfast	ontbyt	ontbeyt'
bun	bolletjie	bohl-let-yee
butter	botter	boht'te(r)r
cake	koek	koo'k
cheese	kaas	kahss
chocolate	sjokolade	tjokolahde(r)
cigar	sigaar	seechahr
claret	klaret	kla(h)rret
cocoa	kakao	ka(h)ka(h)o
cutlet	skaapribbetjie karbonaadjie	skahprib'be(r)yee ka(h)rrbo(h)nah-yee

English.	Afrikaans.	Pronunciation.
Drinks	drank	dra(h)nk
beverage	verskeie soorte	ferskeye(r) sohr-te(r)
brandy	brandewyn	bra(h)nde(r)-veynn
gin	jenewer	yehneyferr
lemonade	lemonade	leemonah'de(r)
minerals	mineraalwater	minnerahlvah-te(r)r
soda water	sodawater, siphon	soda(h)vahte(r)r, seefo(h)n
wine	wyn	veyn
water	water	vahte(r)r
coffee	koffie	kof'fee
cream	room	rohm
dinner	middagmaal	mid'da(h)chmahl
eggs	eiers	ey'e(r)rss
fat	vet	fet
flour	fyn meel	feyn meyl
fowl	hoender	hoo(h)nde(r)r
fried	gebraai	che(r)brah'i
game	wild	vilt
grilled	op rooster gebraai	op rohste(r)r che(r)brah'i
ham	ham	ha(h)m
honey	heuning	hu(r)ning
hunger	honger	hohng'ge(r)r
ice	ys	eyss
iced water	bevriesde water	be(r)freessde(r)-vahte(r)r
jam	konfyt	ko(r)nnfeyt
joint	stuk vleis	stu(r)k fleyss
kidneys	niertjies	neert'yees
lamb	lamvleis	la(h)mfleyss
lean	maer vleis	ma(h)e(r)r fleyss
leg	boud	bout (like boat)
marmalade	marmelade	ma(h)rrme(r)-lahde(r)
meal	meel, maaltyd	meyl, mahl'teyt
menu	spys lys	speys-leys

English.	Afrikaans.	Pronunciation.
meat	vleis	fleyss
—, mince	gemaalde vleis	che(r)mahlde(r) fleyss
—, boiled	gekookte vleis	che(r)koh fleyss
—, roast	gebraaide vleis	che(r)brah'ide(r) fleyss
milk	melk	mel'k
mustard	mosterd	mossterrt
mutton	skaapvleis	skahp'fleyss
oil	olie	ohlee
omelet	eierkoek, ommelet	eyerrkook, o(h)me-let
onion	ui	ui (which see)
pepper	peper	peype(r)r
pork	varkvleis	fa(h)rk'fleyss
pudding	poeding	poo'ding
rice	rys	reyss
rib	rib	rip
roll	broodjie	broht'yee
salad	slaai	slah'i
salt	sout	sout
sausage	wors	vors
shoulder	skouer	skou'err
sirloin	lendestuk	lehnde(r)stuck
slice	skyf	skeyff
soup	sop	sop
sugar	suiker	suike(r)r
supper	aandete	ahnt'eete(r)
tea	tee	tey
thirst	dors	dorss
tobacco	tabak, twak	tahba(h)k', tvahk'
underdone	halfgaar	ha(h)lf chahrr
veal	kalfvleis	ka(h)lf'fleyss
vegetables	groente	chroonte(r)
vinegar	asyn	ahseyn'
water	water	vahte(r)r
well-done	goed gaar	choot chahr
wine	wyn	veyn

House and Furniture (Huis en Huisraad)

English.	Afrikaans.	Pronunciation.
Armchair	leuningstoel	lu(r)ningstool
ashes	as	a(h)ss
basin	kom	ko(h)m
basket	mandjie	ma(h)ntyee
bath	bad	bat
bed	bed	bet
bedroom	slaapkamer	slahp'kahme(r)r
bedstead	ledikant	leydeeka(h)nt
bell	bel	bel
blanket	kombers	kombe(r)rss
blind	rolgordyn	ro(h)lcho(h)rdeyn
book-case	boekrak	book'ra(h)k
box, trunk	doos, koffer	dohss, koffe(r)r
brick	baksteen	ba(h)ksteen
broom	besem	beese(r)m
burner	brander, lamp	bra(h)n'der, la(h)mp
candle	kers	kerss
candlestick	blaker, kandelaar	bla(h)ker, ka(h)n-de(r)lahr
carpet	tapyt	tahpeyt'
ceiling	solder, plafon	sol'de(r)r, plahfon'
cellar	kelder	kel'de(r)r
chair	stoel	stool
chamber-utensil	waterpot	vahte(r)rpot
chest-of-drawers	laaitafel	lah'itahfe(r)l
chimney	skoorsteen	skohrsteyn
clock	klok	klok
coals	kole	kohle(r)
corridor	breë gang	bree'e(r) cha(h)ng
counterpane	sprei	sprey
cupboard	kas	ka(h)s
curtain	gordyn	*chordeyn'
dining-room	eetkamer	eet'ka(h)me(r)r
door	deur	du(r)r
door-bell	deurklokkie	du(r)rklokee
drawer	laai	lah'i
drawing	tekening	teyke(r)ning

*ch : pronounced like the ch in loch

English.	Afrikaans.	Pronunciation.
drawing-room	sitkamer	sitka(h)me(r)r
dresser (kitchen)	kombuistafel met rakke	kombuisstahfe(r)l met ra(h)k'ke(r)
dressing-table	kleedtafel	kleyt'tahfe(r)l
electric light	elektries lig	ele(r)ktrees lich
feather-bed	verebed, bulsak	feyre(r) bet, bûl-sa(h)k
fender	haardskerm	hahrrtske(r)rm
fire-place	vuurherd	feurrhe(r)rt
flat	woonkamers	vohnka(h)mers
floor	vloer	floo'r (the oo in groom)
foot-stool	voetstoel	fohtstohl
garden	tuin	tuin
gas flame	gasvlam	chass'fla(h)m
grate	rooster	rohsste(r)r
hall	saal	sahl
hearth-rug	haardkleedjie	hahrtkleetyee
house	huis	huis
incandescent	gloeiend	chloo'ient
jug, ewer	beker, lampetbeker	beeke(r)r, la(h)m-pet-beeke(r)r
key	sleutel	slu(r)'te(r)l
kitchen	kombuis	ko(r)mbuis
lamp	lamp	la(h)mp
landing	landingsplek	la(h)ndingsple(r)k
larder	spens	spe(r)ns
library	biblioteek	beebleeohteyk'
light	lig	lich
—, electric	elektries lig	elektreess lich
lock	slot	slot
looking-glass	spieël	spee'e(r)l
mantel-piece	kaggel	ka(h)ch'che(r)ll
mattress	matras	mahtra(h)ss
ornament	ornament	orna(h)ment
passage	gang	cha(h)ng
piano	klavier	kla(h)'fee(r)r
picture	prent	pre(r)nt
pillow	kussing	kûss'ing
pillow-case	kussingsloop	kûss'ing·slohp

English.	Afrikaans.	Pronunciation.
poker	vuuryster	fêurr-eysste(r)r
roof	dak	da(h)k
room	kamer	kahme(r)r
rug	reiskombers, vloerkleedjie	reysko(h)mbe(r)rss, floo'rkleet-yee
seat	sitplek	sitple(r)k
sheet	bedlaken	bet'lahke(r)n
shelf	rak	ra(h)k
shovel	skoopgraaf	sko(h)p'chrahff
sideboard	buffet	buffet'
smoke	rook	rohk
soot	roet	root
spark	vonk	fonk
staircase	trap	tra(h)p
storey	verdieping	ferdeeping
switch, electric	skakelaar	ska(h)ke(r)lahrr
table	tafel	tahfe(r)l
table-cloth	tafellaken	tahfe(r)l-lahke(r)n
tongs	tang	ta(h)ng
towel	handdoek	ha(h)n'dook
trunk	koffer	kof'fe(r)r
vase	vaas	fahss
wall	muur	mêur
wash-hand-basin	waskom	va(h)ss-ko(r)m
wash-stand	wastafel	va(h)sstahfe(r)l
window	venster	fenste(r)r
writing-desk	skryftafel	skreyff'tahfe(r)l

Cooking and Eating Utensils (Kombuisgereedskap)

Basin	kom	kom
coals	kole	ko(h)le(r)
coffee-pot	koffiekan	koffeeka(h)n
cork-screw	kurktrekker	kûrk'tre(r)ke(r)r
cup	koppie	ko(h)pee
decanter	kraffie	kra(h)fee
dish	skottel	skoh'te(r)l
— cover	— deksel	— dek'se(r)l
finger-bowl	vingerglas	fing'e(r)rchla(h)ss
firewood	vuurhoud	fêurr'howt
—	brandhoud	bra(h)nt'howt

English.	Afrikaans.	Pronunciation.
fork	vork	forrk
frying-pan	braaipan	braa'ipa(h)n
gas	gas	cha(h)ss
glass	glas	chla(h)ss
gridiron	rooster	rohste(r)r
kettle	ketel	keytel
jug	beker	bee-ke(r)r
knife	mes	mess
lid	deksel	dekse(r)l
matches	vuurhoutjies	vêurhowtyees
milk-jug	melkbeker	melk'bee-ke(r)r
nut-cracker	neutkraker	nu(r)tkrahke(r)r
oven	oond	ohnt
plate	bord	bort
salt-cellar	soutvaatjie	sowtfahtyee
sauce-bowl	souskommetjie	sowskomme(r)tyee
sauce-pan	kastrol	ka(h)stroll
saucer	piering	peer'ring
serviette	servet	serfet'
— ring	— ring	— ring
soup-ladel	soplepel	sople(r)pe(r)l
spoon	lepel	le(r)pe(r)l
—, egg	eierlepeltjie	eyerle(r)pe(r)lt yee
—, tea	teelepeltjie	teele(r)pe(r)lt yee
stove	stoof	stohf
table-cloth	tafellaken	tahfe(r)l-lahke(r)n
tea-pot	teepot	teepot
tray	skinkbord	skinkbort
tumbler	glas	chla(h)ss
water-bottle	waterbottel	vahte(r)rbo(r)tel
wine-glass	wynkelkie	veynn'kel-kee

Religion (Godsdiens)

Aisle	subeuk, vleuel	seybu(r)k, flu(r)e(r)l
altar	altaar	a(h)ltahr
absolution	vergifnis	ferchifniss
angel	engel	ẹng'l
baptism	doop	dohp
belfry	kloktoring	klok'tohring
believing	vertrou	fertro

English.	Afrikaans.	Pronunciation.
Bible	Bybel	beybel
Bible Society	Bybelgenootskap	beybelche(r)noht-ska(h)p
belief	geloof	che(r)lohff
breviary	kort begrip	ko(h)rt be(r)chrip
burial	begrafnis	be(r)chra(h)ffniss
cathedral	domkerk, katedraal	do(h)mmke(r)rk, ka(h)teedrah'l
cemetery	begraafplek, kerkhof	be(r)chrahff'ple(r)k
chancel	koor	kohr
choir-master	koormester	kohr-meysste(r)r
chapel	kapel	kahpell'
charity	liefdadigheid	leefdahdichheyt
choir	koor	kohr
clergy	geestelikheid	cheyss'te(r)likheyt
clergyman (Prot.)	predokant	pre(h)deekahntt
clergyman (Catholic)	priester	pree'sterr
Communion	avondmaal	ah'font-mahl
confirmation	aanneming	ahn'neyming
Creator	Skepper	ske(r)per
creed	geloofsbelydenis	che(r)lohfsbe(r)ley-denniss
divine	goddelik	chod'de(r)lik
— service	godsdiensoefening	chods'deens-oof-e(r)n-ing
divinity	godheid	chotheyt
Eternal	die Ewige	dee eeviche(r)
eternal life	ewige iewe	eeviche(r) leeve(r)
eternity	ewigheid	eevich'heyt
everlasting	ewigdurend	eevichdeurend
faith	geloof	che(r)loof
faithful	getrou	che(r)trou
faithfulness	getrouheid	che(r)trou-heyt
fear	vrees	freyss
font	doopbakkie	dohp'bak-kee
forgive	vergewe	fercheyve(r)
forgiveness	vergifnis	ferchifniss
God	God	chott (ch as in Loch)
gospel	evangelie	ee'fa(h)nn-chee-lee

English.	Afrikaans.	Pronunciation.
grave	graf	chra(h)f
hymn	gesang	che(r)sa(h)ng
— book	— boek	— book
heaven	hemel	heymeyl
hell	hel	hell
Holy	Heilig	heylich
— Week	die stil week	dee stil veyk
— of Holies	die Heilige der Heilige	dee heyliche(r) dair heyliche(r)
— City	Rome	rohme(r)
— Spirit	die Heilige Gees	dee heyliche(r) cheyss
— Writ	die Heilige Skrif	dee heyliche(r) skriff
— day	heiligedag	heyliche(r)da(h)ch
— Thursday	Hemelvaartdag	heymeylfahrtd-da(h)ch
— water	wywater	veyvahte(r)r
hope	hoop	hohp
Jesus Christ	Jesus Kristus	yee'sûss kris'tûss
joy	vreugde	fru(r)chte(r)
joyful	vrolik	frohlik
lectern	koorlessenaar	kohr'lesse(r)nahr
litany	litanie	leetahnee'
liturgy	liturgie	leetursjee
Lord	Here	he(r)re(r)
love	liefde	leefde(r)
marriage	hewelik	hêuve(r)lik
mass	mis	miss
matins	vroegmis	frooch-miss
mercy	genade	che(r)nahde(r)
missal	misboek	miss'book
mission	sending	sending
missionary	sendeling	sende(r)ling
nave	naaf, skip	nahf, skip
offertory	kollekte	kollekte(r)
organ	orrel	or're(r)l
organist	orgelist	or'che(r)list
peace	vrede	freede(r)

(Remember in phonetics ch is always pronounced like the ch in loch)

English.	Afrikaans.	Pronunciation.
penance	boetedoening, straf	boote(r)dooning, stra(h)f
praise	prys, loof	preyss, lohf
prayer	gebed	che(r)bet
— book	gebedboek	che(r)bet'book
preach, to	preek	preyk
preacher	predikant	preyde(r)ka(h)nt
priest	priester	prees'te(r)r
Protestant	Protestant	prote(r)sta(h)nt'
pulpit	preekstoel	preyk'stool
repentance	berou	beh-ro, be(r)ro
Roman Catholic	Rooms-Katolik	rohmss-kahtohleek'
sacrament	sakrament	sahkra(h)ment'
sacred	heilig	heyle(r)ch
salvation	saligheid	sah'le(r)ch-heyt
Salvation Army	Heilsleër	heylss'leye(r)r
Saviour	Saligmaker, Heiland	sahlichma(h)ker, heyla(h)nt
sermon	preek	preyk
service	diens	deynss
—, divine	Godsdiens	chotts'deynss
—, morning	môre . . . oefening	mawre(r) . . . oofe(r)-ning
—, evening	aand	ahnt
sin	sonde	sonde(r)
sinner	sondaar	sondahr
sorrow	droefheid	droof'heyt
soul	siel	seel
tombstone	grafsteen	chra(h)ff'steyn
true	waar	vahrr
trust	vertrou	ferr'tro
verger	koster	ko(h)ste(r)r
vespers	vesper	fesspe(r)r
worship	aanbid	ahnbit

Legal and Judicial Terms (Wettige en Regterlike Terme)

Acquittal	vryspraak, ontslag	freysprahk, o(h)nt'-sla(h)ch
action	hofsaak, proses	ho(r)f'sahk, prosess

English.	Afrikaans.	Pronunciation.
affidavit	beëdigde verklaring	be(r)eed'dichte(r) ferklahring
agreement	ooreenkoms	ohreynkomms
allegation	bewering	be(r)veyrr'ing
allege	beweer	be(r)veyrr
appeal	appeleer	a(h)pel'eyrr
apology	verontskuldiging	fe(r)ont'skuldiching
arbitrate	beslis	be(r)sliss
arbitration	arbitrasie	a(h)rrbeetrah'see
arbitrator	skeidsregter, arbieter	skeyds'rechterr, a(h)rrbee'te(r)r
arbitress	skeidsvrou	skeyts'fro
arrangement	skikking, reëling	skik'ing, reye(r)l-ing
arrest	arresteer, in hegtenis neem	a(h)res'teyrr, in he(r)chte(r)niss neym
attest	verklaar	ferklahrr
attestation	verklaring, bewys	ferklahrr'ing, be(r)veyss
attorney, advocate	prokureur, advokaat	prohke(r)reûr a(h)t-fohkaht'
—, power of	volmag, prokurasie	fol'ma(h)ch, proh-keûrah'see
—, general	staatsprokureur, prokureur-generaal	stahts'prohke(r)reûr prohke(r)reur-che(r)ne(r)rahll
authorise	magtig	machtich
award	toeken	too'ke(r)nn
bail	borgtog	borch'toch
bailiff	balju	ba(h)lyu(r)
barrister	advokaat	a(h)tfohkaht'
bond (for loan)	verband, hipoteek	ferba(h)nt,heepo(h)-teyk
burglary	huisbraak, inbraak	huisbrahk, inbrahk
case for the prosecution	aanklag	ahn'kla(h)ch
case for the defence	verdediging	fe(r)dey'de(r)ching
charge (accusation)	aanklag	ahn'kla(h)ch
charge, to	beskuldig	be(r)skuldich
claimant	eiser	eysser

English.	Afrikaans.	Pronunciation.
client	klient	klee-hent
complaint	klag	kla(h)ch
complainant	klaer	kla(h)e(r)r
conviction	veroordeling	ferohrr-de(r)ling
consent	toestemming	too'ste(r)m-ing
court of justice	geregshof	che(r)rechsho(r)f
crime	misdaad	missdaht
criminal	misdadiger	missdahd'diche(r)r
— case	strafsaak	stra(h)ff'sahk
— code	strafwetboek	stra(h)ff've(h)t book
— law	strafreg	stra(h)ff'rech
decision	beslissing, besluit	be(r)sliss'ing, be(r)-sluit
deed (of sale)	koopbrief	kohp'breef
— (of lease)	pagbrief	pa(h)ch'breef
— (of assignment)	bewys van boedel-oorgawe	be(r)veyss fa(h)n bood'l ohrr-ga(h)ve(r)
deeds office	registrasiekantoor	re(r)chestra(h)see-ka(h)nntoor'
deed stamp	akteseël	a(h)kte(r)seye(r)'l
defence	verdediging	fe(r)rdeyde(r)ching
defend (in court)	verdedig	fe(r)rdeydich
defendant (in a suit)	verweerder	fe(r)rveyrde(r)
deposition (on oath)	beëdigde verklaring	be(r)eed'dichte(r) ferklahring
discharge	ontslag	o(h)ntt'sla(h)ch
effects (goods)	goed, besittings	choot, be(r)sit'ings
equity	billikheid	billikheyt
— of redemption	inlossingsreg	inlossingsre(r)ch
—, in	billikerwys	billike(r)rveys
—, court of	vredegerig	freede(r)'che(r)rich
estate	boedel	boode(r)l
—, personal	persoonlike vermoë	persohn'likke(r) fermooe(r)
—, real	onroerende goedere	onrohr'ende(r) choode(r)re(r)
—, surrender one's	boedel oorgee	boode(r)l ohrrchee
evidence	getuie	che(r)tuie(r)

English.	Afrikaans.	Pronunciation.
evidence, bear	getuienis aflê	che(r)tuie(r)niss a(h)flai(r)
evidence, king's	kroongetuie	krohnn'che(r)tuie(r)
excise	aksyns	a(h)kseynss'
execute (a deed)	akte optrek	a(h)kte(r) optre(r)k
— (a person)	ophang, onthoof	opha(h)ng, onthoof
executioner	laksman	la(h)ks'mann
fee	fooi	foh'i
fine	boete	boote(r)
forgery	vervalsing	fe(r)rfa(h)lsing
fraud	bedrog	be(r)droch
illegal	onwettig	onvettich
imprisonment	tronkstraf	tronkstra(h)ff
information	inligting	inlich'ting
informer	aanklaer	ahnklahe(r)r
injunction	opdrag, bevel	opdra(h)ch, be(r)fell
indictment	aanklag	ahnklahch
injustice	onreg	onre(r)ch
invalid	ongeldig	on'che(r)ldich
inventory	inventaris	infentahriss
jail	gevangenis, tronk	ge(r)fa(h)ng'e(r) niss, tro(h)nk
judge	regter	rechter
judgment, to give	uitspraak doen	uitsprahk doon
jurisdiction	jurisdiksie	yeurisdiksee
jury	jurie	yeuree
justice of the peace	vrederegter	freyde(r)rechte(r)r
law, civil	burgerlike wet	burcherlike(r) vet
—, criminal	strafreg	stra(h)f'rech
— suit	regsgeding	rechs'che(r)ding
lawful	wettig	vettich
lawyer	regsgeleerde	rechsge(r)leyrde(r)
legal	wettig	vettich
— authority	regsmag	rechsma(h)ch
legalisation	legalisasie	lee-cha(h)lee-sa(h)-see
legality	wettigheid	vettich'heyt
lender	lener	leyne(r)r
magistrate	magistraat	ma(h)ch'che(r)-straht

English.	Afrikaans.	Pronunciation.
magistrate's court	magistraats hof	ma(h)ch'che(r)-strahts hohf
magistracy	magistratuur	ma(h)ch'che(r)-strah-teu͡r
non-suit, to	afwys	a(h)fveys
oath	eed	eyt
—, to take an	'n eed aflê	'n eyt a(h)f-lai(r)
—, on	onder ede	onde(r)r eyde(r)
—, breaking	meineed	meyneyt
pardon	kwytskel	kveytskell
—, general	amnestie	a(h)mnestee
parties (in a suit)	partye	pa(h)rtey'e(r)
penal	strafbaar	stra(h)ff'bahrr
— servitude	hardepad	ha(h)rde(r)pat
penalise	beboet	be(r)boot
perjury	meineed	meyneyt
petitioner	petisionaris	petisiona(h)riss
plaintiff	eiser	eyse(r)r
police	poliesie	pohleesee
— force	— mach	— ma(h)ch
— law	— wet	— vet
— man	konstabel	konsta(h)be(r)l
proceedings (legal)	proses	prohsess
procedure	prosedure	prohse(r)dee͡ur(r)
—, legal	regspraktyk	re(r)chs-pra(h)kteyk
process	regsgeding	re(r)chs'che(r)rding
proof	bewys	be(r)veyss
prosecution (in court)	vervolging	fe(r)rfolching
prosecutor	vervolger	fe(r)rfolche(r)r
—, public	publieke aanklaer	pohbleeke(r) ahnn-kla(h)e(r)r
punishment	straf	stra(h)f
record book	verslagboek	fe(r)rsla(h)chbook
release	ontslag	ontsla(h)ch
robbery	diefstal	deefsta(h)l
seal	seël	se(r)'l
—, the Great	die Rykseël	dee rey(r)kseye(r)l
—, the Privy	die geheimseël	dee che(r)heymm-seye(r)l
sentence	vonnis	fonniss

English.	Afrikaans.	Pronunciation.
service	diens	deens
—, church	kerkdiens	kirkdeens
—, civil	siviele diens	se(r)feele(r) deens
sign	teken	te(r)ke(r)n, tey-ke(r)n
statement	verklaring, staat	fe(r)rklahring, staht
statute	wet	vet
— book	statuteboek	sta(h)tẽute(r) book
— law	afgekondigde wet	a(h)fge(r)kondich-de(r) vet
statutory	wetlik	vet'lik
sue	vervolg	fe(r)rfolch
suit	proses, regsgeding	prohsess, rechsge(r)-ding
summons (of court)	dagvaring	da(h)ch'fahrr-ing
surety	borg	borch
tenant (of house)	huurder	hẽurde(r)r
testament (will)	testament, uiterste wil	tesstahment, uiters-ste(r) vill
testator	erflater	e(r)rflahte(r)r
theft	diefstal	deefsta(h)l
thief	dief	deef
trial by jury	verhoor	ferhohrr
under seal	verseël	fe(r)seye(r)l
— secretary	ondersekretaris	onde(r)rse(r)kre(r)-tahris
unlawful	onwettig	onvet'tich
valid	geldig	cheldich
will	wil	vill
witness	getuie	che(r)tuie(r)
writ	lasbrief	la(h)ss'breef
written report	skriftelike rapport	skriffte(r)likke(r) rahport
written language	skryftaal	skreyff tahl

Professions and Trades (Beroepe en Ambagte)

Actor	toneelspeler	tohneylspeyle(r)r
architect	argitek	a(h)rsheetek (see sj under the G, g)

English.	Afrikaans.	Pronunciation.
artisan	handwerksman	ha(h)ntwe(r)rks-ma(h)n
artist	kunstenaar	kunstenahr
author	outeur	o(h)tu(r)r
authoress	skryfster	skreyfste(r)r
baker	bakker	ba(h)k'ke(r)r
banker	bankier	ba(h)nkeer
barber	barbier	ba(h)rbeer
bookbinder	boekbinder	book-binnde(r)r
bookmaker	boekmaker	bookma(h)ker
bookseller	boekhandelaar	book'ha(h)ndelahr
brewer	brouer	bro'e(r)r
butcher	slagter	sla(h)ch'te(r)r
carpenter	timmerman	tim'me(r)rma(h)n
cashier	kassier	ka(h)s'seer
chemist	apteker	ahp'teyke(r)r
clergyman	predikant, priester geestelike	preyde(r)ka(h)nnt, preester cheyss-te(r)lik'ke(r)
clerk	klerk	klerrk
coachman	koetsier	kootseer
commercial traveller	handelsreisiger	ha(h)nde(r)lssrey-se(r)che(r)r
confectioner	suikerbakker	suike(r)rba(h)ke(r)r
cook	kok	kok
cycle-maker	rywielmaker	reyveelmahke(r)r
dairyman	melkboer	melkboor
dentist	tandedokter, tandarts	ta(h)nde(r)dokte(r)r ta(h)nt'ahrtss
diamond merchant	diamant-handelaar	deea(h)ma(h)nt-hahndelahr
draper	handelaar in draperie	ha(h)nde(r)lahr in dreype(r)r'ree
editor	uitgewer, editeur	uitchever, edeetu(r)r
electrical engineer	elektriese-ingenieuer	elecktreesé-ingeneer
engineer	ingenieur	inshe(r)nee-u(r)r
farmer	boer, pagter	bohr, pa(h)chte(r)r
farrier	hoefsmid	hoofsmit
fisherman	visser	fisse(r)r

English.	Afrikaans.	Pronunciation.
fishermonger	viskoper	fiskohpe(r)r
florist	blomkweker, bloemis	blo(h)mkveeke(r)r, bloomis
fruiterer	vrugtehandelaar	fruchte(r)ha(h)nde(r)lahr
gas engineer	gas ingenieur	cha(h)s-inyeneer
glazier	glasmaker	chla(h)ss'mahke(r)r
goldsmith	goudsmid	chout'smitt
governess	goewernante	choeve(r)rna(h)nte(r)
grocer	kruidenier	kruide(r)neer
hairdresser	haarsnyer	hahrsneye(r)r
jeweller	juwelier	yeûve(r)leer'
lady's man	damesvriend	dahme(r)ss'freent
laundress	wasvrou	va(h)ss'fro
merchant	koopman	kohpma(h)n
hosier	koushandelaar	kousha(h)nde(r)lahr
ironmonger	ysterhandelaar	(b)a(y)ster-hahndelahr
messenger	boodskapper	bohtska(h)p'pe(r)r
miller	meulenaar	mu(r)l'e(r)nahr
milliner	modemaakster	mohde(r)mahkste(r)r
miner	mynwerker	meynve(r)rke(r)r
motor engineer	motor-ingenieuer	motor-ingeneer
nursemaid	kindermeid	kinnde(r)rmeyt
optician	gesigskundige	che(r)sichskun'diche(r)
pastry-cook	pasteibakker	pa(h)stey'ba(h)ke(r)r
photographer	afnemer, fotograaf	a(h)fnehme(r)r, fohtochrahf
physician	arts, dokter	ahrtss, dokte(r)r
policeman	poliesieman, konstabel	pohleeseema(h)n, konstah'bill
printer	drukker	druk'ke(r)r
professor	professor, hooglermaar	profe(r)ssor, hohch'leerahr
provisions	lewensmiddele	leyve(r)ns'mid'de(r)l'e(r)

English.	Afrikaans.	Pronunciation.
provision dealer	verkoper van	fe(r)rkohpe(r)r fa(h)n
publisher	uitgewer	uit'che(r)ve(r)r
quack	kwaksalwer	kva(h)ksa(h)lver
Quaker	Kwaker	kvahke(r)r
ranger	boswagter	bossva(h)chte(r)r
reaper	maaier	maa'ie(r)r
receiver	kurator	keuahtorr
registrar	registrateur	re(r)che(r)strah-tu(r)r
renovator	vernuwer	fe(r)rnu(r)ve(r)r
repairer	hersteller	he(h)rrste(r)le(r)r
reporter	stenograaf	sten'o-chrahff
retail-dealer	kleinhandelaar	kleyn'ha(h)nde(r)-lahr
ropemaker	toudraaier	to'draa'i e(r)r
saddler	saalmaker	sahlmahke(r)r
schoolmaster	skoolmeester	skohl'meyste(r)r
servant	diensbode	deensbohde(r)
shoemaker	skoenmaker	skoon'mahke(r)
shopkeeper	winkelier	vinke(r)l'lee(r)r
smith	smid	smit
soldier	soldaat	soldaht
stationer	handelaar in skryf-behoeftes	ha(h)nde(r)lahrr in skreyf'be(r)hoof-te(r)s
student	student	steude(r)nt
surveyor	landmeter	la(h)ntmeyte(r)r
tailor	kleermaker	kleyr'mahke(r)r
teacher	onderwyser, leeraar	onde(r)rveyse(r)r, leyrahr
tobacconist	tabakhandelaar	ta(h)ba(h)kha(h)n-de(r)lahr
watchmaker	oorlosiemaker	ohrlohseemahke(r)r
wireless engineer	draadlose-in-genieuer	dra(h)tloose-ingeneer
workman	werksman	ve(r)ks'ma(h)n

Ships and Shipping (Skepe en Verskeping)

Anchor	anker	a(h)nke(r)r

English.	Afrikaans.	Pronunciation.
boat	boot	boht
bow	boeg	booch
cabin	kajuit, hut	kahyuit, hut
cable	kabel	kahbe(r)l
captain	kaptein	kahpteyn
compass	kompas	kompa(h)ss
course	koers	koorss
crew	bemanning	be(r)ma(h)nning
deck	dek	dek
flag	vlag	fla(h)ch
harbour (port)	hawe	hahve(r)
helm	roer	roor
keel	kiel	keel
landing-stage	landingsplek	la(h)ndings-ple(r)k
lighthouse	vuurtoring	fe͡ur'tohring
mast	mas	ma(h)ss
man-of-war	oorlogskip	ohr'loch-skip
merchantman	koopvaardyskip	kohp'fahrdeyskip
oar	roeispaan, roeiriem, roeier	roo'i'spahn, roo'-i'reem, roo'i'e(r)r
pilot	loods	lohts
rope	tou	to (like toe)
sail	seil	seyl
seaman (sailor)	matroos	ma(h)trohss
ship	skip	skip
steersman	stuurman	ste͡urma(h)n
stern	agterstewe	a(h)chte(r)rstey-ve(r)
tug	sleepboot	sleyp'boht
wharf	werf, kaai	verrf, kah'i

Travelling (Reisend). **By Rail and Road** (per trein en oorland)

Apartments	kamers	ka(h)me(r)rs
arrival	aankoms	ahnkoms
bill	rekening	reyke(r)ning
boarding-house	losieshuis, koshuis	lo(h)sees'huis, kos-shuis
booking-office	bespreekplek	be(r)spre(r)k'ple(r)k
boot-cleaning	skoenbepoetsing	skoon'be(r)pootsing
" boots " (hotel)	skoenpoetser	skoon'poots e(r)r

English.	Afrikaans.	Pronunciation.
brake (on wheel)	briek	breek
bridle	toom	tohm
bus	bus	bus
cab	keb	kep
cabman	kebryer	kep'reye(r)r
carriage	rytuig	reytuich
chambermaid	kamermeisie	ka(h)me(r)rmeysee
cloak-room	kleedkamer	kleytka(h)me(r)r
coach	koets	koots
coachman	drywer	dreyve(r)r
compartment	afdeling, komparte-ment	a(h)f-deeling, kom-pa(h)rte(r)me(r)nt
coffee-room	koffiekamer	koffeeka(h)me(r)r
cushion	kussing	kus'sing
custom-house	doeanekantoor	duahne(r)ka(h)n-tohr
customs-officer	doeane-amptenaar	duahne(r)-a(h)mp-te(r)nahrr
departure	vertrek	fe(r)rtre(r)r
drive	rytoertjie, ritjie	reytooryee, rityee
engine	lokomotief	lohkohmohteef'
excursion	ekskursie	ekskkursee
fare	vraggeld, passa-siers-geld	fra(h)ch'che(r)lt, pa(h)ssa(h)seers-che(r)lt
foot-warmer	voetwarmer	footva(h)rme(r)r
" Gentlemen "	Here	heyre(r)
guard	kondukteur	konduktu(r)r'
guide	gids	chits
guide-book	reisgids	reyss'chitts
hall-porter (door-keeper)	deurwagter	du(r)rva(h)chte(r)r
hat-box	hoededoos	hoode(r)dohss
hotel	hotel	hoh'tel
interpreter	tolk	tol'k
" Ladies "	Dames	dahme(r)s
landlord	huisbaas	huisbahss
landlady	eienares	eyenahr'e(r)ss'
lavatory	toiletkamer was-kamer	toy'lett-kahme(r)r va(h)ss'kahme(r)r

English.	Afrikaans.	Pronunciation.
lift, elevator	hystoestel, lift	heyss'tooste(r)l, lift
lodgings, furnished	kamers, gemeubileerd	kahme(r)s, che(r)mu(r)be(r)leyrrd
office	kantoor	ka(h)ntohr'
—, lost property	—, verlore begasie	—, ve(r)rlohre(r), bah'chah'see
luggage	bagasie	bah-chah'see
— label	— adres kaart vir die-	a(h)dre(r)ss kahrtt fe(r)r dee bah-chah'see
— van	bagasiewa	bah-chah'see-wa
manager	bestuurder	be(r)steūr'de(r)r
motor-bus	moterbus	mohte(r)r'buss
motor-car	moterkar, outo	mohte(r)r ka(h)rr, o(h)toh
newspaper	koerant, nuusblad	koo'ra(h)nt, neūs-bla(h)tt
omnibus	omnibus	om'neebuss
ostler (stable-boy)	staljong	sta(h)l'yo(h)ng
package	pakkie	pa(h)kee
payment	betaling	be(r)tahling
platform	platform	pla(h)t'for(r)m
porter (railway)	portier	porteer'
railway	spoorweg	spohrwe(r)ch
—, tube	ondergrond spoorweg	onde(r)rchront spohrwe(r)ch
— carriage	spoorwa	spohrwah
— station	(spoorweg) stasie	(spohrwe(r)ch) stah'see
receipt	kwitansie	kvitt'tahn'see
reins	teuels, tome	tu(r)e(r)ls, toh'me(r
ride (on horse back)	perdry	pe(r)rt'rey
riding-whip	sambokkie, rysweep	sa(h)mbok'kee, rey'sveyp
road	pad, weg	pa(h)t, vech
saddle	saal	sahl
signal (railway)	sein	seyn
signal-box (cabin)	sienjaalhuisie	seenjahl'huisee
sleeping-car	slaap(spoorweg)wa	slahp(spoorve(r)ch)-vah

English.	Afrikaans.	Pronunciation.
smoking-room	rookhamer	rohk'kahme(r)r
smoking-carriage	rookwa	rohk'vah
station-master	stasiemeester	stahsee-meyste(r)r
strap	platriem, band	pla(h)tt'reem, ba(h)nt
subway	onderaardse deurgang, duikweg	onde(r)rahrtse(r) du(r)cha(h)ng, duikve(r)ch
ticket, single	eenpersoons reiskaartjie	eynpe(r)rsohns reys'-kahrt'yee
—, first-class	eersteklas kaartjie	eyrste(r)kla(h) skahrtyee
— office	kaartjieskantoor	kahrtyeeska(h)ntohr
—, return	retoerkaartjie	re(r)toor'ka(h)rtyee
time-table (railway)	spoorwegboek	spohrwe(r)ch'book
tip, gratuity	tip, loon, drinkgeld	tip, lohn, drink'che(r)lt
train	trein	treynn
tramway (electric)	elektriese trem	ehle(r)ktree'se(r) tre(h)m
travelling rug	reisdeken	reyssdeyke(r)n
trunk	koffer	kof'fe(r)r
waiter	tafelbediende	ta(h)fe(r)l-be(r)-deende(r)
waiting-room	wagkamer	va(h)chkahme(r)r
walk	loop, wandel	lohp, va(h)nde(r)l
whip	sweep, piets	sveyp, peets

Travelling by Sea (Oor see reis)

Aft, after	agter	a(h)chte(r)r
amidships	in die middelskip	in dee mid'de(r)l-skip
anchor	anker	a(h)nke(r)r
berth	lêplek, skipskooi	lai(r)ple(r)k, skipps'koh'i
boat	boot	boht
—, rowing	skuit	skuit
boat-hook	boothaak	boht'hahk

English.	Afrikaans.	Pronunciation.
boatman	skipper, roeier	skip'pe(r)r, roo'i-e(r)r
boiler	ketel, stoomketel	keyte(r)l, stohm-keyte(r)l
bow	boeg	booch
bridge (of ship)	skeepsbrug	skeyps'bruch
buoy	baken (in see), boei	ba(h)ke(r)m [in sey] boo'i
cabin	kajuit, hut	ka(h)'yuit, hut
cable	kabeltou, ankertou	ka(h)be(r)l'tou, a(h)n'ke(r)r-tou
captain	kaptein	ka(h)pteynn'
compass	kompas	ko(h)mm'pa(h)ss
crew	skeepsbemanning	skeyps-be(r)ma(h)n-ing
deck	dek	dek
decks, between	tussendeks	tûs'se(r)n-deks
deck, gun	geskutdek	che(r)skûtt'de(r)k
—, main	bodek	boh'de(r)k
—, lower	onderdek	onde(r)r'de(r)k
—, quarter	halfdek	ha(h)lf'de(r)k
— chair	dekstoel	de(r)kstool
— hand	dekmatroos	de(r)kma(h)trohs
dock	dok	dok
—, dry	droogdok	drohchdok
—, floating	dryfdok	dreyff'dok
dockage (charges)	dokgeld, hawegeld	dok'che(r)lt, hah-ve(r)che(r)lt
dockyard	skeepswerf	skeypsve(r)rff
embark, to	inskeep	inskeyp
engineer	ingenieur, masjinis	insje(r)neye(r)r, ma(h)sheen'niss
engine-room (house)	masjieneloods	ma(h)sheene(r)lohts
fishing-boat	vissersboot	fis'se(r)rs-boht
fishing-net	visnet	fisnett
flag	vlag	fla(h)ch
fog-horn	mishoring	missho(h)r'ring
fore	voor	fohr
fore and aft	van die een end na die ander	fa(h)n dee eyn e(h)nt na(h) dee a(h)nde(r)r

English.	Afrikaans.	Pronunciation.
funnel	skoorsteenpyp	skohrr'steyn-peyp
gangway	loopplank	lohp'pla(h)nk
harbour, port	hawe	hahve(r)
helm, rudder	roer	roor
land, to	aan wal stap	ahn vahl sta(h)p
landing-stage place	landingsplek	la(h)ndingsple(r)k
leeward, to drift to	lyswaard se kant toe afdryf	leysvahrrt se(r) ka(h)ntt too a(h)fdreyff
lifebelt	reddingsboei	red'dings-boo'i
lifeboat	reddingsboot	red'dings-boot
lifebuoy	reddingsboei	red'dings-boo'i
lighthouse	vuurtoring	feûrr'tohring
mast	mas	mas
mate	stuurman	steûrma(h)n
oar	roeispaan, roeiriem, roeier	roo'ispaan, roo'ireem, roo'i'e(r)r
paddle wheel	skeprad	skepp'ra(h)tt
pier	hawehoof, pier	hahve(r)hohf, peer
pilot	gids, stuurman	chitts, steûrr'ma(h)n (port side)
port (side)	bakboord	ba(h)k'bohrt
port-hole	geskutspoort	che(r)skûtts'pohrt
pump	pomp	po(h)mp
quay	kaai	kah'i
rope, hawser	tou, sleepkabel	to, sleyp'kahbe(r)l (to—o as in toe)
sail	seil	seyl
sailing-ship	seilskip	seylskip
saloon	salon	sa(h)lonn
— carriage	salonwa	sa(h)lonn va'
screw- (propeller)	skroef	skroof
seaman (sailor)	matroos	ma(h)tro(h)s
sea-sickness	seesiekte	seyseekte(r)
sea-sick	seesiek	seyseek
ship	skip	skip
signals, to make	seine maak	seyne(r) mahk
skylight	dakvenster	da(h)kfenste(r)r
starboard (side)	stuurboord (kant)	steûrr'boort (ka(h)nnt)

English.	Afrikaans.	Pronunciation.
steamboat	stoomboot	stohm'boht
steamer	stoomskip	stohmskip
steersman	stuurman	steurma(h)n
stern	agterstewe	a(h)chte(r)rsteyye(r)
steward	hofmeester, opsigter	ho(r)fmeyste(r)r, opsichte(r)r
stewardess	hofmeesteres	ho(r)fmeyste(r)ress
stoker	stoker	stohke(r)r
tug	sleepboot	sleyp'boht
ventilator	lugvervarser	luchferfa(h)rse(r)r
voyage	seereis	seereyss
watch (aboard)	wag	vach
windward	loeisy	loo'isey

Aviation (Lug(skeep)vaart)

English	Afrikaans	Pronunciation
Area	oppervlakte	op'per-fla(h)kte(r)
Aerodrome	vliegbaan	fleechbahn
aviator	vlieër	flee'e(r)r
aeronaut	lugskipper	luchskippe(r)r
aeronautical	lugskeepvaart	luch-skeyp-fa(h)rrt
aviation	lug(skeep)vaart	luch(skeyp)fa(h)rrt
aeroplane	vliegmasjien, lugskip	fleech'ma(h)sheen, luch'skipp
aileron flap	afhangende rand	a(h)ff'ha(n)ng-e(r)nde(r) ra(h)nt
aeroplane fabric	fabrikaat, materiaal	fa(h)bree'kahtt, ma(h)teyr're(r)hah'l
balloon	lugballon, ballon	luch'ba(h)l'lonn, ba(h)l'lonn
balloonist	lugreisiger	luch'reysiche(r)r
babbit metal	witmetaal	vitt me(h)tahl
bed, the	plek	plek
—, engine	masjiene lê plek	masheene(r) le(h) ple(h)k
bi-plane	tweedekker	tvey'de(r)k'ke(r)r
brace	koppel	ko(r)p'pe(r)l
bracing wires	koppeldrade	ko(r)pp'pe(r)l drahde(r)
body	liggaam	lich'ahm

English.	Afrikaans.	Pronunciation.
body fuselage	liggaamsverstywing	lich'ahms-fe(r)rsteyving
boatshaped	bootsfatsoen	bohtsía(h)tsoon
bracing strut	koppelstut	ko(r)p'pe(r)lstutt
bar	bout	bo't
cam	kam	ka(h)m
cam shafts	kamaste	ka(h)mm'a(h)ste(r)
certificate	sertifikaat	se(r)rtiff'fe(r)kaht
—, a pilot's	'n stuurman *se* sertifikaat	(h)in steȗrma(h)n se(r) se(r)rte(r)fe(r) kaht
	die sertifikaat van 'n stuurman	dee se(r)rte(r)fe(r)kaht fa(h)n(h)in steȗrma(h)n
cockpit	hanemat	ha(h)ne(r)ma(h)t
crank	slinger	slinge(r)r (i as in din)
case, box	kas, doos	ka(h)ss, dohs
crank case	slingerdoos	slinge(r)r'dohs
cover	deksel, bedekking	dek'sell, be(r)dek'ing
control lever	hefboom beheer	he(h)ffbohm be(r)heyr
chord	koord	kohrt
climbing	klimmend	klimm'(h)ind
capacity	kapasiteit, bevoegdheid	ka(h)pa(h)'see-teyt, be(r)foh chd-heyt
dirigible (adj.)	bestuurbaar	be(r)steȗrbahr
dirigible (a.)	'n bestuurbare lugballon	(h)in be(r)steȗrbahre(r) luchba(h)l'lonn
dope	vernis	fe(h)rniss
engine	masjien	ma(h)sheen
— bed	masjiene lê plek	ma(h)sheene(r) le(h) ple(h)k
elevator	ligter	lich'te(r)r
fuel	brandstof	bra(h)nt'sto(r)ff
— pipe	— pyp	— -peyp
frame	raam	rahm
fin	vin	finn

English.	Afrikaans.	Pronunciation.
feed	perspomp, aanvoer-pyp	pe(r)rss'pomp, ahnfoorpeyp
fan	waaier	vaa'i-e(r)r
fittings	toebehore, bybehore	too'be(r)hohre(r), bey'be(r)hohre(r)
flying-school	vlieënde skool	flee'e(r)nde(r) skool
fuselage	verstywing	ferstey'ving
glider	glyer	chleye(r)r
gravity	swaartekrag	svahrte(r)kra(h)ch
hood	hoofdeksel	hohf'deksell
hinge	skarnier	ska(h)rr'neer
hand	hand	ha(h)nt
hand steering control	handstuurrad	ha(h)ntsteu͡r'ra(h)t
hydro-aeroplane	watervliegtuig	va(h)ter'fleechtuich
hub	naaf	nahff
landing gear	landing gereedskap	la(h)nd'ing-chereydska(h)p
machinery	masjienerie	ma(h)s'yeen-e(r)ree
monoplane	eendekker	eyndek'ke(r)r
minute	minuut	mineu͡t
needle	naald	nahlt
— valve	naaldklap	nahlt'kla(h)p
pipe	pyp	peyp
plug	prop	pro(h)p
pilot	stuurman	steu͡rma(h)n
propeller	drywer, skroef	dreyver, skroof
plane	vliegtuig	fleech-tuich
pulley	katrol	ka(h)tro(h)l
pressure	druk, aandrang	druk, ahndra(h)ng
rudder	roer	roor
rib	rib	rip
rudder-bar	roerbout	roor-bo't
revolutions	rewolusies	revoh'loo'-sees
shaft, axle, axis	as	a(h)ss
support	stut	stut
skid	briek	breek
seat	sitplek	sit'ple(r)k
sparking	vonk-ontsteking	fo(h)nk'o(h)nt-steeking

English.	Afrikaans.	Pronunciation.
sparking plug	vonkontsteking-prop	fo(h)nko(h)ntsteek-ingprop
steering-control	stuurrad, stuurwiel	steȗrr'rat, steȗr'veel
span	span	spa(h)nn
side-slip	syloslaat	sey'lohss-laht
stay wires	stutdrade	stutt'dra(h)de(r)
seaplane	watervliegtuig	va(h)te(r)r'fleech-tuich
spars (of plane)	sparre	spa(h)r re(r)
strut	stut	stut
single-seater	vir een persoon	fe(h)r eyn pe(r)r-sohn
shield	skerm	ske(r)r'm
stabiliser	stabiliseerder	sta(h)bill'ee-seyr-de(r)r
seat	sitplek	sit'ple(r)k
stay	stut	stut
steering wheel	stuurrad	steȗr'ra(h)tt
tail	stert	ste(r)rt
— skid	stert briekblok	ste(r)rt breek'blo(h)k
two-seater	'n tweesitplek vliegmasjien	i(h)n tvey-sitple(r)k -fleech-ma(h)-shee'n
throttle	lugpyp	luch'peyp
tail	stert	ste(r)rt
— fin	stertvin	ste(r)rt finn
tank	tenk, waterbak	tenk, va(h)ter-ba(h)k
tail area	stertoppervlakte	ste(r)rt'opper-fla(h)kte(r)r
tube	pyp	peyp
three-seater	'n lugskip met drie sitplekke	i(h)n luchskipp met dree sitplek'ke(r)
tri-plane	driedekker	dree'de(r)k'ke(r)r
valve	klap	kla(h)pp
wing	vlerk	flerr'k
— support	vleuelstut	flu(r)e(r)l-stutt
— spar	vleuelspar	flu(r)e(r)l-spa(h)rr

English.	Afrikaans.	Pronunciation.
wire	draad	draht
wing span	vleuelspan	flu(r)e(r)l-spa(h)nn
wind	wind	vint
— shield	windskèrm	vint'ske(r)r'm

Countries and Nations (Lande en Volke)

Africa	Afrika	a(h)f'reekah
Africander	Afrikaner	a(h)f'reekahner
African	Afrikaans	a(h)f'reekahns
America	Amerika	ahmey'reekah
American	Amerikaans	ahmey'reekahns
Asia	Asië	ah'see-e(r)
Australia	Australië	ohstrahlee-e(r)
Australian	Australiër	ohstrahlee-e(r)r
Belgium	België	bel'chee-e(r)
Belgian	Belgies	bel'chees
Canada	Kanada	kahnahdah
Cape, the	die Kaap	dee kahp
China	Sjiena	sheenah
Chinese	Sjinees	sheenees
country	land	la(h)nt
Cuba	Kuba	keûbah
Dane	Deen	deyn
Denmark	Denemarke	deyne(r)ma(h)rke(r)
Dutchman	Hollander	hol'la(h)n-de(r)r
empire	ryk	reyk
England	Engeland	eng'e(r)la(h)nt
English, the	die Engelse	dee'eng'e(r)lse(r)
Englishman	Engelsman	eng'e(r)lsma(h)n
Europe	Europa	u(r)rohpah
France	Frankryk	frahnk'reyk
French, the	die Franse	dee fra(h)nse(r)
Frenchman	Fransman	fra(h)nssma(h)n
Free State	Vrystaat	frey'staht
German	Duitser	duit'se(r)r
Germany	Duitsland	duits'la(h)nt
Great Britain	Groot Brittanje	chroot brit'ta(h)-nye(r)
Holland	Holland	hol'la(h)nt
Hungarian	Hongaar	honchahr

English.	Afrikaans.	Pronunciation.
Hungary	Hongarye	hongahrey'e(r)
India	Indië	indee-e(r)
Indian	Indiër, Indiaan	indee-e(r)r, indeehahn
Indies, East	Oos-Indië	ohs-indee-e(r)
—, West	Wes-Indië	ves-indee-e(r)
Ireland	Ierland	eer'la(h)nt
Irish	Iere	eer'e(r)
Irishman	Ier	eer'
Italian	Italiaan	eetahleeahn
Italy	Italië	eetahlee-e(r)
Japan	Japan	yahpa(h)n
Japanese	Japanees	yahpa(h)nees
kingdom	koninkryk	kohninreyk
New Zealand	Nu-Seeland	nu-seela(h)nt
Norway	Noorweë	nohrveye(r)
Norwegian	Noor	nohr
Russia	Rusland	russ'la(h)nt
Russian	Rus	russ
Scotchman	Skot	skot
Scotland	Skotland	skot'la(h)nt
Spain	Spanje	spa(h)n'ye(r)
Spaniard	Spanjaard	spa(h)n'yahrt
Swede	Sweed	sveyt
Sweden	Swede	sveyde(r)
Swiss	Switser	svit'se(r)r
Switzerland	Switserland	svit'se(r)rla(h)nt
Turk	Turk	turk
Turkey	Turkye	turkaye(r)
Transvaal	Transvaal	trans'fahl
Union of South Africa	Unie van Suid Afrika	eunee fa(h)n suit ahfrika(h)
United States of America	Verenigde State van Amerika	fereenichte(r) stahte(r) fa(h)n a(h)meyreekah

Towns, etc. (Stede, ens.). **(South Africa**—Suid Afrika)

Aberdeen	Aberdeen	a(h)be(r)rdeyn
Alice	Alice	a(h)l'lis
Aliwal North	Aliwal Noord	a(h)leeva(h)l nohrt

English.	Afrikaans.	Pronunciation.
Barberton	Barberton	ba(h)rr'be(r)rto(h)n
Beaconsfield	Beaconsfield	beeko(h)nsfeeld
Beaufort West	Beaufort Wes	beaufort ves
Bedford	Bedford	bet'fo(h)rt
Bethlehem	Bethlehem	be(r)tleehemm
Bethulie	Bethulie	be(r)too'lee
Bloemfontein	Bloemfontein	bloom'fonteyn
Bloemhof	Bloemhof	bloom'ho(r)ff
Bulawayo	Bulayayo	boola(h)waa'i'ho(h)
Butterworth	Butterworth	butterr'worth
Caledon	Caledon	ka(h)le(r)do(h)nn
Cape Town	Kaapstad	kahpsta(h)t
Cathcart	Cathcart	kethka(h)rt
Charlestown	Charlestown	sjahrlstown
Christiana	Christiana	kriss'tee-ah-ma(h)
Colenso	Colenso	ko(h)lens'oh
Colesberg	Colesberg	ko(h)ls-berr-ch
Cradock	Cradock	kra(h)dok
Dordrecht	Dordrecht	dorr'dre(r)rch
Dundee	Dundee	dunn'dee
Durban	Durban	durr'bann
East London	Oos Londen	ohss' london
Edenburg	Edenburg	eyde(r)n'berch
Ermelo	Ermelo	e(r)rme(r)lo
Estcourt	Estcourt	est'ko(r)rt
Fauresmith	Fauresmith	faw're(r)-smith
Ficksburg	Ficksburg	fiksburch
Fort Beaufort	Fort Beaufort	fort'bo(h)fo(r)rt
Fort Victoria	Fort Victoria	fo(r)rt'fiktooree-ah
Fouriesburg	Fouriesburg	fooreesburch
George	George	cher(r)orch
Germiston	Germiston	chermisstonn
Glencoe	Glencoe	gle(r)nn'ko
Graaffreinet	Graaffreinet	chrahff'ree-nett
Grahamstown	Grahamstown / Gramstad	chra(h)mms'sta(h)t
Greytown	Greytown	greytown
Gwelo	Gwelo	gvel'low
Harrismith	Harrismith	ha(h)rree'smith

English.	Afrikaans.	Pronunciation.
Heidelberg	Heidelberg	heyde(r)l'berch
Hopefield	Hopefield	hohpfeeld
Howick	Howick	how'ik
Indwe	Indwe	i(h)nn'dwee
Irene	Irene	eye'reen-e(r)
Jagersfontein	Jagersfontein	ya(h)che(r)rs'-fo(h)nteyn
Johannesburg	Johannesburg	yo(h)a(h)n'ne(r)ss-burrch
Keetmanshoop	Keetmanshoop	keytma(h)nshohp
Kimberley	Kimberley	kimbe(r)rley
Kingwilliamstown	Kingwilliamstown	kingwilliamstown
Klerksdorp	Klerksdorp	kle(r)rks'do(r)rp
Kroonstad	Kroonstad	krohn'sta(h)t
Krugersdorp	Krugersdorp	kreûche(r)rs-do(r)rp
Ladybrand	Ladybrand	leydee'bra(h)nt
Ladysmith	Ladysmith	leydee'smith
Lichtenburg	Lichtenburg	lich'te(r)n-burch
Lydenburgh	Lydenburg	leyde(r)n'burch
Machadadorp	Machadodorp	ma(h)sja(h)doh-do(r)rp
Mafeking	Mafeking	ma(h)fe(r)-king
Malmesbury	Malmesbury	ma(h)lms-burree
Maseru	Maseru	ma(h)ss'ee-roo
Middelburg	Middelburg	mid'de(r)l-burch
Molteno	Molteno	mo(r)l'teen-o
Mosselbay	Mosselbaai	mosse(r)l-baa'i
Newcastle	Newcastle	newka(h)sse(r)l
Oudtshoorn	Oudtshoorn	ohtshohrr'n
Paarl	(Paarl) Perel	perr'e(r)l
Parys	Parys	pa(h)rr'eyss
Pietermaritzburg	Pietermaritsburg	peeter-ma(h)rits-burch
Pietersburg	Pietersburg	peete(r)rsburch
Port Alfred	Port Alfred	port-a(h)lf're(r)t
Potchefstroom	Potchefstroom	pot'jefs'stro(h)m
Pretoria	Pretoria	pree-to(h)r'ree-ha
Prieska	Prieska	prees'ka(h)
Prince Albert	Prince Albert	prinss a(h)lbe(r)rt
Queenstown	Queenstown	kveens'town

English.	Afrikaans.	Pronunciation.
Richmond	Richmond	risjmont
Riversdale	Riversdale	riversdeyll
Robertson	Robertson	rob'be(r)rts-so(h)nn
Rustenburg	Rustenbyrg	russ'te(r)n-burch
Salisbury	Salisbury	sawls'burree
Senekal	Senekal	senn'nee-ka(h)l
Somerset East	Somerset Oos	sohmersett-ohss
Somerset West	Somerset Wes	sohmersett-vess
Standerton	Standerton	sta(h)nderto(h)nn
Stellenbosch	Stellenbos	ste(r)lle(r)nbo(h)ss
Swellendam	Swellendam	svelle(r)n'da(h)mm
Tarkastad	Tarkastad	tarrka(h)sta(h)tt
Uitenhage	Uitenhage	uit'te(r)n-ha(h)-che(r)
Upington	Upington	upington
Victoria West	Victoria Wes	fiktoreeah wes
Volksrust	Volksrust	fo(r)lksruss
Vrede	Vrede	freyde(r)
Vryburg	Vryburg	freyburch
Vryheid	Vryheid	frey'heyt
Warrenton	Warrenton	va(h)rentonn
Wellington	Wellington	vel'ling-tonn
Wepener	Wepener	vep'pe(r)nahr
Willowmore	Willowmore	vill'o-mohr
Winburg	Winburg	vinn'burch
Windhoek	Windhoek	vint'hook
Worcester	Worcester	voos'terr
Zastron	Zastron	sa(h)ss'tro(h)nn
Zeerust	Zeerust, Seerus	seeruss

Commercial and Trading Terms (Handels- en Koopmansterme)

Account, to settle an	'n rekefenning vereffeni	-(h)n reyke(r)ning fe(r)reffe(r)n
—, to close an	— rekening afsluit	i(h)nreyke(r)ning(h) fsluit
—, current	— lopende rekening	i(h)nlohpe(r)nde(r) reyke(r)ning
—, joint	gesamentlike rekening	che(r)sahme(r)nt-like(r) reyke(r)n-ing

English.	Afrikaans.	Pronunciation.
account of sale	verkooprekening	ferkohpreyke(r)n-ing
acknowledgment	ontvangsberig	ontfa(h)ngsber'rich
advice, letter of	adviesbrief	a(h)tfeessbreef
advance (of money)	voorskot	fohrskot
agency	agentskap	a(h)chentska(h)p
agent	agent	a(h)chent
apprentice	leerjonge	leyryo(h)nge(r)
arrangement	skikking	skik'king
arrear, in	agter	a(h)chter
assets	boedel, bate	boode(r)l, ba(h)te(r)
authorise, to	magtig	ma(h)chtich
average (to ships)	avery	a(h)fe(r)rey
balance	balans, saldo	ba(h)la(h)ns, sa(h)l-doh
— of account	saldo, rekening	sa(h)ldoh reyke(r)n-ing
— sheet	kasrekening ba-lans rekening	ka(h)ss'reyke(r)ning ba(h)la(h)nsreyk-ke(r)ning
banking	bankwese, ban-kier sake	ba(h)nkveyse(r), ba(h)nkeer'sah-ke(r)
bearer (of cheque)	toonder	tohnde(r)r
bill, accommodation	formawissel	formahvisse(r)l
— at sight	wissel op sig	visse(r)l op sich
— at three month's date	—, drei maande na sig	—, dree mahnde(r) nah sich
— of exchange	wisse l(brief)	visse(r)l (breeff)
— of lading	vragbrief	fra(h)chbreeff
— of fare	spyslys	speyss'leyss
— of credit	skatkisbiljet	ska(h)tkissbilyet
— of parcels	faktuur	fa(h)ktêûr
— of sale	koopbrief	kohpbreef
— of health	gesondheidspas	che(r)sontheyts-pa(h)ss
— book	wisselboek	visse(r)lbook
— broker	makelaar in wissels	ma(h)ke(r)lahr in visse(r)ls
bond, in	in entrepot	in a(h)ntre(r)poh

English.	Afrikaans.	Pronunciation.
bonded goods	goedere in 'n pakhuis	choode(r)re(r) in i(h)n pa(h)khuis
book-keeper	boekhouer	boo'khoe(r)r
brokerage	makelaarsloon	ma(h)ke(r)lahrs-lohn
business, wholesale	groothandel	chroht'ha(h)nde(r)l
—, retail	kleinhandel	kleyn'ha(h)nde(r)l
buyer	kooper	kohpe(r)r
carriage-(post)-paid	vragvry	fra(h)chfrey
cartage	vrag, vraggeld	fra(h)ch, fra(h)ch'-chelt
catalogue	katalogus	kahtahloh'chuss
charter a ship, to	'n skip huur	i(h)n skip heūr
claim, to send in a	'n eis instel	i(h)n eyss instel
	'n aanspraak maak op	i(h)n ahnsprahk mahk op
—, to make good a	'n eis goedmaak	i(h)n eyss goht-ma(h)k
clearing-house	verrekeningskantoor	ferreyke(r)nings-ka(h)ntohr
clerk	klerk	kle(r)rk
company, limited	maatskappy, beperk	mahtska(h)ppey, be(r)perk
—, joint-stock	—, op aandele	—, op ahndeyle(r)
complaint	klag	kla(h)ch
contract	kontrak	kontra(h)k
cost, insurance and freight	koste, versekering en vrag	koste(r), fe(r)rsey-kering en fra(h)ch
credit balance	batige saldo	ba(h)tiche(r) sa(h)l-doh
creditor	krediteur	krey'deetu(r)r
custom-house	doeanekantoor	dooahne(r)ka(h)n-tohr
customs-officer	doeane amptenaar	dooanne(r) a(h)mp-te(r)nahr
customs duties	doeaneregte	dooahne(r)rechte(r)
damages	skadevergoeding	ska(h)de(r)ferchood-ing
—, to claim	eis vir skadevergoeding	eyss fir ska(h)de(r)-ferchooding

English.	Afrikaans.	Pronunciation.
dated at three months'	drie maande na dato	dree mahnde(r) na(h) da(h)too
debit and credit	debet en krediet	de(h)be(r)t en kre(r) deet
debtor	skuldenaar, debiteur	skulde(r)nahr, de(r) beetu(r)r
deliver, to	lewer	leve(r)r
delivered free	posvry aflevering	possfrey a(h)fley-ve(r)ing
demurrage (days of)	lêdae	lai(r)da(h)e(r)
director	bestuurder, direkteur	be(r)steũrde(r)r, deere(r)ktu(r)r
discount	korting, afslag	korting, a(h)fs-la(h)ch
—, to	inwissel, diskonteer	invisse(r)l, dis-ko(h)nteyrr
dividend warrant	diwident waarborg	deeveedent vahr-borch
dock and harbour dues	dokgeld	dok'chelt
double entry	dubbel boekhou	dubbe(r)l boo'khou
drawer	trekker	trek'ke(r)r
duty, export	uitvoerreg	uitfoorrech
— free	vry van invoer-regte	frey fa(h)n in'foor'-rechte(r)
—, import	invoerreg	in'foorrech
—, liable to	onderhewig aan in-voerreg	onderhevich ahn infoorrech
enclosed	ingeslote	inge(r)slohte(r)
enclosure	bylae	beylahe(r)
endorse, to	endosseer	endosseyrr
endorsement	endossement	e(h)ndosse(r)ment
exchange (the)	beurs	bu(r)rss
firm	firma	firmah
forwarding	versending, afsend-ing	fe(r)rsending, a(h)f-sending
— agent	ekspediteur	ekspeydeetu(r)r
free on board (f.o.b.)	vry aan boord	frey ahn bohrt
gross weight	brutogewig	breũtoh-che(r)vich
guarantee	waarborg	vahrrborch

English.	Afrikaans.	Pronunciation.
guarantor	borg	borch
I.O.U.	ek is aan jou verskuldig	e(r)k iss ahn yoo fe(r)rskuldich
import and export	invoer en uitvoer	infoor en uit'foor
information	informasie	informahsee
inquire, to	vra	frah
inquiry	navraag	nahfrahch
insurance, marine	seeversekering	seyferseykering
— broker	assuransie-makelaar	a(h)sseura(h)nsee-mahke(r)lahr
— company	versekering-maatskappy	ferseykering-mahtska(h)ppey
— policy	versekering-polis	ferseykering-pohliss
— premium	versekering-premie	ferseykering-preymee
insure against, to	versekering teen	ferseykering teyn
interest, rate of	rentekoers, rentevoet	rente(r)kohrs, ren'te(r)foo-t
introduce, to	invoer	infoor
introduction	introduksie	introduksee
landing charges	koste van landing	kosste(r) fa(h)n la(h)nding
liabilities	verpligtinge	fe(r)rplichting-e(r)
lighterage	ligtergeld	lichterchelt
load, to	laai	laa'i
loss	verlies	fe(r)leess
manager	bestuurder, direkteur	be(r)steurde(r)r, deerektu(r)r
market	mark	ma(h)rk
—, cattle	veemark	feyma(h)rk
— day	markdag	ma(h)rkda(h)ch
— dues	mark-gelde	ma(h)rk-che(r)lde(r)
—, foreign	buitelandse mark	buite(r)la(h)ndse(r) ma(h)r-k
—, home	binnelands verkeer	binne(r)la(h)nts fe(r)rkeyr
—, London	Londense mark	londe(r)nse(r) ma(h)rk
— master	markmeester	ma(h)rk meyste(r)r
— place	markplein	ma(h)rkpleyn

English.	Afrikaans.	Pronunciation.
market price	markprys	ma(h)rkpreyss
negotiable, saleable	gangbaar	cha(h)ngbahr
offer (for sale), to	te koop aanbied	te(r) kohp ahnbeet
offers	aanbiedinge	ahnbeedinge(r)
order, to	bestel	be(r)ste(r)l
packing	inpak	inpa(h)k
partnership	vennootskap	fe(r)nnohtska(h)p
payable at sight	betaalbaar op sig	be(r)tahlbahr opsich
port of delivery	losplek	lossple(r)k
price, cost	inkoopsprys	inkohps'preyss
— list	pryslys	preysleys
—, selling	verkoopsprys	fe(r)rkohpspreyss
—, wholesale	groothandelsprys	chrohtha(h)nde(r)l-spreys
quotation (of price)	pryskwotasie	preysskwo(h)ta(h)-see
—, lowest	uiterste prys	uite(r)rste(r) preyss
receipt	ontvangs	ontfa(h)ngs
reduction	vermindering	ferminde(r)ring
register, to	registreer	re(r)che(r)streyrr
registered letter	geregistreerde brief	ge(r)re(r)che(r)-streyr de(r) breeff
registered tonnage	tonneinhoud	tonne(r)inhout
rent	huur	hêûr
representative	verteenwoordiger	ferteynvohrdiche(r)r
salesman (seller)	verkoper, winkel-bediende	ferkohpe(r)r, vin-ke(r)lbe(r)deen-de(r)
settling days	betaal-dae	be(r)tahlda(h)e(r)
shares, debenture	aandele, skuldbe-wyse	ahndeyle(r), skult-be(r)veyse(r)
shares, ordinary	aandele, gewone	ahndeyle(r) che(r)-vohne(r)
—, preference	preferensie aandele	preyferrensee ahn-deyle(r)
—, railway	spoorwegaandele	spohrve(r)chahn-de(r)le(r)
ship, to	inskeep, verskeep	inskeyp, ferskeyp
ship-broker	skeepsmakelaar	skeypsma(h)ke(r)-lahr

English.	Afrikaans.	Pronunciation.
shipping charges	inskepingskoste	inskeypingskosste(r)
-- house	seehandel	seyha(h)nde(r)l
solvent	in staat om te betaal solvent	in staht om te(r) be(r)tahl
speculator	spekulant	spekéula(h)nt
stock	voorraad, kapitaal	fohr'raht, ka(h)pee-tahl
stock-broker	makelaar in effekte	ma(h)ke(r)lahr in e(r)ffe(r)kte(r)
stowage	bêreplek, bêregeld	bai(r)e(r)plai(r)k, bai(r)e(r)che(r)lt
telegraphic address	telegram-adres	te(r)le(r)chra(h)m'-andres
towing charges	sleeploon	sleyplohn
underwriter	versekeraar	ferseyke(r)r'rahr
unloading	aflaai	a(h)fflaa'i
wharf	werf	verf
wharfage	kaaigeld	kaa'ichelt
wholesale prices	groothandelspryse	chrohtha(h)nde(r)ls preyse(r)
winding-up	likwidasie	lik'vee-dahsee

Gold and Diamond Industries Terms (Terme in dic Goud en Diamant industriee)

[Term en dee ghote en deea(h)ma(h)nt industreee(r)]

alluvial diamond	aliuwiaal diamant	a(h)looveea(h)l deea(h)ma(h)nt
— diggings	— delwerye	— delverayeh
amalgam	amalgama ; metaal-mengsel	a(h)ma(h)lghama ; meta(h)lmengsill
amalgamator	metaalmenger	meta(h)lmeng-er
battery	battery	ba(h)tteray
carat	karaat	ka(h)ra(h)t
diamond cutter	diamantslyper	deea(h)ma(h)nt-slayper
dynamite	dinamiet	deenameet
engine-room	masjienekamer	machinaka(h)mer

English.	Afrikaans.	Pronunciation.
flaw	reet ; bars	reet ("ee" sound as in *deer*); ba(h)rs
fuse	lont	lont
gold	goud	ghote or chote
level	vlak ; waterpas	fla(s)k ; va(h)ter-pass
mine	myn	mane
— manager	mynbestuurder	manebesteûrder
— surveyor	mynmeter	manemey(h)ter
— captain	mynkaptein	maneka(h)ptane
miner's phthisis	myntering	manetearing
— — Board	mynteringraad	manetearingra(h)d
mining commissioner	mynkommissaris	manekommisa(h)ris
mining plant	mynapparaat	manea(h)pera(h)t
overwind	oorwinding	(m)oarvin/ding
polish	opwrywing	opvrayving
props	stutte	stutte ("u" sounded like "u" in *ultra*)
prospecting	prospekteer	prospekteer
reduction works	reduksiewerke	reduckseeverke(r)
— officer	reduksie offisier	— offe(r)sea-r
rough diamond	ru diamant	reû deea(h)ma(h)nt
shaft	disselboom ; skag	disselboom ("oo" like "oo" in *moor*; scha(h)ch ("ch" sound as "ch" in Scotch *loch*)
shift	skof	scoff
skip	mynkarretjie	maneka(h)retyee
sort	uitsoek	uitsook
stopes	myntonnel	manetonnel
strike	staking	sta(h)keng
surface	oppervlakte	opperfla(h)kte(r)
tanks	tenks	tenks
timekeeper	tydregelaar	taitrechlaar(d)
wash	was	vas
winding gear	hystoestel	hays-too-stel

Cycling (Ry met 'n Fiets)

[Ray met i(h)n feets]

English.	Afrikaans.	Pronunciation.
Acetylene	asetileen	a(h)se(r)teeleyn
axle	as	a(h)s
ball bearings	koeëlasse, koeël-draers	koo'e(r)la(h)sse(r), koo'e(r)ldrahe(r)rs
bearings	draagplekke	drahchple(r)kke(r)
bell	bel, klokkie	bell, klok'kee
bicycle, " bike "	rywiel, fiets	rey'veel, feets
bolt	bout	boat
brake	briek	breek
caution	waarsku	vahrskeû
cement	sement	se(r)ment
chain	ketting	ketting
chainless	sonder ketting	so(h)nde(r)r ketting
chain-wheel	kettingrad	kettingra(h)t
cone	kegel	keyche(r)l
connection	koppeling, verbind-ing	koppe(r)ling, fer-binding
crank	slinger, handvatsel	slinge(r)r, ha(h)nt-fa(h)tse(r)l
cyclist, lady	fietster	feetste(r)r
cyclist	fietser	feetser
cycle, to	fiets	feets
cycle-maker	rywielmaker	reyveelma(h)ke(r)r
cycle-shop	rywielhandelsplek	reyveelha(h)nde(r)l-splek
cycle race	fietswedstryd	feetsve(r)tstreyt
cycle-tour	fietstoer	feetstoor
cycling-track	fietsbaan	feetsbahn
cyclometer	sieklometer	seeklohmeyte(r)r
danger	gevaar	che(r)fahr
dismount, to	afklim	a(h)fklim
dress-guard	kleedbeskermer	kleydbe(r)skerme(r)
electro-plate, to	versilwer, vernikkel	fersilver, fernikkel
enamel	enemmel	enem'me(r)l
foot-rest	voetstut	footstut
foot-step	trapper	tra(h)p'pe(r)r

English.	Afrikaans.	Pronunciation.
fork	vork	fork
frame	raam	rahm
friction	wrywing	vreyving
gear, gearing	tandrat, versnelling	ta(h)ntra(h)t, ferse(r)ling
—, high	hoë versnelling	hoher(r) fersne(r)l'-ling
—, low	lae versnelling	la(h)e(r) fersne(r)l'-ling
gear-case	kettingkas	kettingka(h)s
handles, grips	handvatsels	ha(h)ntfa(h)tse(r)ls
handlebar	stuurstok	steursto(r)k
hub	wielnaaf	veelnahff
indiarubber	gomlastiek, rubber	chom-la(h)steek, rubbe(r)r
— solution	solusie	so(h)lu(h)see
inner tube	binneband	binne(r)ba(h)nt
knapsack	knapsak	k-na(h)psa(h)k
lamp	lamp	la(h)mp
— bracket	hakie vir die lamp	hahkee fer dee la(h)mp
— wick	lamppit	la(h)mp'pitt
link	skakel	ska(h)ke(r)l
lighting-up time	lamp opsteek tyd	la(h)mp op steyk teyt
light-up, to	lig-maak	lich-ma(h)k
lubricator	smeepot	smeyrr'po(h)tt
— protector	— deksel	— de(r)kse(r)l
leather (chamois)	leer, (gems-)	leyr (che(r)ms-)
luggage-carrier	bagasiedraer	ba(h)chah'see-dra(h)e(r)r
map	landkaart	la(h)nt-kahrt
mount	opklim	opklimm
mudguard	modderskerm	mod'de(r)r-ske(r)rm
nut	moer	moor
oil for burning	brandolie	bra(h)nt'ohlee
oil for lubricating	smeerolie	smeyrr'ohlee
oilcan	oliekan	ohleeka(h)n
outer-cover	mantel	ma(h)nte(r)l

English.	Afrikaans.	Pronunciation.
pedal	pedaal, trap	pe(r)dahl, tra(h)p
pedal-rubber	pedaal gomlastiek	pe(r)dahl chom-la(h)steek
pump	pomp	pomp
pump-tube	pompslang	pomp-sla(h)ng
pump up, inflate	oppomp	oppo(h)mp
rags, old	ou lappe	oh la(h)p'pe(r)
removable	afneembaar, verplaasbaar	a(h)fneymbahr, ferplahsbahr
repair, to	repareer	re(r)pa(h)reyr
repairing outfit	reparasiedoos	re(r)pa(h)rahsee-dohs
rim	rand	ra(h)nt
saddle	saal	sahl
saddle-bag	saalsak	sahlsa(h)k
saddle-pillar (-tree)	saalboom	sahlbohm
screw	skroef	skroof
screw-bolt of the chain	kettingboutjie	ke(r)t'tingboutyee
screwdriver	skroewedraaier	skroove(r)drah'i-e(r)r
screw, to	vasskroef	fa(h)sskroof
spanner	skroefsleutel, skroefhamer	skroofsleûte(r)l, skroofha(h)me(r)r
speed-gear	dryfwerk	dreyfve(r)rk
spokes	speke	speyke(r)
spring	veer	feyrr
start off	vertrek	fertrek
steer, to	stuur	steûr
strap (leather)	leer-riem	leyr'reem
take to pieces	uitmekaarhaal	uitme(r)kahrhahl
tighten-up	vaster maak	fa(h)ste(r) mahk
toe clip	toonhak	tohnha(h)k
tricycle	driewieler	dree'veeler
trousers' clips	broek vere	broo'k-feyre(r)
tube, inner	binneband	binne(r)ba(h)nt
— (outer cover)	buiteband	buite(r)ba(h)nt
tyre (pneumatic)	lugband	luchba(h)nt
unscrew, to	losskroef	loss'skroof
valve	klappie, klep	kla(h)pee, kle(r)p

English.	Afrikaans.	Pronunciation.
valve-cap	klepkappie	kle(r)pka(h)p'pee
valve-tubing	klappie buiswerk	kla(h)pee buis-ve(r)rk
wallet	sak	sa(h)k
wheels	wiele	veele(r)
wheel (front)	voorwiel	fohrr'veel
— (back)	agyerwiel	a(h)chte(r)r-veel

Motoring Terms (Moter benamings)

Accumulator	akkumulator	a(h)kkeûmeûlah tor
battery	battery	ba(h)tterey
brake collar (steel)	remband (staal)	remba(h)nt (stahl)
cam	kam	ka(h)m
carburettor	karburateur, vergasser	ka(h)rbeûrah'tu(r), fercha(h)ss-e(r)r
chain adjustment	die ketting span	dee ke(r)tting spa(h)nn
claw	tang, vork	ta(h)ng, fork
contact breaker (trembler)	automatiese stroomsluiter	o(h)to(h)ma(h)-teese(r) strohm-sluite(r)r
driver, chauffeur	moterdrywer	mo(h)te(r)rdrey-ve(r)r
driving pinion	dryfkamwiel	dreyf' ka(h)mveel
elbow	elmboog	elmbohch
electric (-al)	elektries	elektreess
electricity	elektrisiteit	elektreeseeteyt
electric motor	elektriese moter	elektreese(r) mohter
evaporate, to	uitwasem, verdamp	uitva(h)se(r)m, ferda(h)mp
exhaust	uitlaat	uitlaht
exhaust-box, silencer	knalpot, skokdemper	kna(h)lpo(h)t, skok'demper
exhaust cam	afvoerkam	a(h)f-foor-ka(h)m
exhaust-valve	afvoerklappie	a(h)f-foor-kla(h)p'-pee
feed-pump	perspomp	persspo(h)mp
fill, to	vol maak, vul	fo(h)l mahk, fu(r)l

English.	Afrikaans.	Pronunciation.
flaw	spleet, bars	spleyt, ba(h)rs
fly-wheel	vliegwiel	fleechveel
garage	moterhuis	mohterhuis
gas	gas	cha(h)s
generator	gassuier	cha(h)s-suie(r)r
goggles	stofbril	sto(h)fbrill
gradient	styging	steyching
handle, starting	die in beweging-bring handvatsel	dee in be(r)vey-chingbring ha(h)ntfa(h)ts-se(r)l
hooter, horn	toeter, fluit	tooter, fluit
horse-power	perdekrag	pe(r)rde(r)kra(h)ch
ignition	ontbranding, ont-steking	ontbra(h)nding, ontsteyking
leakage	lekkasie	le(r)k-ka(h)see
lever handle	hefboomhandvatsel	he(r)fbohmha(h)nt-fa(h)tse(r)l
lever	hefboom	he(r)fbohm
light up!	draai aan die lig!	drah'ia(h)n dee lich
motor	moter	mohte(r)r
packing	digmaak goed	dichmahk choot
petrol	petroleum, bensien	petrohlyum,benseen
pressure	druk	druk
—, high	hoë drukking	hc(h)e(r) drukking
—, low	lae druk	la(h)e(r) druk
rack	pynbank, rak	peynba(h)nk, ra(h)k
reservoir	vergaarbak, reservoir	ferchahrba(h)k, re-se(r)rvaw(r)r
reversing gear	agterwaartse ver-snelling	achtervahrtse(r) fersne(r)ling
sparking-plug	vonkontsteking-prop	fo(h)nko(h)ntsteyk-ingprop
speed, full	volle mag, volle vaart	fo(h)le(r) ma(h)ch, fo(h)le(r) fahrt
—, high	hoë snelheid	hohe(r) sne(r)lheyt
—, low	minder (snelheid) vaart	minder fa(h)rt
speed-changing	snelheidsverander-ing	sne(r)lheydsfer-a(h)ndering

English.	Afrikaans.	Pronunciation.
speed-changing gear	gangwissel	cha(h)ngvisse(r)l
starting gear	dryfwerk	dreyfverk
steering bar	stuurstang	steu͡rsta(h)ng
tap	tap, kraan	ta(h)p, krahn
trembler	triller	triller

Wireless and Electrical Terms (Draadlose en Elektriese Terme)

accumulator	ophoper	ophooper ("oo" has "oo" sound as in *moor*)
aerial	in die lug ; opvanger	en dee luch ; opfa(h)nger
— circuit	lugomtrek	luchomtrek
alternating current	afwisselende stroom	a(h)fvissellende(r)
ammeter	ammeter	a(h)mmeter
amperage	amperkrag	a(h)mperkra(h)ch
ampere	amper	a(h)mper
amplifier	vergroter	ferchrohter
anode	anode	a(h)no(h)de(r)
atmospherics	dampkringe	da(h)mpkrenge(r)
cable	kabel	ka(h)bel
capacity	inhoud	inhoud
carrier wave	dragolf	dra(h)cholf
choke	verstik	ferstik
condenser	kondensator	kondensa(h)tor
conductor	afleier	a(h)flayer
coupling	verbinding	ferbinding
crystal detector	kristal ontdekker	krista(h)l ontdecker
current	stroom	stro(h)m
direct current	direktestroom	deerekte(r)stro(h)m
dynamo	dinamo	deena(h)mo
electrode	elektrode	elektro(h)de(r)
electrolyte	elektroliet	elektro(h)leet
electron	elektron	electron
ether	eter	eeter
farad	farad	farad

English.	Afrikaans.	Pronunciation.
filament	draadjie	dra(h)dyee
— resistance	weerstand draadjie	veersta(h)nd dra(h)-dyee
frame aerial	raamopvanger	ra(h)mopfa(h)nger
frequency	vermenigvuldigheid	fermenichfilldich-hate
galvanometer	galvanometer	cha(h)lfa(h)no(h)-meter
generator	voortbrenger	fohrtbrenger
grid	rooster	ro(h)ster
— circuit	— omtrek	omtrek
— condenser	— kondensator	kondensa(h)tor
— control	— kontrole	controlle(r)
— current	— stroom	strohm
— leak	— lek	leck
— rectification	— rektifikasie	rectifika(h)see
heterodyne	heterodiene	heterodeene
high frequency	hoogherhaaldheid	hoochherha(h)ld-haid
— — amplifier	versterker	ferst(h)erker
— — choke	verstikker	verstikker
— — transformer	vervormer	ferform-mer
— tension	hoëspanning	hooehspa(h)nning
— — battery	battery	ba(h)tteray
hydrometer	hidrometer	heedro(h)meter
impedance	vertrager	fertra(h)cher
inductance	induksie	inducksee
insulation	insolasie	eesola(h)see
insulator	insolator	eesola(h)tor
interference	inmenging	inmenging
jamming	klemming	klemming
kilowatt	kilowat	keelovat
loading coil	ladingdraad	la(h)dingdra(h)t
loose coupling	losseverbinder	losse(r)ferbin-der
loud speaker	luidspreker	luidspreeker
low frequency	laagherhaaldheid	la(h)chherha(h)ld-hade
— — amplifier	laagversterker	la(h)chferste(h)rker
magnetism	magnetiesekrag	machnea(r)teese(r)-kra(h)ch

English.	Afrikaans.	Pronunciation
mast	mas	mass
megohm	megoom	mechoom
microfarad	mikrofarad	meecrowfa(h)ra(h)d
microphone	mikrofoon	meecrohfohn
milliampere	milliamper	milliea(h)mper
modulation	stemwisseling ; modulasie	ste(h)mvisse(r)iling modula(h)sie
morse code	morskode	morsek(h)ode(r)
natural	natuurlike	nateurlike(r)
— wave length	— golflengte	cholflengte(r)
negative	negatief	nechateef
— pole	negatiewe pool	nechateevah pohl
— potential	— potensiaal	potenseeahl
— resistance	— weerstand	veersta(h)nd
note magnifier	nootversterker	nootferst(h)erker
ohm	ohm	ohm
open circuit	opeomtrek	ohpe(r)omtrek
oscillate	slinger	sling(h)er
oscillation	slingering	sling(h)ering
period	periode	peereeohde(r)
phone	foon	fohn
plate	plaat	pla(h)t
— current	— stroom	strohm
— voltage	elektriese krag in wolts uitgedruk	elektree se(r)krach i(h)n vots uitchedruk ("u" like "u" in *mud*)
plug	prop	prop
positive	positief	posseeteef
power	krag	kra(h)ch
— valve	klep	kl(h)ep
primary cell	primêresel	preemarecell
radio	straal	stra(h)l
reaction	reaksie	reea(h)ksee
— condenser	kondensator	condensa(h)tor
rectifier	verbeteraar	ferbeytera(h)r
reflection	refleksie	refleksee
regeneration	regenerasie	rechenera(h)see
relay station	wisselstasie	visselsta(h)see
resonance	weerklank	veerkla(h)nt

English.	Afrikaans.	Pronunciation.
rheostat	reostat	rheostat
self-capacity	selfinhoud	selfi(h)nhoud
— -inductance	self-induksie	self-inducksee
short circuit	kortomtrek	kortomtrek
— waves	kort golfies	kort cholfees
simultaneous broadcasting	tegelyktydige uitsaaiing	te(r)che(r)laketaydiche(r) uitsighing
smoothing circuit	gladde omtrek	chla(h)dde(r) omtrek
studio	atelier	a(h)telleer
telephone	telefoon	telle(r)fohn
television	televisioen	telefeeseeoon
tight coupling	nou koppelketting	no koppelketting
time signal	tyd sein	taid sane
tone	toon	tohn
transmission	versending	fersending
transmitter	versender	fersender
tuner	stemmer	ste(h)mmer
tuning coil	stemdraad	ste(h)m dra(h)d
ultra short waves	baie kort golfies	bye-e(r) court cholfees
unidirectional	eenrigtend	eynrichtinned
unit	eenheid	eynhade
vacuum	lugledig	luchleydich
valve	klep	clep
— amplifier	versterker	fe(h)rste(h)rker
— detector	ontdekker	ontdekker
— oscillator	slinger	slinger
— receiver	opvanger	opva(h)nger
variometer	variometer	variometer
velocity	snelheid	snelhate
vernier	vernier	fernier (like "ier" in *bier*)
volt	wolt	volt
voltmeter	woltmeter	voltmeter
watt	wat	va(h)t
watt-hour	uurwat	uurva(h)t

English.	Afrikaans.	Pronunciation.
watt-meter	watmeter	va(h)tmeter
waves	golwe	cholve(r)
wavelength	golflengte	cholflengte(r)
wavemeter	golfmeter	cholfmeter
wet battery	nat battery	na(h)t ba(r)teray
wireless	draadloos	dra(h)dlohs
zero	sero ; nul.	sero ; nul(ler)

Photography (Fotografie)

The amateur	die amateur	dee a(h)ma(h)tu(r)r
backgrounds	agtergronde	a(h)chte(r)r-chronde(r)
—, cloth	—, laken	—, lahke(r)n
backing paper	fotografiepapier	fohtohchrahfee'-pahpeer
bulging	uitpeulpapier	uitpu(r)l'pahpeer
burnisher	blinkmaker	blinkmahke(r)r
camera	kamera	ka(h)me(r)rah
camera-bellows	kamera blasbalk	ka(h)me(r)rah blahsba(h)lk
camera-portrait	kamera portret	ka(h)me(r)rah portre(r)t
cutting-moulds	synvorms	sneyfo(h)rms
dark-room lamp	donkerkamer lamp	donkerka(h)me(r)r la(h)mp
dark slide, double	donker skuifpla-atjie (dubbel)	donker skuifplaht-yee
develop, to	ontwikkel	ontvikke(r)l
dipper	skepper	ske(r)pper
dipper plate-clip	skepper plaatkny-per	ske(r)pper plaht-kneyper
dishes for develop-ing	skottels om te ontwikkel	sko(h)t'te(r)ls om te(r) o(h)ntvik-ke(r)l
— — fixing	fikseerskottels	fikseyrrskotte(r)ls
draining rack	droogrek	drohchre(r)k
dry plates	droë plate	dro(h)e(r) plahte(r)
enlargement	vergroting	ferchrohting

English.	Afrikaans.	Pronunciation.
exposure	beligting	be(r)lichting
— meter	— meter	— meyte(r)r
—, over	te sterk belig	te(r) sterk be(r)-lich
—, under	te swak belig	te(r) sva(h)k be(r)-lich
—, snap	'n momente be-ligting	i(h)n mohme(r)n-te(r) be(r)lichting
—, time	belighting op tyd	be(r)lichting op teyt
fade, to	verbleek	ferbleyk
film	film	film
film side	die lig kant	dee lich ka(h)nt
fix, to	fikseer	fikseer
flash-lamp (light)	magnesium skit-ter lamp (lig)	ma(h)chneyseûm skitterla(h)mp (lich)
focus	brandpunt, fokus	bra(h)ntpunt, fo(h)-kuss
focussing glasses	instelloep, fokus-glase	inste(r)l'loop, fo(h)-kuss glahse(r)
funnels	tregters	tre(r)chte(r)rs
glass measure	glasmaat	chla(h)ssmaht
half-plate	halwe plaat	ha(h)lve(r) plaht
half-length, bust	borsbeeld, kniestuk	bo(h)rssbeylt, k-neestuck
half-tone	halfkleurig (sepia)	ha(h)lfkleu(r)rich (se(r)peehah)
intensifying	versterking	ferste(r)rking
iris diaphragm	ieris mantelvlies	eeris ma(h)nte(r)l-flees
lamp, dark-room	lamp ver die don-ker-kamer	la(h)mp ferr dee do(h)nkerr-ka(h)-me(r)r
lens	lens	lens
—, the cap of	doppie van die lens	do(h)pee fa(h)n dee lens
—, portrait	protret	po(h)rr'tre(r)tt
mount	opplak (kaart)	o(h)p'pla(h)k-(kahrt)
—, to	opplak	o(h)p'pla(h)k

English.	Afrikaans.	Pronunciation.
mount, slip-in	skuiweropplak-kaart	skuiver-o(h)p'-pla(h)kkahrt
mounting-roller	portret roller	po(h)rr'tre(r)tt ro(h)l'le(r)r
paste, mountant	pasta, gom, smeer-sel	pa(h)sta(h), cho(h)m, smeyr-se(r)l
paste-brush	styselkwas	steyse(r)lkva(h)ss
negative	negatief	ne(r)cha(h)teef
—, on paper	—, op papier	—, op pa(h)peer
photographer	afnemer	a(h)f'ne(h)me(r)r
plate-holder	plaatvashouer	plahtfa(h)ssho(h)-e(r)r
plate-lifter	plaatligter	plahtlichte(r)r
platinotype	platinadruk	pla(h)teenahdruk
positive	positief	posse(r)teef
— bath	— bad	— bat
printing (photos)	afdrukke maak	a(h)fdru(r)k'ke(r) mahk
printing-frame	kopieerpers	ko(h)pee'eyr-pe(h)rs
printing paper	drukpapier	drukpa(h)peer
prints	prente	prente(r)
quarter-plate	kwartplaat	kva(h)rt'plaht
re-touching	bywerking	beyverking
scales and weights	weegskale en ge-wigte	veychskahle(r) e(r)n che(r) vichte(r)
shutter	sluiter	sluiter
shutter, instant-aneous	sluiter, oombliklik	sluiter, ohmbliklik
time	—, op tyd	—, op teyt
silver bath	silwerbad	sillverrba(h)t
speed-indicator, -ometer	snelheidsmeter	sne(r)lheytsmee-te(r)r
spirit-level	waterpas	va(h)terpa(h)ss
spot, stain	vlek	fle(r)k
squeegees with solid rubber roller	persrolle van soliede gomlastiek	persro(h)lle(r) fa(h)n so(h)leede(r) cho(h)mla(h)-steek

English.	Afrikaans.	Pronunciation.
swing-back apparatus	terugwaaitoestel	te(r)ruchvah'i-too-ste(r)l
toning-bath	kleurbad	klu(r)rba(h)t
tripod (twofold)	drievoet wat dubbel toevou	dreefoot va(h)t dub-be(r)l toofoh
varnishing	prente vernis	prente(r) ferniss
view-finder	soeker	sookerr
—, square	—, vierkante	—, feerka(h)nte(r)
—, oblong	—, langwerpege	—, la(h)ngverpe(r)-che(r)
washing tanks	spoelbakke	spoolba(h)k'ke(r)
— rack	afdroog rak	a(h)fdrohch ra(h)k

Fishing and Shooting (Visvang en Skiet (Jag))

bait	aas	ahs
fishing	visvang	fissfa(h)ng
— basket	vismandjie	viss'ma(h)ntyee
— boat	vissersboot	fisse(r)rsboht
— gear	visgereedskap, vistuig	fiss'che(r)reyts-ka(h)p'fiss'tuich
— hook	(vis) hoek	(fiss) hook
— line and wheel	vis-snoer	fiss'snoor
— line	vislyn	fiss'leyn
— net	visnet	fiss'net
— rod	visstok	fiss'sto(h)k
— spear	harpoen	ha(h)rpoon
— tackle	visgereedskap, vistuig	fiss'che(r)reyt-ska(h)p, fiss'tuich
— wheel on rod	visswiel aan stok	fisswiel ahn sto(h)k
float	dobber	dobbe(r)r
fly	kunsvlieg vir visvang	kuns'fleech fir fiss'-fa(h)ng
game-bag	jagsak	ya(h)ch'sa(h)k
gimlet	skroefboor, drilboor	skroofbohr drilbohr
axe	byl	beyl
bullet	koeël	koo'e(r)l, (short, koo'(h)l)
cartridges	patrone	pahtrohne(r)
— extractor	patroontang	pahtrohn-ta(h)ng

English.	Afrikaans.	Pronunciation.
big game	grootwild	chrohtvilt
game	wild	vilt
— bag	jagsak	ya(h)ch'sa(h)k
— keeper	wildopsigter boswagter	vilt'opsichter bo(h)ss'va(h)ch-terr
— law	jagwet	ya(h)ch'vett
— licence	jaglisensie, jaglik-sens	ya(h)ch'lee-sen-see, ya(h)ch'lik-se(r)ns
— park, preserve	wildtuin	vilt'tuin
gun	geweer, roer	che(r)veyrr, roo(h)r
gunpowder	buskruit	buskruit
gunshot	geweerskot	che(r)veyrr-skott
gun stick, ramrod	laaistok	lah'i-sto(h)k
gunstock	geweerkolf	che(r)veyrr-ko(h)lf
guts	derms	de(h)rms
hammer	hamer	hahme(r)r
hunt, hunting	jag	ya(h)ch
hunter	jagter	ya(h)chte(r)r
hunting-box	jaghuis	ya(h)ch'huis
— dog	jaghond	ya(h)ch'hont
— ground	jagveld	ya(h)ch'fe(r)lt
— knife	jagmes, grootmes	ya(h)ch'mess, chroht'mess
— permit	jaglisensie	ya(h)ch'lee-sen-see
— season	jagtyd	ya(h)ch'teyt
knife	mes	mess
match	vuurhoutjie	feûr'hoht-yee
nail	spyker	speyke(r)r
pincers	knyptang	kneypta(h)ng
range	koeëlafstand	koo(h)'e(r)l-a(h)f-sta(h)nt
—, out of	buiten bereik van die geskut	buite(r)n be(r)reyk fa(h)n dee che(r)-sku(r)t
—, within	onder skot	o(h)nde(r)r sko(h)t
— finder	afstandsmeter	a(h)fsta(h)nts-meyte(r)r

English.	Afrikaans.	Pronunciation.
rifle	geweer, roer	che(r)veyrr, roo(h)r
— barrel	geweerloop	che(r)veyrr'lohp
— club	skietklub, skietvereniging	skeet'klup, skeet'fereyniching
— range	skietbaan	skeet-bahn
— man	skerpskutter, skut	skerpskutter, skut (u as in nut)
— shot	geweerskoot	che(r)veyrrskoht
screwdriver	skroewedraaier	skroover-drah'i-e(r)r
sheath	skede, skild	skeyde(r), skilt
tools	gereedskap	che(r)reytska(h)p
whetstone	slypsteen	sleypsteyn
wire-nippers	draadknippers	drahtknip'pers

Amusements (Vermake)

Admission	toegang	too'cha(h)ng
— (charge for)	toegangsgeld	too'cha(h)ngs-chelt
aeroplane	vliegmasjien	fleechma(h)syeen
air-ship	lugskip	luchskip
aviator	vlieër, lugskipper	flee'e(r)r, luch, skipper
ball	bal	ba(h)l
—, fancy dress	gekostumeerde bal	che(r)kostêumeyrde(r) ba(h)l
—, masked	gemaskerde bal	che(r)ma(h)skeyrde(r) ba(h)l
— room	danssaal	dahns'sahl
balloon	lugballon	luch'ba(h)l-lon
—, dirigible	bestuurbare lugballon	be(r)stêurba(h)re(r) luch-ba(h)l'lon
balloonist	lugreisiger	luch'reys'e(r)cher
band (of music)	musiekkorps	mêuseek'korps
bandsman	musikant	mêuseeka(h)nt
band-master	kapelmeester	ka(h)pe(r)l'meyster
band stand	kiosk	kee-osk'

English.	Afrikaans.	Pronunciation.
cinematograph	kienema, bioskoop	keene(r)ma(h), bee-oo(h)skohp
circus	sirkus	sirkus
concert	konsert	konsert'
accompanist	begeleier	be(r)che(r)leye(r)r
choir	koor	kohr
— boy	— knaap	— knahp
— master	— leier	— leye(r)r
— leader	voorsinger	kohrsinger
— music	koormusiek	kohrmeūseek
— singer	koorsanger	kohrsa(h)nger
chorus	refrein	re(r)freyn
conductor	geleier	che(r)leyer
gramophone	praatmasjien, grammofoon.	pra(h)t'masheen, chra(h)m'moh-fohn
instruments	instrumente	instrumente(r)
—, brass	metaal instrumente	metahl instru-mente(r)
—, string	snaarinstrumente	snahr'instrumen-te(r)
—, brass band	blaasorkes	blahs'orkess
—, string band	strykorkes	streyk'orkess
pianist	pianis	peeahniss
piano	klavier	kla(h)feer
— stool	musiekstoel	museek'stool
— tuner	klavierstemmer	kla(h)feer'ste(h)m-me(r)r
recital	musiekvoordrag	museek'fohr-dra(h)ch
singer, the	die sanger, sangeres	sa(h)ng'e(r)r, sa(h)ng'e(r)re(r)ss
violin	viool	fee'ohl
violinist	vioolspeler	fee'ohl-speyler
song	lied	leet
voice	stem	ste(r)m
entrance (door, etc.)	ingang	incha(h)ng
exhibition	tentoonstelling	te(r)ntohn'ste(r)l-ing
exit	uitgang	uitcha(h)ng

English.	Afrikaans.	Pronunciation.
flower-show	blomtentoonstelling	blo(h)mte(r)ntohn'ste(r)ling
flying-machine	vliegmasjien	fleech'ma(h)sheen
games and pastimes	speel en tydverkorting	speyl en teytferko(h)rting
billiards	biljartspel	bilya(h)rt'spe(r)l
— ball	biljartbal	bilya(h)rt'ba(h)l
— cue	biljartstok	bilya(h)rt'sto(h)k
— room	biljartkamer	bilya(h)rt'ka(h)mer
— table	biljarttafel	bilya(h)rt'ta(h)fe(r)l
boating (rowing)	vaar met 'n boot	fahr met i(h)n boht
row, to	roei	roo'i
rowing club	roeiklub	roo'i-klup
cards	karte	ka(h)rte(r)
cardplayer	kaartspeler	ka(h)rt'speyler
card playing	kaartspeel	ka(h)rtspeyl,
— table	kaarttafel, speeltafel	ka(h)rt'ta(h)fe(r)l, speyl'ta(h)fe(r)l
chess	skaakspel	skahk'spe(r)l
— board	skaakbord	skahk bo(h)rt
— man	skaakman	skahk'ma(h)n
— player	skaakspeler	skahk'speyler
cricket	krieket	kree'ket
— bat	— stok	— stok
cricketer	krieketspeler	kree'ketspeyler
cricket field	krieket veld	kree'ket'felt
— match	— wedstryd	— vetstreyt
— pitch	— baan	— bahn
— team	— span	— spa(h)n
draughts	damspel	da(h)m'spe(r)l
driving and riding	drywe en ry	dreyve(r) en rey
fishing	visvang	fiss'fa(h)ng
football	voetbal	foot'ba(h)l
— season	voetbalseisoen	foot'ba(h)lseysoon
golf	kolf, gholf	ko(h)lf, cho(h)lf
— links	gholfbaan	cho(h)lf'bahn
grand-stand	groot pawiljoen	chront pa(h)vilyoon

English.	Afrikaans.	Pronunciation.
hunting	jag	ya(h)ch
match, the	die wedstryd	dee ved'streyt
races	reisies	reysees
race-course	reisiebaan, renbaan	reyseebahn, ´ renbahn
race-horse	reisieperd	reysee'pe(h)rt
rowing	roei	roo'i
skating	skaatsry	skahtsrey
skittles	kegels	keyche(r)ls
swimming	swem	sve(r)m
tennis	tennis	ten'nis
museum	museum	musêûm
music-hall	konsertsaal	konsertsahl
picture gallery	skilderysaal	skilder'rey sahl
reading-room	leeskamer, leessaal	leyskahmer, leys'-sahl
subscription	subskripsie, intekengeld	subskripsee, inteykenche(r)lt
theatre	teater	teeah'te(r)r
act	voordrag, spel	fohrdra(h)ch, spe(r)l
actor	toneelspeler	tohneylspeyler
ballet	ballet, toneeldans	ba(h)let, tohneyl'-da(h)ns
box-office	sitplekbureau	sitple(r)kbêûroh
cloak-room	kleedkamer	kleyt'kahmer
comedian	komediant	ko(h)meydeea(h)nt
comedy	komedie	ko(h)meydee
curtain	gordyn	chordeyn
dancer	danser	da(h)n'ser
farce	klug	kluch
footlights	voetligte	footlichte(r)
manager	bestuurder	be(r)stêûrder
—, stage	toneeldirekteur	tohneyl-de(r)re(r)k
opera glasses	toneelkyker, benokel	tohneylkeyker, beenok'l
—	toneel	tohneyl
— house	operahuis	o'-prah-huis
performance	voorstelling	fohr'stelling
play	spel, toneelstuk	spe(r)l, tohneylstuk

English.	Afrikaans.	Pronunciation.
programme	program	pro(h)chra(h)m
proprietor	eienaar	ey-e(r)-nahr
refreshment-room	verversingskamer	ferfersingskahmer
scene	toneel	to(h)neyl
seats	sitplekke	sitple(r)kke(r)
boxes	loges, kamertjies	lohshe(r)ss, kah-mer-yees
dress-circle	eerste galery	eyrste(r) cha(h)le(r)-rey
gallery	galery	cha(h)le(r)rey
pit	onder die galery	onder dee cha(h)-le(r)rey
reserved	bespreekte	be(r)spreykte(r)
stalls	stalles	sta(h)l'less
stage	toneel	tohneyl
tickets	biljette	bilyette(r)
tragedy	treurspel	treurspel
tragedian	treurspelspeler	treurspelspeyler
orchestra	orkes	orkess
clarinet	klarinet	kla(h)reenett
clarion	klaroen, trompet	kla(h)roon, tro(h)m-pet
cornet	kornet	ko(h)rnet
cello	sello	sello
drum	tamboer	ta(h)mboor
kettle-drum	keteltrom	keyteltro(h)m
violin	viool	feeohl
walking	loop	lohp
walking-stick	kierie, wandelstok	kee'ree, va(h)nd'l-sto(h)k

Correspondence (Briefwisseling)

Address	adres	a(h)dress
address, to	adreseer	a(h)dres-seyr
re-address	ooradreseer	ohr-a(h)dres-seyr
blotting-paper	vloeipapier	floo'i-pahpeer
blotting-pad	vloeiblok	floo'i-blo(h)k
book	boek	boo'k

English.	Afrikaans.	Pronunciation.
copy, to take a	afskrywe, kopieer	a(h)fskreyve(r), kopee'eyr
date	datum, dagteken-ing	da(h)tum, dach-teyke(r)ning
desk, writing-	lessenaar, skryfta-fel	lesse(r)nahr, skreyf-ta(h)fe(r)l
enclosure	bylage	beyla(h)che(r)
envelope	omslag. konvert	o(h)msla(h)ch, kon-fe(r)rt
fountain-pen	vulpen	vul'pen (u as in furl)
herewith	hierby	heer'bey
immediate	dadelik, onmid-delik	dahde(r)lik, o(h)n-midde(r)lik
ink	ink	ink
ink-stand, -well	inkpot	inkpot
letter	brief	breef
letter-box	briewebus	breeve(r)buss
letter-card	poskaart	poss'ka(h)rrt
note	briefie	bree-fee
paper	papier	pa(h)peer
—, note-	skryfpapier	skreyf'pa(h)peer
pen, steel (nib)	staal pen	stahl pen
— holder	pennouer	penn'ho-e(r)r
pencil	potlood	potloht
penknife	pennemes, knipmes	penne(r)mess, knip'-mess
post	pos	poss
—, by	per pos	per poss
—, by return of	per kerende pos	per keyre(r)nde(r) pos
postage	posgeld	posche(r)lt
— stamp	posseël	poss'seye(r)l
postal guide	posgids	poss-chits
order	posorder, poswissel	poss-order, poss'-vissel
post-bag	possak	poss'sa(h)k
— -man	posman	poss'ma(h)n
— -mark	posmerk, posstem-pel	poss'merk, poss'-stempe(r)l

English.	Afrikaans.	Pronunciation.
post-master	posmeester	poss'meyste(r)r
— -master-general	posmeester-generaal	poss-meyste(r)r-che(r)ne(r)rahl
— office	poskantoor	poss'ka(h)ntohr
— -office box	posbus	poss'bus
quire, a	'n boek papier	i(h)n boo'k pa(h)-peer
scissors	skêr	skai(r)r
seal	seël	sey'e(r)l
sealing-wax	lak	la(h)k
sheet (of paper)	vel (papier)	fel (pa(h)peer)
signature	handtekening	ha(h)nt'teyke(r)n-ing
typewriter	tikmasjien	tik'ma(h)sheen
type (-write), to	met tikmasjien skrywe	met tikma(h)sheen skreyve(r)
typist	tikster, tipiste	tik'ste(r)r, tee'-piste(r)
writing	skrywe, skryf	skreyve(r), skreyf
— materials	skryfgereedskap	skreyf'che(r)reyt-ska(h)p

Post Office and Telegrams (Pos- en Telegraafkantoor)

Book-post	drukwerk	drukverk
called for, to be	poste restante	po(h)ste(r) rest-a(h)nte(r)
collection	versamel	fersa(h)me(r)l
contents	inhoud	inho't
counterfoil	teenblad, kontra-bewys	teyn'bla(h)t, kon-tra(h)be(r)veyss
customs declaration	doeane deklarasie	dooahne(r) de(r)k-le(r)rahsee
deliver, to	aflewer	a(h)fleyver
delivery (letters)	lewering, uitgee	leyvering, uitchey
description	beskrywing	be(r)skreyving
despatch-note	afsending briefie	a(h)fsending breefee
destination	bestemming	be(r)stem'ing
directory	adresboek	a(h)dress'boo'k
excess postage	strafport	stra(h)fport

English.	Afrikaans.	Pronunciation.
insured value	versekerde waarde	ferseyke(r)rde(r) vahrde(r)
label	kaártjie	kahrt'yee
letter	brief	breef
—, by	per brief	per breef
— -bag	briewesak	breeve(r)sa(h)k
— -balance	brieweskaal	breeve(r)skahl
— -book	brieweboek	breeve(r)boo'k
— -box	briewebus	breeve(r)bus
— -carrier	posman	po(h)ss'ma(h)n
— -case	briewekas	breeve(r)ka(h)s
— -file	brieweryer, brief-lias	breeve(r)'reye(r)r, breef'leea(h)ss
lettered	geletter	che(r)letterr't
letter-head	briewehoof	breeve(r)hohft
lettering	merk	merk
letter-lock	letterslot	letterslo(h)t
— -paper	briefpapier	breef'pa(h)peer
— scales	briefweër	breef'vey-e(r)r
— -writer	briefskrywer	breef'skretve(r)r
— -post	briewepos	breeve(r)poss
— —, foreign	— buitelandse	— buite(r)la(h)nt-se(r)
— —, inland	— binnelandse	— binne(r)la(h)nt-se(r)
mail	pos, mail	poss, mail
— bag	possak	poss'sa(h)k
— boat	passasierskip	pa(h)s'se(r)-seer-skip
— packet	posstoomboot	poss'stohm-boht
— service	posdiens	poss'deens
— train	passasierstrein	pa(h)s'se(r)-seers-treyn
money order	poswissel	poss'visse(r)l
nature of contents	aard van die inhoud	ahrt fa(h)n dee in-ho't
news	nuus	neûss
— -cable	— -kabel	— -kahbe(r)l
— -paper	koerant, nuusblad	koo'ra(h)nt, neûs-bla(h)t

English.	Afrikaans.	Pronunciation.
newspaper-wrapper	koerantomslag	koo'ra(h)nt'oms-la(h)ch
number	nommer, getal, klomp	no(h)mer, che(r)-ta(h)l, klo(h)mp
parcel post	pakkiespos, pak-ketpos	pa(h)kees'poss, pa(h)ket'poss
" printed matter "	drukwerk	drukve(r)rk
registered letter	geregistreerde pos, aangetekende pos	che(r)rich'che(r)-streyrde(r), ahn-che(r)teykende(r) poss
reply paid	antwoord betaal	a(h)ntvohrt be(r)-tahl
stamp, the	die briefmerker	dee breef'merker
telegraph, to	telegrafeer	tele(r)chrahfeer
telegram	telegram	tele(r)chra(h)m
—, wireless	draadlosetelegram	drahtlohse(r)-tele(r)chra(h)m
—, cable	kabel	ka(h)be(r)l
—, cablegram	— gram	— chra(h)m
telegraph form	telegramvorm	tele(r)chra(h)m-for'm
telegraphist	telegrafis	tele(r)chra(h)fiss
telegraph messenger	telegraaf bode	tele(r)chrahf bohde(r)
— office	telegraaf kantoor	tele(r)chrahf ka(h)n-tohr
— circulating office	— sirkulasie kan-toor	— sirkeula(h)see-ka(h)ntohrr
telephone	telefoon	tele(r)fohn
—, to	telefoneer	tele(r)fohneyr
— — exchange	sentrale telefoon	sentrahle(r) tele(r)-fohn
engaged	besig wees, beset	beysich veys, be(r)-set
telephone call office	oproep kantoor, oproep hutjie	oproop ka(h)ntohr, oproop hutyee
— number	telefoon nommer	tele(r)fohn nommer
weight	gewig	che(r)vich
—, over	oor die gewig	ohr dee che(r)vich

English.	Afrikaans.	Pronunciation.
weight, under	onder die gewig	onder dee che(r)-vich

Washing List (Wasgoedlys)

Aprons, pinafores	voorskote	fohrskohte(r)
blankets	komberse	ko(h)mbe(r)rse(r)
bodices	lyfies	leyfees
bonnets, caps	musse	muss'se(r)
chemises	vrouenshemde	fro'e(r)ns-hemde(r)
collars	boordjies	bohrtyees
—, lace	dames kant boortjies	dahmess ka(h)nt boort-yees
combinations	hempbroeke	hemp'brooke(r)
coverlets	dekens	deyke(r)ns
cuffs	los handboortjies	loss ha(h)nt'bohrt-yees
drawers, pairs of	onderbroeke	onderbrooke(r)
dresses, gowns (night)	slaaprokke	slahp'rokke(r)
dressing-gown	huiskleed, kamerkleed	huis'kleyt, ka(h)-merkleyt
fronts (linen)	voorhemde (linne)	fohrhemde(r) (lin'-ne(r))
night-caps	nagmusse	na(h)ch'musse(r)
night-shirts (gowns)	naghemde	nach'hemde(r)
pants	onderbroeke	onderbrook'e(r)
petticoats	onderrok	onder'rok
pillow-cases	kussingslope	kussing'slohpe(r)
pocket-handkerchiefs	sakdoeke	sa(h)k'dooke(r)
—, silk	sysakdoeke	sey'sa(h)k-dooke(r)
serviettes	servette	serfet'te(r)
sheets	lakens	lahkens
shirts	hemde	hemde(r)
pyjamas	slaapklere	slahpkleyre(r)
socks, pairs of	sokkies, kouse	sokkeys, ko'se(r)
stockings, pairs of	vrouenskouse	fro'ns-ko'se(r)
table-cloths	tafeldoeke, -kledjies	tahfe(r)ldo'ke(r), kleyt'yees
towels	handdoeke	ha(h)nt'dooke(r)

English.	Afrikaans.	Pronunciation.
under-vests	onderhempies	onder'hempees
waistcoats (flannel)	flennie onderbaadjies	flennee onderbaht-yees

Bodily and Mental Powers, Physical Qualities
(Liggaamlike en geestelike kragte ; fiesiese eienskappe)

Age (of persons)	ouderdom (van mense)	o'der-do(h)m
art	kuns	kuns
beginning	begin, aanvang	be(r)chin, ahn-fa(h)ng
bottom	boom	bohm
character	karakter	ka(h)ra(h)k'ter
dimensions	grootte	chroht'te(r)
breadth, width	breedte	breyt'te(r)
depth	diepte	deep'te(r)
height	hoogte	hohchte(r)
length	lengte	leng'te(r)
thickness	dikte	dik'te(r)
emotions, feelings	aandoening, gevoeltes	ahndo'ning, che(r)-foolte(r)s
anger	toorn, gramskap	tohrn, chrahms'-ka(h)p
dislike	afkeer, teensin	a(h)f'keyr, teyn'sin
envy	afguns, nyd	a(h)f'chuns, neyt
hatred	haat	haht
pleasure	vergenoeging	ferche(r)nooching
surprise	oorrassing	ohr'ra(h)ss-ing
end	end, doel, oogmerk	ent, dool, ohch-me(r)k
foolishness, folly	dwaasheid	dvahs'heyt
gentleness	sagsinnigheid, minsaamheid	sa(h)ch'sinnich-heyt, minnsahm'-heyt
goodness	goedheid	choot'heyt
greatness, size	grootte, grootheid	chroh'theyt, chroht'te(r)
honesty	eerlikheid	eyrlik'heyt
honour	eer	eyr

English.	Afrikaans.	Pronunciation.
idea	idee, denkbeeld	ee'dey, denkbeylt
intelligence	verstand	fersta(h)nt
judgment	oordeel	ohrdeyl
knowledge	kennis	kennis
laughter, laughing	gelag, lag	che(r)la(h)ch, la(h)ch
learning	geleerdheid	che(r)leyrt'heyt
middle, midst	middel, te midde van	midde(r)l, te(r) midde(r) fa(h)n
mind, intellect	gees, verstand	cheyss, fersta(h)nt
oration	redevoering	reyde(r)fooring
patience	geduld	che(r)dult
reason (power of)	rede, verstand	reyde(r), fersta(h)nt
science	wetenskap	veyte(r)nska(h)p
senses	sinne	sinne(r)
feeling, touch	gevoel	che(r)fool
hearing	gehoor	che(r)hohr
seeing, sight	sien, gesig	seen, che(r)sich
smell (-ing)	ruik	ruik
taste, tasting	smaak, proef	smahk, proof
side	sy, kant	sey, ka(h)nt
smile, smiling	lag	la(h)ch
sneeze	nies	nee's
snore	snork	sno(h)rk
speaking, speech	praat	praht
strength	krag	kra(h)ch
thinking, thought	dink, gedagte	dink, che(r)da(h)-chte(r)
top	top, toppunt, bo-kant	top, toppunt, bo'-ka(h)nt
voice	stem	ste(r)m
weakness	swakheid, swakte	sva(h)k'heyt sva(h)kte(r)
weeping	huil, ween, treur	huil, veyn, tru(r)r
wisdom	wysheid	veysheyt

Ranks and Titles (Rang en Titel)

Ambassador	gesant, ambassa-deur	che(r)sa(h)nt, am-ba(h)sadu(r)r
chairmen	voorsitter	fo(h)r'sitte(r)r

English.	Afrikaans.	Pronunciation.
Chancellor	kanselier	ka(h)nse(r)leer
crown	kroon	krohn
deputy	plaasvervanger	plahsferfa(h)nger
duke	hertog	hertoch
duchess	hertogin	hertochin
earl, count	graaf	chrahf
countess	grafin	chra(h)fin
emperor	keiser	keyser
empress	keiserin	keyserin
government	regering, goewerment	re(r)cheyring, chooverment
heir	erfgenaam	erfche(r)nahm
heiress	erfgename	erfche(r)nahme(r)
his, her majesty	sy, haar majesteit	sey, hahr maa'i-e(r)steyt
his, her royal highness	sy, haar koniklike hoogheid	sey, hahr kohniklike(r) hohchheyt
King	koning	ko(h)ning
Queen	koningin	ko(h)ning'inn
mayor	burgemeester	burche(r)meyste(r)r
mayoress	burgemeestersvrou	burche(r)meystersfro
member	lid	lit
minister	minister	minister
ministry	ministerie	ministeyree
nobility	adel, adeldom	ahde(r)l, ahde(r)l-do(h)m
parliament	parlement, volksraad	pa(h)rle(r)ment, folksraht
president	president	preseedent
prince	prins	prins
princess	prinses	prinses
Royal Family	koninklike familie	koninklike(r) fa(h)meelee
secretary	sekretaris	sekreta(h)ris
Throne	troon	trohn
treasurer	skatbewaarder, penningmeester	ska(h)tbe(r)vahrde(r)r, penningmeyste(r)r

Naval and Military Titles (See- en Militêre Tittels)

English.	Afrikaans.	Pronunciation.
Adjutant	adjutant	a(h)d-yoo-ta(h)nt
admiral	admiraal	a(h)tmee rahl
boatswain	bootsman	bohtsma(h)n
bugler	trompetter	tro(h)mpet'ter
captain (navy)	seekaptein	seyka(h)pteyn
— (infantry)	kaptein van die voetvolk	ka(h)pteyn fa(h)n dee foot'folk
— (cavalry)	kaptein van die ruitery	ka(h)pteyn fa(h)n dee ruite(r)ey
chaplain (army)	veldprediker	feltpreyde(r)ke(r)r
colonel	kolonel	kolo(h)ne(r)l
commandant	kommandant	komma(h)n-da(h)nt
commander-in-chief	opperbevelhebber	opper-be(r)fe(r)l-he(r)bbe(r)r
commanding-officer	bevelhebber	be(r)fe(h)lhebber
corporal	korporaal	korporahl
doctor	dokter	dokter
drummer	tamboerslaner	ta(h)mboorsla(h)ner
engineer	ingenieur	insje(r)nu(r)r
field-marshal	veldmaarskalk	feldmahrska(h)lk
general	generaal	chenerahl
lieutenant	luitenant	luite(r)nahnt
major	majeur	mahyu(r)r
marine	seesoldaat	seysoldaht
mate	maat, kameraad, stuurman	maht, ka(h)meraht, steurma(h)n
midshipman	seekadet	seykahde(r)t
nurse	verpleegster	ferpleychster
officer	offisier	o(h)f'fe(r)seer
orderly	lyfdienaar	leyf'dee-nahr
paymaster	betaalmeester	be(r)tahl'meyste(r)r
private	gewone soldaat	che(r)vo(h)ne(r) soldaht
quartermaster	kwartiermeester	kva(h)rteermeys-te(r)r
sailor, bluejacket	matroos	mahtro(h)ss
sergeant	sersjant	se(r)rs'yahnt, sah(r)rs'yah-nt

English.	Afrikaans.	Pronunciation.
trumpeter	trompetblaser	tro(h)m'pe(r)t-blahser

Naval and Military Terms (See- en Militêre uitdrukkings)

English.	Afrikaans.	Pronunciation.
Ambulance	ambulans	a(h)mbeûla(h)ns
ammunition	skietvoorraad, ammuniesie	skeetfohrr'raht, a(h)m'eûnee-see
army	leër, krygsmag	ley'e(r)r, kreychs'-ma(h)ch
artillery	geskut, artillerie	che(r)skut, a(h)rtil-leree
band	musiekkorps	meûseek'korps
barracks	kaserne, barakke	ka(h)se(r)rne(r), ba(h)ra(h)k'ke(r)
battalion	bataljon	ba(h)ta(h)l'yo(h)n
battery	battery, geskut	ba(h)ter-rey, che(r)-skut
battle	veldslag	feltsla(h)ch
bayonet	bajonet	ba(h)yo-nett'
brigade	brigade	breecha(h)'de(r)
bugle	beuel	bu(r)'l
camp	kamp	ka(h)mp
cannon, gun	kanon, geskut	ka(h)non,che(r)skut
cartridge	patroon	pa(h)trohn
cavalry	ruitery	ruite(r)rey
cease fire!	houop met skiet	ho-op met skeet
colours (of a regiment)	vaandels	fahnde(r)ls
column	kolonne	kolo(h)n'ne(r)
commissariat	kommissariaat	ko(h)m'mee-sahree-aht
communications, line of	verbindings (kommunikasie) lienie	ferbind'ings (kom-munika(h)see) lee-nee
court-martial	krygsraad	kreychs-raht
crew (navy)	skeepsbemanning	skeyps'be(r)ma(h)n-ing
defence	verdediging	ferdeydiching
deserter	deserteur	de(r)se(r)rteûrr
detachment	afdeling	a(h)f'deyling

English.	Afrikaans.	Pronunciation.
discipline	discipliene	deese(r)pleene(r)
disembarkation	ontskeping, landing	ontskeyping, la(h)n-ding
dismiss (discharge), to	ontslaan, afdank, laat gaan	ontslahn, a(h)f-da(h)nk, laht-chahn
dismount, to	afklim, afstyg	a(h)fklim, a(h)f-steych
dockyard	skeepswerf	skeypsverff
drill, to	militêre oefening	mil'ee-tai(r)r-e(r) oof'e(r)-ning'
drum	tamboer, trommel	ta(h)m'boor, tro(h)mmel
duty, on	op diens	op deens
embarkation	inskeping	inskeyping
enemy	vyand	feyahnt
engagement	geveg	che(r)fe(r)ch
enlistment	inskrywing, aan-werwing	inskreyving, ahn-verving
entrenchment	verskansing	ferska(h)nsing
equipment	uitrusting	uitrusting
escort	geleide, eskort	che(r)leyde(r), eskort
expedition (military)	veldtog, ekspe-diesie	felt'toch, expe(r)-dee-see
fatigue duty	arbeidsdiens	a(h)rbeyts'deens
field-day	velddiensoefeninge	feltdeensoofe(r)n-inge(r)
field-glass	verkyker	ferr'keyke(r)r
field-gun	veldgeskut, veld-stuk	feltche(r)skut, felt-stuk
field-hospital	militêre veld-hos-pitaal	meele(r)tai(r)e(r) felt-hospeetahl
file, in single	agtermekaar	a(h)chterme(r)kahr
flag	vlag	fla(h)ch
flank	flank, sy	fla(h)nk, sey
fleet	vloot	floht
formation	vormasie	forma(h)see
fort	fort	forrt

English.	Afrikaans.	Pronunciation.
fortify, to	versterk	fersterk
furlough, on	verlof	ferlo(h)f
garrison	garnisoen	cha(h)rneesoon
guard, advance	voorhoede	fohrr'hoode(r)
—, rear	agterhoede	a(h)chte(r)r'hocde(r)
gunner	kanonier	ka(h)non'neer
head-quarters	hoofkwartier	hohf'kva(h)rteer
infantry	infanterie	infa(h)nteyree
—, mounted	berede infanterie	be(r)reyde(r) in-fa(h)nteyree
intelligence department	informasieburo	info(h)rr'mahsee-beuro(h)
ironclad	pantserskip	pa(h)nse(r)rskip
knapsack	bladsak, knapsak	blahtsa(h)k, kna(h)p-sa(h)k
lance	lans, harpoen	la(h)ns, ha(h)r-poon
line of battle	slagorde	sla(h)ch'orde(r)
manœuvre	maneuwer, krygs-oefening	ma(h)nu(r)ver, krey hs oofe(r)n-ing
man-of-war	oorlogskip	ohrloch'skip
military service	militêrediens	meele(r)tai(r)e(r)-deens
mine	myn	meyn
muster, to	oproep, versamel	oproop, fersahme(r)l
navy	seemag, floot	seyma(h)ch, floht
non-combatant	nie-strydend	nee-streydent
parade	parade	pa(h)ra(h)de(r)
patrol	patrollie	pahtrollee
picket	pikett	peekitt
prisoner of war	krygsgevangene	kreychs'che(r)-fa(h)nge(r)ne(r)
quarters	huisies	huisees
rank-and-file	die minderes, klomp	dee mindere(r)s, klo(h)mp
rations	rantsoen	ra(h)nt'soon
recruit	rekruut	re(r)kreut
regiment	resjiment	re(r)sheement
regulations	regelment	reche(r)lment

English.	Afrikaans.	Pronunciation.
reserves (reserve forces)	reserwe korps	reserve(r) korps
rifle	geweer	che(r)veyrr
salute	saluut, groet	salêut, chroot
scout	verkenner, spioen	ferkenner, spee'oon
sentry	brandwag, skildwag	bra(h)ntva(h)ch, skilt'va(h)ch
shell	bom	bom
shot (cannon ball)	kanonkoeël	ka(h)non-koo'e(r)l
skirmish, to	skermutseling	skerr-mêut-se(r)ling
soldier	soldaat	soldaht
spy	spioen	spee'oon
squadron (military)	eskadron	eska(h)dro(h)n
— (naval)	seeeskadron	seyeska(h)dro(h)n
staff (military)	staf	sta(h)f
submarine boat	duikboot	duikboht
sword	sabel, swaard	sa(h)be(r)l, svahrt
torpedo-boat	torpedoboot	torpeydohboht
transport (ship)	transpo.tskip	tra(h)nspo(h)rtskip
trenches	loopgrawe	lohpchra(h)ve(r)
troops	troepe	troope(r)
uniform	uniform	êuneeform
volley	sarsie, salwo	sa(h)rsee, sa(h)lvo
volunteer	vrywilliger	freyvillicher
wing, left	linker vleuel	linker flu(r)'l
—, right	regter vleuel	rechter flu(r)'l
wounded (men)	gekweste, gewonde	che(r)kve(r)ste(r), che(r)vo(h)nde(r)

Cardinal Numbers (Hooftelwoorde)

1 **one**	een	eyn
2 **two**	twee	tvey
3 **three**	drie	dree
4 **four**	vier	feer
5 **five**	vyf	feyf
6 **six**	ses	sess
7 **seven**	sewe	seyve(r)
8 **eight**	ag	a(h)ch
9 **nine**	nege, neë	neyge(r), ney'e(r)
10 **ten**	tien	teen

English.	Afrikaans.	Pronunciation.
11 eleven	elf	elf
12 twelve	twaalf	twahlf
13 thirteen	dertien	derr'teen
14 fourteen	veertien	feyrteen
15 fifteen	vyftien	feyfteen
16 sixteen	sestien	sesteen
17 seventeen	sewentien	seve(r)nteen
18 eighteen	agtien	a(h)chteen
19 nineteen	negentien (neëntien)	neyge(r)nteen(ney - e(r)nteen)
20 twenty	twintig	tvinte(r)ch
21 --- -one	een-en-twintig	eyn-e(r)n-tvinte-(r)ch
22 — -two	twee-en-twintig	tvey-e(r)n-tvin-te(r)ch
23 — -three	drie-en —	
24 — -four	vier-en —	
25 — -five	vyf-en —	
26 — -six	ses-en —	
27 — -seven	sewe-en —	
28 — -eight	ag-en —	
29 — -nine	neën-en —	
30 thirty	dertig	derr'te(r)ch
40 forty	veertig	feyrte(r)ch
50 fifty	vyftig	veyfte(r)ch
60 sixty	sestig	seste(r)ch
70 seventy	sewentig	seyve(r)nte(r)ch
80 eighty	tagtig, taggentig	ta(h)chte(r)ch, ta(h)ch'che(r)n-te(r)ch
90 ninety	neëntig, negentig	ney'e(r)nte(r)ch, neyge(r)nte(r)ch
100 hundred	honderd	honder(r)t
101	— (en) een	
110	— (en) tien	
120	— (en twintig	
130	— (en) dertig	
200	tweenhonderd	
300	driehonderd	
400	vierhonderd	

English.	Afrikaans.	Pronunciation.
500	vyfhonderd	
600	seshonderd	
700	sewenhonderd	
800	aghonderd	
900	negehonderd	
1,000 thousand	duisend	duise(r)nt
2,000	twee —	
3,000	drie —	
10,000	tien —	
20,000	twintig —	
30,000	dertig —	
40,000	veertig —	
50,000	vyftig —	
60,000	sestig —	
70,000	sewentig —	
80,000	tagtig —	
	taggentig —	
90,000	neëntig —	
	negentig —	
100,000	honderd —	
1,000,000 million	millioen (miljoen)	mil'li-oon
1905	een duisend nege honderd en vyf, *or* negentienhonderd en vyf	eyn duise(r)nt neyge(r) hondert e(r)n feyf, *or* neyge(r)nteenhon-dert e(r)n feyf

Ordinal Numbers (Rangtelwoorde)

The 1st	die eerste	dee eyrste(r)
— 2nd	— tweede	— tveyde(r)
— 3rd	— derde	— derrde(r)
— 4th	— vierde	— feerde(r)
— 5th	— vyfde	— feyfde(r)
— 6th	— sesde	— sesde(r)
— 7th	— sewende	— sevende(r)
— 8th	— agste	— a(h)chste(r)
— 9th	— negende,	— negende(r),
	— neënde	— ney'e(r)nde(r)
— 10th	— tiende	— teende(r)
— 11th	— elfde	— elfde(r)

English.	Afrikaans.	Pronunciation.
The 12th	die twaalfde	dee tvahlfde(r)
— 13th	— dertiende	— derrteende(r)
— 14th	— veertiende	— feyrteende(r)
— 15th	— vyftiende	— feyf'teende(r)
— 16th	— sestiende	— sess'teende(r)
— 17th	— sewentiende	— seyve(r)nteende(r)
— 18th	— agtiende	— a(h)chteende(r)
— 19th	— neëntiende	— ney'e(r)nteende(r)
— 20th	— twintigste	— tvin'te(r)chste(r)
— 21st	— eenentwintigste	— eyn'e(r)ntvinte(r)chste(r)
— 30th	— dertigste	— derr'te(r)chste(r)
— 40th	— veertigste	— feyr'te(r)chste(r)
— 50th	— vyftigste	— feyf'te(r)chste(r)
— 60th	— sestigste	— sess'te(r)chste(r)
— 70th	— sewentigste	— seyve(r)nte(r)chste(r)
— 80th	— tagtigste	— ta(h)ch'te(r)chste(r)
— 90th	— negenste	— ney'ge(r)nte(r)chste(r)
— 100th	— honderdste	— hon'dertste(r)
— 1,000th	— duisendste	— dui'se(r)ndste(r)

N.B.—Where pronunciation is omitted, it will be found given previously.

Collective and Fractional Numbers, etc.

(Versamelname en Breuke)

All, the whole	alles, die ganse	a(h)l'le(r)s, dee cha(h)nse(r)
Century	eeu	ee'w
—, half-a-	'n halwe eeu	i(h)n ha(h)lve(r) ee'w
couple (pair)	paar	pahr
crowd	gedrang, menigte	che(r)dra(h)ng, meyne(r)chte(r)
decade	tiental	teenta(h)l
double	dubbel	dub'be(r)l

English.	Afrikaans.	Pronunciation.
dozen	dosyn	dohseyn
a fifth	'n vyfde	i(h)n feyfde(r)
one fifth	een vyfde	eyn feyfde(r)
firstly	ten eerste, eerstens	te(r)n eyrste(r), eyrste(r)ns
four-fifths	vier vyfdes	feer feyfde(r)s
a gross	'n gros, twaalf dosyn	i(h)n chross, tvahlf-dooseyn
half	(adj.) half, (noun) helfte	hahlf, helfte(r)
half-a-dozen	'n halfdosyn	i(h)n hahlfdooseyn
the last	die laaste	dee lahste(r)
once	eens, eenmaal	eyns, eynmahl
one at a time	een vir een	eyn fer eyn
one by one	een na die ander	eyn na(h) dee a(h)n-de(r)r
a pair	'n paar	i(h)n pahr
a part, portion	'n deel, porsie, gedeelte	i(h)n deyl, po(h)r-see,che(r)deylte(r)
quarter, fourth part	kwart, vierde-deel	kva(h)rt, feerde(r)-deyl
score	twintigtal	tvin'te(r)chta(h)l
secondly	ten twede	te(r)n tveyde(r)
single, singly	alleen	a(h)lleyn'
tens, by	by tiene	bey teene(r)
tenths	tiendes	teende(r)s
tenfold	tiendubbel, tien-voudig	teendubbe(r)l, teen-fode(r)ch
ten times	tienmaal	teenmahl
of ten lines	tienreëlig	teenrey'e(r)lich
a third, one third	'n derde, een derde	i(h)n de(r)rde(r) eyn de(r)rde(r)
three-fold	drievoudig	dreefode(r)ch
three-quarters	driekwart	dreekva(h)rt
an eighth	ag(t)ste	a(h)ch(t)ste(r)
eighth (of an inch)	aks	a(h)ks
three-eighths	drieaks	dreea(h)ks
several, severally	verskeie, afsonder-lik	ferskeye(r), a(h)f-sonde(r)rlik
threes	drieë	dree'e(r)

English.	Afrikaans.	Pronunciation.
three-sevenths	driesevendes	dreeseyve(r)nde(r)s
triple, triply	drievoudig	dree'fo-de(r)ch
twice	tweemaal	tveymahl
two-fold	tweefoud	tveyfo(h)t
two-thirds	tweederdes	tveyderrde(r)s

Adjectives (Byvoeglike Naamwoorde)

Able, un-	bekwaam, onbekwaam	be(r)kvahm, on-
active, in-	werksaam, werkloos	verksahm, verklohs
agreeable, dis-	aangenaam, on-	ahnche(r)nahm, on-
angry	kwaad	kvaht
anxious	angstig	a(h)ng'stich
arrogant	aanmatigend, verwaand	ahn'ma(h)te(r)-che(r)nt, fervahnt
awkward, inconvenient	ongeleë	o(h)nche(r)l'eye(r)
bad	sleg	sle(r)ch
beautiful, fine	skoon	skohn
bitter	bitter	bitter
blind	blind	blinnt
blunt	stomp	stomp
bold	vrypostig	freypos'-tich
brave	dapper	da(h)per
breadth	breedte	breydte(r)
bright	helder	helde(r)r
brisk	lewendig	leyve(r)ndich
broad	breed	breyt
busy	besig	beysich
calm	kalm, rustig, stil	ka(h)lm, rustich, still
careful, careless	sorgvuldig, sorgeloos	sorch'fuldich, sorch'e(r)lohs
certain, un-	seker, onseker	seyker, onseyker
cheap	goedkoop	chootkohp
cheerful	vrolik, opgeruimd	frohlik, opche(r)-ruim'd
civil, un-	beleef, onbeleef	be(r)leyf, onbe(r)-leyf
clean	skoon, rein	skohn, reyn

English.	Afrikaans.	Pronunciatiou.
clear	helder	heller
clear, distinct	duidelik	dui'de(r)lik
clever	slim, knap	slim, kna(h)p
cold	koud	ko(h)t (pron. as coat)
comfortable, un- (of persons)	gemaklik, ongemaklik	che(r)ma(h)klik, onche(r)ma(h)lik
— — (of things)	lê lekker, lê sleg	lai(r) le(r)k'ke(r)r, lai(r) sle(r)ch
common, un-	gewoon, ongewoon	che(r)vohn, onche(r)vohn
complete, in-	volkome, onvolkome	folkohmer(r), onfolkohme(r)
content	tevrede	te(r)frede(r)
continual	voortdurend	fohrt'dure(r)nt
cool (weather, etc.)	koel	kool
correct, in-	juis, foutief korrek, verkeerd	yuis, fo'teef kor're(r)k, ferrkeyrt
cruel	wreedaardig	vreyt'ahrdich
curious	nuuskierig	nu(r)skeer'ich
damp	vogtigheid	fo(h)chtich'heyt
dangerous	gevaarlik	che(r)fahr'lik
dark	donker	donkerr
dead, deceased	dood	doht
deaf	doof	dohf
dear	lief, also duur (expensive)	lẹef, du(r)rr
deep	diep	deep
different	verskillend	ferskil'le(r)nt
dirty	vuil	fuil
disagreeable	onaangenaam	onahnche(r)nahm
dishonest	oneerlik	oneyrlik
drunken	dronk	dronk
dry	droog	drohch
dull (of weather)	betrokke	be(r)trok'ke(r)
dumb	stom	stom
dusty	stowwerig	stovve(r)rich
eager	begerig, ywerig	be(r)cheyrich, eyverich
early	vroeg	frooch

English.	Afrikaans.	Pronunciation.
easy	gemaklik	che(r)ma(h)klik
equal, un-	gelyk, ongelyk	che(r)leyk, onche(r)-leyk
empty	leeg	leych
every	ieder	eede(r)r
extraordinary	buitengewoon	buite(r)nche(r)vohn
fair	skoon, gunstig, blonde	skohn, chunstich, blo(h)nt
faithless	troueloos	tro'e(r)lohs
false	vals	fa(h)ls
famous	beroemd	be(r)roomt
fashionable, un-	modies, ouderwets, nie na die mode nie	mohdees, nee na(h) dee mohde(r) nee, o-de(r)r-ve(r)ts
fast (quick)	vinnig	fin'ne(r)ch
— (firm)	standvastig	sta(h)ntfa(h)stich
fat	vet	fe(r)t
favourable, un-	gunstig, ongunstig	chunste(r)ch, on-
few	weinig	veynich
fierce	wild, wreed	vilt, vreyt
fine	mooi, fyn, fraai	moh'i, feyn, frah'i
fit	bekwaam, geskik	be(r)kvahm, che(r)-skik
flat	plat	pla(h)t
foolish	dwaas	dvahss
fortunate, un-	gelukkig, ongelukkig	che(r)luk'kich, on-
free	vry	frey
frequent	herhaaldelik	he(r)hahlde(r)lik
fresh	vars, vris, koel	fa(h)rs, fris, kool
full	vol	fo(h)l
gay	vroolik	frohlik
— (many coloured)	bont	bo(h)nt
general, usual	gewoonlik	che(r)vohnlik
generous	grootmoedig	-chroht'moode(r)ch
gentle	minsaam, sagsinnig	minsahm, sa(h)ch'sinnich
glad	bly	bley
good	goed	choo't
grand	groot, vernaam	chroht, fernahm

English.	Afrikaans.	Pronunciation.
great, big, large	groot	chroht
hairy	harig	hahre(r)ch
handsome	mooi, aansienlik	moh'i, ahnseenle(r)k
happy, un-	gelukkig, ongelukkig	che(r)luke(r)ch, on-
hard	hard, moeilik	ha(h)rt, mooile(r)k
heavy	swaar	svahr
height	hoogte	hohchte(r)
high	hoog	hohch
hilly	bergagtig, bulterig	berch-ah)ch-te(r)ch,(bul-te(r)-re(r)ch
hollow	hol	ho(h)l
honest	eerlik	eyrlik
hot	warm	va(h)rm
hungry	hongerig	hong-e(r)re(r)ch
idle, unoccupied	lui, niksdoende	lui, niksdoon'de(r)
ill	kwaad, sleg, siek	kvaht, slech, seek
immediately	dadelik, onmiddelik	dahde(r)lik, onmid-de(r)lik
impolite	onbeleefd	onbe(r)leyft
important, un-	belangrik	be(r)lahng'rik
injurious	skadelik, nadelig	skahde(r)lik, na(h)-deylich
innocent	onskuldig	onskuldich
interesting, un-	interessant, on-	inte(r)re(r)s-sa(h)nt
just, un-	regvaardig, on-	re(r)chfahrdich
kind, kindly	vriendelik, minsaam	freende(r)lik, min-sahm
lame	lam, mank, kruppel	la(h)m, ma(h)nk, krup'pe(r)l
large	groot, ruim	chroht, ruim
late	laat	laht
lean	maer, skraal	mah'e(r)r, skrahl
length	lengte	le(r)ng'te(r)
light	lig	lich
little	klein	kleyn
long	lang (lank)	la(h)ng (la(h)nk)
loose	los	loss

English.	Afrikaans.	Pronunciation.
loud	luid, hard, uitgelate	luit, ha(h)rt, uit-che(r)lahte(r)
low (of position)	nederig	neyde(r)ich
many	baie, veel	bah'i-e(r)
mild (weather, climate)	koel, 'n sagte klimaat	kool, i(h)n sa(h)ch-te(r) klee'maht
miserable	ellendig	eh'le(r)ndich
modern	modern	modai(r)rn'
muddy	modderig	modde(r)re(r)ch
narrow	nou, smal	no', sma(h)l
natural, un-	natuurlik, onnatuurlik	na(h)teûrlik, on-
necessary	nodig, onnodig	nohde(r)ch, onnoh-de(r)ch
new	nuut	neût
nice (to taste)	lekker	le(r)k'ke(r)r, lai(r)'-ke(r)r
— (pretty)	gaaf, lief	chahf, leef
noble, ig-	edel, veragtelik	eyd'l, fera(h)ch'-te(r)lik
numerous	talryk. baie	ta(h)l'reyk, bah'-i-e(r)
oblong	langwerpig	la(h)ngver'pe(r)ch
old	oud	o't (the same sound as *oa* in coat)
open	open	ohpen
ordinary	gewoon, gebruiklik	che(r)vohn, che(r)-bruiklik
pale	bleek	bleyk
patient, im-	geduldig, ongeduldig	che(r)dulde(r)ch, on-
perfect, im-	volmaak, onvolmaak	fo(h)l'mahk, on-fo(h)lmahk
plain (clear)	eenvoudig	eynfo'de(r)ch
plain (evident)	duidelik	duide(r)lik
pleasant, un-	aangenaam, on-	ahnche(r)nahm, on-
poisonous	giftig	chif'tich
polite	beleefd	be(r)leyft
poor	arm	a(h)rm

English.	Afrikaans.	Pronunciation.
possible, im-	moontlik, onmoontlik	mohntlik, onmohntlik
practical, un-	prakties, onprakties	pra(h)ktees, onpra(h)ktees
present	teenwoordig	teynvohrde(r)ch
pretty	mooi, bevallig	moh'i,be(r)fa(h)'lich
principal	vernaamste	fernahmste(r)
private	privaat, vertroulik	preefaht, fertro'lik
probable, im-	waarskynlik, on-	vahrskeynlik
proud	trots, hoogmoedig	tro(h)ts,hohch'me͡ude(r)ch
public	publiek, openbaar	pe͡ubleek, ohpe(r)nbahr
pure	suiwer, rein	suiver, reyn
queer, strange	snaaks	snahks
quick, rapid	lewendig, gou, vinnig, rats	leve(r)nde(r)ch, cho, fin'nich, ra(h)ts
quiet	rustig, stil, bedaard	ru(h)ste(r)ch, still, be(r)dahrt'
rare	seldsaam, skaars	seltsahm, skahrs
raw	rou	ro (as in roe)
ready (prepared)	klaar, bereid, gereed	klahr, be(r)reyt, che(r)reyt
real, un- (legitimate)	eg, oneg	ech, onech
real (genuine)	regtig, reëel	rechtich, re(r)ey'(r)l
reasonable, un-	billik, onbillik	billik, onbillik
regular, ir-	gereeld, ongereeld	che(r)reylt, on-
reliable	vertroubaar	fertro'bahr
remarkable, striking	opmerklik, merkwaardig	opme(r)rklik, merkvahrde(r)ch
rich	ryk	reyk
right (correct)	reg, juis	re(r)ch, yuis
ripe	ryp	reyp
rough (in manners)	onmanierlik	onma(h)neyr'lik
— (uneven)	grof, rof	chrof, roff
round	rond	ront
rude, impolite, insolent	onbeleef, onbeskof	onbe(r)leyf, onbe(r)skoff
rural	landelik	la(h)nde(r)lik

English.	Afrikaans.	Pronunciation.
sacred	heilig	heylich
sad	treurig, droewig	tru(r)rich, droovich
safe, secure	veilig	feylich
same (the same)	selfde (die selfde)	selfde(r), (dee selfde(r))
satisfactory, un-	bevredigend, on-	be(r)freyde(r)-che(r)nt, on-
serious	ernstig	e(r)rns-tich
severe (pain)	heftig	he(r)ftich
sharp	skerp	skerp
short	kort	ko(h)rt
silent	stil	stil
simple	eenvoudig, onnosel	eynfo'de(r)ch, ohn-nohse(r)l
single	enkeld	enke(r)lt
slow	stadig, langsaam	sta(h)dich, la(h)ng-sahm
small	klein	kleyn
smooth	glad	chla(h)t
soft	sag	sa(h)ch
solid (metals, etc.)	solied, massief	so(h)leet, ma(h)sseef
sound	gesond	che(r)sont
sour	suur	seur
square	vierkantig	feer'ka(h)ntich
stormy	stormagtig	sto(h)rma(h)ch-te(r)ch
straight	reguit, direk, eerlik	re(r)chuit,deere(r)k, eyrlik
strange	vreemd	freymt
strong	sterk	ste(r)rk
stupid	dom, lomp	dom, lomp
sufficient, in-	genoeg, ongenoeg-saam, nie genoeg nil	che(r)nooch, on-che(r)noochsahm, nee che(r)nooch nee
suitable	geskik, voegsaam	che(r)skik, fooch-sahm
sure	seker	seyker
sweet	soet	soot
swift	vinnig, rats, gou	finnich, ra(h)ts, cho

English.	Afrikaans.	Pronunciation.
tall (of persons)	groot, lang (lank)	chroht, la(h)ng, (la(h)nk)
tedious, tiresome	vervelig, langdradig	ferfeylich, la(h)ng-drahde(r)ch
tender (of food)	sag, mals	sa(h)ch, ma(h)ls
terrible	verskriklik, yslik, vreeslik	ferskrikle(r)k, eyslik freyslik
thick	dik	dik
thickness	dikte	dikte(r)
thin	dun	dun
thirsty	dors, dorstig	do(h)rs, do(h)rstich
tight (taut)	styf, gespan	steyff, che(r)-spa(h)nn
tight (of clothes)	nou	no
tight (water-tight)	waterdig	va(h)terdich
torn	geskeur	che(r)sku(r)r
total	totaal	tohtahl
tough	taai	tah'i
timely	tydig	teydig
troublesome	lastig, neulerig	la(h)ste(r)ch, nu(r) le(r)rich
true	waar	vahr
ugly	leelik	leylik
uncertain	onseker	onseyke(r)r
unequal	ongelyk	oncherleyk
unfit	ongeskik, onbe-kwaam	onche(r)skik, on-be(r)kvahm
unsettled	onseker, onbepaald	onseyke(r)r, on-be(r)pahlt
unsound (bad)	bederf	be(r)de(r)f
urgent	dringend	dringe(r)nt
useful	nuttig	nut'te(r)ch
usual, un-	gewoonlik, onge-woon	che(r)vohnlik, on-che(r)vohn
vain	ydel, vergeefs	eyde(r)l, fercheyfs
valuable	kosbaar	kossba(h)r
various	verskillend, ver-skeie	ferskille(r)nt, fer-skeye(r)
violent	geweldig, hewig	che(r)ve(r)ldich, heyvich

English.	Afrikaans.	Pronunciation.
visible, in-	sigbaar, onsigbaar	sichbahr, onsichbahr
warm	warm	va(h)rm
weak	swak	sva(h)k
well	wel, gesond	vel, ge(r)sont
wet	nat	na(h)t
whole	heel	heyl
wholesome, un- (of food)	gesond, voedsaam, ongesond, skadelik	che(r)sont, footsahm onche(r)sont, skah-de(r)lik
wicked	goddeloos, sondig, sleg	chod'de(r)lohs, sondich, sle(r)ch
wide	wyd	veyt
wild	wild	wilt
willing, un-	gewillig, ongewillig	che(r)villich, on-
windy	winderig	vinde(r)rich
wise	verstandig, slim	fersta(h)ndich, slim
wonderful	wonderlik	vonde(r)rlik
wooden	van hout	fa(h)nho't
worthless	waardeloos, niks-werd	vahrde(r)lohs, nix-ve(r)t
wretched	ellendig	e(r)le(r)ndich
wrong (erroneous)	verkeerd, foutief	ferkeyrt, fo-teef
yearly, annual	jaarliks	yahrliks
young	jong, jeugdig	yong, yu(r)chdich

Verbs (Werkwoorde)

To accept	aanneem	ahnneym
— admire	bewonder	be(r)vonn'de(r)r
— affirm	bevestig	be(r)festich
— answer	antwoord	a(h)ntwohrt
— approve	goedkeur	chootku(r)r
— arrive	aankom	ahnkomm
— ascend	klim, opvaar	klim, opfahrr
— ask	vra	fra(h)
— assure	verseker	ferseyke(r)r
— awake	wakkerlewendig	va(h)k'ke(r)r, leyve(r)ndich
— be	wees	veys
— be able	kan	ka(h)n

English.	Afrikaans.	Pronunciation.
To be afraid of, fear	bang vir	ba(h)ng fir
— be angry with	kwaad wees met	kvaht veys met
— be fine	mooi, keurig wees	moh'i, ku(r)rich veys
— be hungry	honger wees	honger veys (*hong-e(r)r*)
— be ignorant of	onbekend wees me	tonbe(r)kent veys met
— be injurious	skadelik, nadelig wees	skahde(r)lik, nah-deylich weys
— be mistaken	verkeerd wees	ferkeyrt veys
— be quiet, silent	stil wees	stil veys
— be thirsty	dorstig, dors wees	dorstich, dors veys
— beat	slaan	slahn
— begin	begin	be(r)chin
— believe	glo	chloh
— blame	blameer	blahmeyr
— boil	kook	kohk
— borrow	leen	leyn
— breakfast	ontbyt eet	ontbeyt eyt
— bring	bring	bring
— build	bou	bo
— button, un-	vasknoop, losknoop	fa(h)sknohp, loss-knohp
— buy	koop	kohp
— calculate	reken, bereken	reyke(r)n be(r)rey-ke(r)n
— carry	dra	drah
— chat	gesels	che(r)se(r)ls
— cheat	bedrieg, mislei	be(r)dreech, missley
— compare	vergelyk	ferche(r)leyk
— consent	toestem, inwillig	tooste(r)m, invil-lich
— continue	voortsit, aanhou	fohrtsit, ahnho
— cook	kook	kohk
— cough	hoes	hoos
— count	tel, reken	te(r)l, reyke(r)n
— cover	bedek	be(r)de(r)k
— dance	dans	da(h)ns
— deliver	verlos, lewer	ferloss, leyver

English.	Afrikaans.	Pronunciation.
To decide	beslis, vasstel	**be(r)sliss, fa(h)s-ste(r)l**
— deny	ontken	ontke(r)n
— depart, go away	vertrek, verlaat	fertre(r)k, ferlaht
— descend	afklim, afstam	a(h)fklim, a(h)f-sta(h)m
— desire (wish for)	begeer	be(r)cheyrr
— despise	verag	fera(h)ch
— draw (pull)	trek	tre(r)k
— draw (picture)	teken	teyke(r)n
— dream	droom	drohm
— dress (oneself)	aantrek	ahntre(r)k
— drink	drink	drink
— dwell, live	woon	vohn
— eat	eet	eyt
— esteem	ag, hoogag	a(h)ch, hohcha(h)ch
— exchange	wissel, ruil	visse(r)l, ruil
— exclaim	uitroep, uitskreeu	uitroop, uitskree'w
— excuse	verontskuldig	ferontskuldich
— explain	uitlê, verklaar	uitlai(r), ferklahr
— fall	val	fa(h)l
— feel (in mind)	voel	fool
— find	vind	fint
— finish	klaarmaak ophou	klahrmahk, opho (*ho* as in hoe)
— follow	volg, navolg	fo(h)lch, na(h)-fo(h)lch
— forget	vergeet	ferr-cheyt
— gather, collect	vergader, versamel	ferchahde(r)r, fer-sahme(r)l
— get, obtain	kry, verkry, bekom	krey, ferkrey, be(r)-kom
— get up	opstaan	opstahn
— give	gee	chey
— go	gaan	chahnn
— go in	ingaan	inchahnn
— go out	uitgaan	uitchahnn
— grow	groei	chroo'i
— guide	lei, bestuur	ley, be(r)stu(r)r
— hate	haat	haht

English.	Afrikaans.	Pronunciation.
To have	hê	hai(r)
— hear	hoor	hohr
— hesitate	aarsel, draai	ahrse(r)l, drah'i
— hide	wegsteek, verberg	ve(r)ch-steyk, ferbe(r)rch
— honour	eer, respekteer	eyr, re(r)spe(r)kteyr
— hope	hoop, verwag	hohp, fervahch
— ignore	verbysien, misken	ferbeyseen, miske(r)n
— imagine	verbeel	ferbeyl
— imitate	namaak	nahmahk
— insult	beleedig	be(r)leydich
— insure	verseker	ferseyke(r)r
— intend	van plan wees	fa(h)n pla(h)n veys
— introduce (one)	voorstel	fohrste(r)l
— — (a thing)	inlei	inley
— jump	spring	spring
— know	ken, weet	ke(r)n, veyt
— laugh	lag	la(h)ch
— lay the tablecloth	die tafel dek	dee tahfe(r)l de(r)k
— learn	leer	leyr
— lend	leen	leyn
— lie down	lê	lai(r)
— live (be alive)	lewe	leyve(r)
— look for	soek na	sook nah
— lose	verloor	ferlohr
— love	liefhê, bemin	leefhai(r), be(r)minn
— marry (take in marriage)	trou	tro (as in *tro*phy)
— meet	ontmoet	ontmoot
— mention	meld, noem	me(r)lt, noom
— object	beswaar maak, objekteer	be(r)svahr mahk, obye(r)kteyr
— obtain	verkry	ferkrey
— offend	beledig, aanstoot gee	be(r)leydich, ahnstohtchey
— offer	aanbied, offer	ahnbeet, offer
— open	oopmaak, inlei	ohpmahk, inley
— order (goods, etc.)	bestel	be(r)ste(r)l
— pack up	pak, inpak	pa(h)k, inpa(h)k

English.	Afrikaans.	Pronunciation.
To paint (a picture)	skilder	skilde(r)r
— pardon	vergewe	ferche(r)ve(r)
— pay	betaal	be(r)tahl
— picture, painting	prente skilder	prenter(r) skilder
— plant	plant	pla(h)nt
— play	speel	speyl
— pluck, pick	pluk	pluk
— praise	loof, prys	lohf, preys
— prove	bewys	be(r)veys
— put (place)	n ɛrsit, stel	neyrsit, ste(r)l
— put (lay)	lê	lai(r)
— put on (dress)	aantrek	ahntre(r)k
— quarrel	twis, russie maak	tviss, reusee, mahk
— read	lees	leys
— reap	oes	oos
— receive	ontvang	ontfa(h)ng
— refrain	bedwing	be(r)dving
— refute	weerlê	veyrlai(r) (*ai* in air)
— rejoin	weer aansluit	veyr ahnsluit
— remember	onthou	ontho
— repay	terugbetaal	te(r)ruchbe(r)tahl
— repeat	herhaal	herhahl
— reply	antwoord	a(h)ntwohrt
— rest	rus	rus
— return	terugkom	te(r)ruchko(h)m
— return (give back)	teruggee	te(r)ruch-chey
— ring the bell	lui die klok(kie)	lui dee klok(kee)
— roast	braai	brah'i
— run	hardloop	ha(h)rtlohp
— say, tell	sê, vertel	sai(r), ferte(r)l
— search	deursoek	du(r)sook
— see	sien	seen
— sell	verkoop	ferkohp
— serve	dien	deen
— sew, stitch	naai	nah'i
— shave (oneself)	skeer	skeyrr
— show	wys, toon	veys, tohn
— sigh	sug	such
— sign (letter, etc.)	teken	teyke(r)n
— sit down	gaan sit	chahn sit

English.	Afrikaans.	Pronunciation.
To sleep	slaap	slahp
— sneeze	nies	nees
— sow	saai	sah'i
— speak	praat, gesels	praht, che(r)se(r)ls
— spin	spin	spin
— steal	steel	steyl
— study	studeer	studeyrr
— swear	vloek	flook
— take	neem	neym
— take off, away	neemah, -weg	neyma(h)f, -vech
— taste	proe, smaak	proo, smahk
— tell (a tale)	sê, vertel, meedeel verhaal	sai(r), verte(r)l, meydeyl ferhahl
— tell the tale	dit navertel	dit nahferte(r)l
— thank	dank, bedank, dankie sê	da(h)nk, da(h)nkee sai(r) be(r)da(h)nk
— think	dink, nadink, bedink	dink, na(h)dink, be(r)dink
— throw	gooi, werp	choh'i, verp
— touch	voel, aanraak, aanroer	fool, ahnrahk, ahnroor
— translate	vertaal, oorsit	fertahl, ohrsit
— travel	reis	reys
— unbutton	losmaak	loss'mahk
— uncover	oopmaak	ohpmahk
— unpack	uitpak	uitpa(h)k
— want, require	nodig hê, wens, verlang	nohde(r)ch hai(r), vens, ferlahng
— wash (oneself)	was	va(h)s
— weep	huil, ween, treur	huil, veyn, tru(r)r
— weigh	weeg	veych
— wish	wens	ve(r)ns
— wish, be willing	wil, gewillig wees	vill, che(r)villich veys
— work	werk, arbei	ve(r)rk, a(h)rbey
— wrap	inrol, toemaak	inro(h)l, toomahk
— write	skrywe	skreyve(r)

Adverbs, Conjunctions, and Prepositions
(Bywoorde, Voegwoorde, Voorsetsels)

English.	Afrikaans.	Pronunciation.
About	ongeveer, omtrent	onche(r)feyr, omtre(r)nt
above	bo, hoer, meer	boh, hoh-e(r)r, meyr
above all	bowenal, veral	bohve(r)na(h)l, fera(h)l
accordingly	ooreenkomstig, gevolglik, duss	ohreynkomste(r)ch, che(r)folchlik, duss
according to	na, volgens	nah, folche(r)ns
across	oor, dwars, deur, anderkant	ohr, dva(h)rs,du(r)r, a(h)nde(r)rhant
after	agter, naderhand, na, later	achter, nahde(r)rhahnt, nah, lahte(r)r
afterwards	daarna, later	dahrnah, lahte(r)r
again	weer, opnuut, nog, verder	veyr, opnéût, noch, fe(r)de(r)r
against	teen	teyn
all	geheel, almal, alles	che(r)heyl, a(h)lma(h)l, a(h)l'le(r)s
all at once, suddenly	plotseling, meteens	plo(r)tse(r)ling, meteyns
almost	amper, byna	a(h)mpe(r)r, beynah
alone, solely	alleen	a(h)l-leyn'
already	al, reeds, alreeds	a(h)l, reyts, a(h)lreyts
also, too, besides	ook, eweneens, buitendien	ohk, eyve(r)neyns, buite(r)ndeen
although	ofskoon, hoewel, almaskie	ofskohn, a(h)lhuve(r)l, a(h)lma(h)skee'
altogether	almal, heeltemal, tesame, volkome	a(h)lma(h)l, heylte(r)ma(h)l, te(r)sahme(r), folkohme(r)
always	altyd, gedurig	a(h)lteyt, che(r)dêûrich

English.	Afrikaans.	Pronunciation.
among	onder, tussen, by	onde(r)r, tu(r)s-se(r)n, bey
and	en	en
anywhere	orals, op enige plek	ohra(h)la, op ey-niche(r) ple(r)k
around	om, om en om, ron-dom, in die rondte	o(h)m, o(h)m e(r)n o(h)m, ro(h)nt-o(h)m, in dee ro(h)nt-te(r)
as	as, soos, gelyk as	a(h)s, sohs, che(r)-leyk a(h)s
as many, as much	net soveel	nett sohfeyl
as . . . as	so . . . as	soh . . . a(h)s
as soon as	so gou as	soh chou a(h)s
at	tot, te, op, in, aan, by, teen, met, na, oor	tot, te(r), op, in, bey, teyn, met, nah, ohr
at first	eers	eyrs
at last	eindelik	eynde(r)lik
at least	tenminste	te(r)nminste(r)
at (the) most	hoogtens, uiters	hohchte(r)ns, uit-e(r)rs
at once	dadelik	da(h)de(r)lik
at present	teenswoordig	teynsvohrde(r)ch
badly	erg, sleg	e(r)rch, sle(r)ch
because	omdat, want, daar	omda(h)t, va(h)nt, dahr
before	voor, vantevore, vroeër	fohr, fa(h)nte(r)foh-re(r), frue(r)r
behind	agter, van agter, agteraan	a(h)chte(r)r, fa(h)n a(h)chte(r), a(h)chte(r)ahn
below	onder, benede, om-laag	onde(r)r, be(r)ney-de(r), omlahch
besides	bowendien, behalwe buiten	bovendeen, be(r)-hahlve(r) bui-te(r)n
better	beter	beyte(r)r
between	tussen, tussenin, onder	tûsse(r)n, tûsse(r)n' in, o(h)nde(r)

English.	Afrikaans.	Pronunciation.
beyond	bo, buite, verder, verby	boh, buite(r), ferder, ferbey
but	maar, dog, egter, behalwe	mahr, doch, êchte(r)r, be(r)hahlve(r)
by	deur, tot, met, na, by, op, langs, naby	du(r)r, tot, me(r)t, nah, bey, op, lahngs, nahbey
by turns	een na die ander	eyn nah dee ahnde(r)r
certainly	sekerlik, beslis	seyke(r)rlik, be(r)sliss
consequently	gevolglik, by gevolge	cherfolchlik, bey che(r)folche(r)
daily	daagliks	dahchliks
down, downwards	neer, na ondertoe	neyr, nah onder-too
during	gedurende	che(r)dȇurende(r)
early	vroeg	frooch
either, or	òf, òf	of, of
elsewhere	erens, elders, anders	ai(r)e(r)ns, e(r)lde(r)s, a(h)nde(r)s
enough, sufficiently	genoeg	che(r)nooch
even if	selfs indien	se(r)lfs indeen
every	elke, ieder	e(r)lke(r), eede(r)r
everywhere	oral(s)	ohra(h)l(s)
except	behalwe	be(r)hahlve(r)
far	ver	fe(r)r
firstly	ten eerste, in die eerste plek	te(r)n eyrste(r), in dee eyrste(r) ple(r)k
foolishly	dwaaslik	dvahslik
for (prep.)	vir	firr
for (conj.)	want	vahnt
formerly	voorheen, eertyds, vanmelewe, vroeër	fohrheyn, eyrteyts, fa(h)nme(r)leyve(r), frooe(r)r
from	van, vandaan, uit, vanuit	fa(h)n, fa(h)ndahn, uit, fa(h)nuit
fully	volkome, heeltemal	fo(h)lkohme(r), heylte(r)ma(h)l

English.	Afrikaans.	Pronunciation.
further	verder, bowendien, buitendien	ferde(r)r, bohven-deen, buiten-deen
gladly, readily	graag, met genoeë, bly, blymoedig	chrahch, met che(r)-nooe(r), bley, bleymoodich
hardly	nouliks, skaars, met moeite	no-liks, skahrs, met moo'ite(r)
here	hier	heer
herewith	hiermee, hierby	heermey, heerbey
how	hoe, wat	hoo, va(h)t
however	egter, nogtans, hoewel	e(r)chte(r)r, noch-ta(h)ns hoove(r)l
how much ?	hoeveel ?	hoo-feyl ?
if	indien, as, so, ingeval	indeen, a(h)s, soh, inche(r)fa(h)l
if not	so nie	soh nee
if only	indien slegs, indien maar net	indeen sle(r)chs, in-deen mahr nett
immediately	dadelik, onmiddellik	da(h)de(r)lik, on-midde(r)lik
in, within	in, binne-in	in, binne(r)-in (*in* in bin)
in case	in geval	in che(r)fa(h)l
indeed	inderdaad, regtig	indai(r)daht, re(r)ch te(r)ch
in future	voortaan, in vervolg	fohrtahn, in ferfolch
inside	binnekant	binne(r)ka(h)nt
in spite of	ten spyte van	te(r)n speyte(r) fa(h)n
instead of	in plaas van	in plahs fa(h)n
kindly	op 'n vriendelike manier	op i(h)n freende(r)-like(r) ma(h)neer
late	laat	laht
less	minder	minde(r)r
like (adj.)	gelyk, eners	che(r)leyk, eyn-e(r)rs
like, as (adv.)	ewenas, soos	eyve(r)na(h)s, sohs
little	klein, min, 'n bietjie	kleyn, minn, i(h)n beetyee

English.	Afrikaans.	Pronunciation.
little by little	stadig, langsamerhand	stahdich, la(h)ngsahmerha(h)nt
more	meer	meyr
much	baie, seer, veel	bah'i-e(r), seyrr, feyl
near	naby, digby, aan, by	na(h)bey, dichbey, ahn, bey
nearly	amper, byna	a(h)mper, beynah
neither . . . nor	nòg . . . nòg ; nie . . .nie	noch . . . noch ; nee . . . nee
never	nooit, nimmer	noh'i-t, nimmer
next to	langsaan	la(h)ngsahn
not	nie	nee
not at all	gladnie	chla(h)t-nee
nothing	niks, niemendal	nix, neeme(r)ndahl
not yet	nog nie	noch nee
now	nou, tans, teenswoordig	no, ta(h)ns, teynsvohrde(r)ch
nowhere	nêrens, niewers	nai(r)'e(r)ns, neevers
of	van, uit, aan	fa(h)n, uit, ahn
of course	natuurlik	na(h)teûrlik
often	dikwels, baiemaal	dikvills, bah'i-e(r)mahl
on, upon	op, aan, by, bo-op	op, ahn, bey, boh-op
on account of	omrede, as gevolg van	omreyde(r), a(h)s che(r)fo(r)lch fa(h)n
on the contrary	inteendeel, daarenteen	inteyndeyl, dahre(r)nteyn
on the left	links om, na die linkerkant	links o(r)m, na(h) dee linkerka(h)nt
on the opposite side	aan die anderkant oorkant	ahn dee a(h)nderka(h)nt, ohrka(h)nt
on the right	regs	re(r)chs
on this side	aan hierdiekant	ahn heerdeeka(h)nt
once	eendag, eenkeer, eens, eenmaal	eynda(h)ch, eynkeyr, eyns, eynmahl

English.	Afrikaans.	Pronunciation.
only	enigste, alleen, slegs, maar net	eynichste(r)r, a(h)l-leyn, sle(r)chs, mahr nett
opposite	teenoorgestel, teen-oor	teynohrche(r)ste(r)l, teynohr
or	of	of
otherwise	anders, origens	a(h)nde(r)rs, ohriche(r)ns
out of	uit	uit
outside	buitekant, buite	buite(r)ka(h)nt, buite(r)
over	oor, uit, bo, op, aan	ohr, uit, boh, op, ahn
perhaps	miskien, dalk, straks	miskeen, da(h)lk, stra(h)ks
presently, soon	netnou, aanstons, aans	nett-no, a(h)ns-to(r)ns, ahns
previously	vantevore	fa(h)nte(r)fohre(r)
quickly	gou, vinnig	cho, finne(r)ch
quietly	stilletjies	stil-le(r)t-yees
quite, altogether	heeltemal, glad	heylte(r)mahl, chla(h)t
rather	liewer(s), taamlik, alte seker, danig	leever(s), tahmlik, a(h)lte(r) seyker, da(h)nich
round	rondom, in die rondte	ro(r)ntom, in dee ro(r)ntte(r)
same (the)	selfde, eners	se(r)lfde(r), eyners
scarcely	nouliks, ternouer-nood	no-liks, ternoe(r)r-noht
secondly	in die twede plaas, ten twede	in dee tveyde(r)-plahs, te(r)n tveyde(r)
seldom, rarely	selde, min	se(r)lde(r), minn
since (adv.)	sinds, sedert	sints, seyde(r)rt
since (conj.)	omdat, daar, aan-gesien	omda(h)t, dahr, ahnche(r)seen
since (prep.)	sedert, sinds	seyde(r)rt, sints
so	so, dus, sodanig	soh, duss, sohdah-nich

English.	Afrikaans.	Pronunciation.
so much, so many	so veel	soh feyl
so much the better, all the better	des te beter	des te(r) beyte(r)r
some (adj.)	enige	eyniche(r)
— (adv.)	ongeveer	onche(r)feyr
somehow	op een of ander manier	op eyn of a(h)nde(r)r ma(h)neer
sometimes	soms, somtyds, partymaal	so(r)ms, so(r)m-teyts, pa(h)rtey-mahl
soon	gou, spoedig, wel-dra, binnekort	cho, spoode(r)ch, veldrah binne(r)-ko(r)rt
suddenly	plotseling, skielik	plo(h)tse(r)ling, skeelik
that (con.)	dat, omdat	da(h)t, omda(h)t
then	dan, toe, daarna, dus vervolgens, destyds	da(h)n, too, dahr-na(h), ferfolch-e(r)ns, desteyts
thence	daarvandaan, van toe af, vandaar	dahrfa(h)ndahn, fa(h)n too a(h)f, fa(h)ndahr
thenceforth	van die tyd af	fa(h)n dee teyt a(h)f
there	daar	dahr
therefore	daarom	dahro(r)m
thirdly	ten derde, in die derde plaas	te(r)n dai(r)rde(r), in dee dai(r)rde(r) plahs
through	deur	du(r)r
thus	dus, so, aldus	dus,, soh, a(h)lduss
till, until	tot, totdat	tot, totda(h)t
to	tot, na, na . . . toe, om, aan, op, vir, om te	tot, nah, nah . . . too, om ahn, op, fir, om te(r)
too	ook	ohk
too much	te veel	te(r) feyl
together	tesaam, bymekaar, gesamentlik	te(r)sahm, bey-me(r)kahr, che(r)-sahme(r)ntlik

English.	Afrikaans.	Pronunciation.
towards	na, tot, teen, jeens	**na(h), tot, teyn, yeyns**
under	onder	**onder**
undoubtedly	ongetwyfeld	**onche(r)tveyfe(r)lt**
unless	tensy, so nie, behalwe	**te(r)nsey, soh nee, be(r)ha(h)lve(r)**
until	tot, totdat	**tot, totda(h)t**
up, upwards	op, bo, na bo, boontoe	**op, boh, na(h) boh, bohntoo**
very	baie, danig, regtig	**bah'i-e(r) da(h)nich, rechte(r)ch**
well	wel, goed, gesond	**vel, choot, che(r)-so(h)nt**
when	wanneer, toe. as	**va(h)n-neyr, too. a(h)s**
where ?	waar ?	**vahr**
whether, if	hetsy, of	**he(r)tsey, of**
while, whilst	terwyl, onderwyl, solank	**terrveyl, onderveyl, sola(h)nk**
why ?	waarom ?	**vahrom**
willingly	graag	**chrahch**
with	met, saam met, saam, mee	**met, sahm met, mey, sahm**
within	binne-in	**binne(r)-in**
without	sonder, buite	**sonder, buite(r)**
yearly	jaarliks	**yahrliks**
yet, still	nog, egter, nogtans, tot, darem	**noch, echter, noch-ta(h)ns, tot, da(h)re(r)m**

rr, reminder to sound r; ch hard guttural

ELEMENTARY GRAMMAR

The Articles (Die Lidworde)

Like their equivalents in English, the Afrikaans Articles are indeclinable; that is to say, they are not subject to inflexion.

There are two Articles:

(*a*) DEFINITE (Bepaalde): die (the),
(*b*) INDEFINITE (Onbepaalde): 'n (a, an).

They are classed as Adjectives (Byvoeglike Naamwoorde) which are likewise not inflected to show difference in gender.

NOTE.—The Definite Article is often used in Afrikaans where there is no article in English, as: van *die* hand in *die* tand, from hand to mouth; though *van hand tot mond* (from hand to mouth) is also heard in some parts, and is not necessarily wrong.

There are phrases, however, in which the definite article used in English is not used in Afrikaans as: Piano speel, to play the piano; Eerlik speel, to play the game.

The Noun (Die Selfstandige Naamwoord)

. Afrikaans nouns are not declined, i.e. they have no cases and, therefore, do not have different terminations.

Gender (Geslag)

There is no "Grammatical" gender in Afrikaans. Sex indicates the distinction in gender. All living beings are, therefore, either masculine, feminine, or common gender; while all inanimate objects are neuter.

In the case of living beings the feminine may be distinguished from the masculine in the following three ways:

1. By SUFFIXES:

(*a*) -IN:

koning	(king)	koningin	(queen)
vriend	(friend)	vriendin	(female friend)
heiden	(heathen)	heidin	(female heathen)

(*b*) -ES:

prins	(prince)	prinses	(princess)
onderwyser	(teacher)	onderwyseres	
digter	(poet)	digteres	(poetess)

(*c*) -STER:

weker	(worker)	werkster	
spreker	(speaker)	spreekster	
voorsitter	(chairman)	voorsitster	

(*d*) -E:

sekretaris	(secretary)	sekretaresse	
president	(chairman)	presidente	
eggenoot	(husband)	eggenote	(wife)

(*e*) -IESE :

eksaminator	(examiner)	eksaminatriese
inspekteur	(inspector)	inspektriese

2. By PREFIXES : mannetjie (male) and wyfie (female)

mannetjievolstruis	(cock ostrich)
volstruiswyfie	(the hen)
mannetjieleeu	(lion)
leeuwyfie	(lioness)
mannetjie-eend	(drake)
wyfie-eend	(duck)

3. By using DIFFERENT WORDS for the masculine and the feminine :

buurman	(neighbour)	buurvrou
baas	(master)	nooi or nôi
heer	(gentleman)	dame
neef	(cousin)	niggie
seun	(son)	dogter
bul	(bull)	koei
vader	(father)	moeder
haan	(cock)	hen
oom	(uncle)	tante
jongetjie	(boy)	meisie

4. Nouns of COMMON GENDER, i.e. those that are either masculine or feminine :

vreemdeling	(stranger)
leerling	(student)
tweeling	(twin)
weeskind, wees	(orphan)
lidmaat	(member)
perd	(horse)
skaap	(sheep)
hond	(dog)

5. The difference in gender may also be brought out by the pronouns hy (he), sy (she), dit (it) ; sy (his), haar (her) ; syne (his), hare (hers) : Die musikant het sy boogdraad (sy strykstok se draad) gebreek (the musician snapped his bow-string) i.e. it is a male. Die weeskind ken haar les goed (the orphan knows her lesson very well). Hierdie speelgoed is nie syne nie ; dit is hare (these toys are not his ; they are hers).

NOTE.—In certain cases feminine endings are gradually being dropped in Afrikaans, as :

boerin (farmer's wife) is now boervrou.

se and sê

Great care must be exercised that se is not confounded with sê. se (pronounced—se(r)) denotes possession, and represents the English apostrophe ; while sê (pronounced—sai(r)) means say :

Jan se perd (John's horse) ; Jan sê Piet se hoed se band is af (John says Peter's hat-band is off).

Die skolier sê vir sy onderwyser dat sy boetie en sussie se oë seer is, dus kan hulle nie skool-toe kom nie.

(The pupil informs (tells) his teacher that his little brother and little sister's eyes are sore consequently they cannot attend school).

Die wa se een wiel (die een wiel van die wa) waggel (one of the wheels of the wagon wobbles).

Number (Getal)

There are two numbers :

(*a*) Singular (enkelvoud) (*b*) Plural (meervoud)

Formation of Plural

Afrikaans nouns do not form their plural in the same way as English nouns, by adding s to the singular.

The plural is formed in various ways, and these must be carefully studied, i.e. by adding :

-e, -te, -s, -ers, -ere to the singular.

1. Plurals in -e :

(*a*) Nouns with the accent on the last syllable form their plural by adding -e :

lemoen (orange) lemoene manél (frock-coat) mannelle

Under this rule are also included nouns of one syllable :

pen (pen) boom (tree)
penne bome

When the final syllable is unaccented, they take -s :

táfel (table) bédelaar (beggar) láfaard (coward)
tafels bedelaars lafaards

(*b*) Nouns ending in -aris take -e in the plural :

sekretaris (secretary) sekretarisse
notaris (notary) notarisse

2. Plurals in -te :

Some nouns ending in f, g, p, s, ended in -t in Dutch, and have lost this final t in Afrikaans, but in the plural it is found again before -e : vrug (fruit)—vrugte ; drif (passion)—drifte ; amp (profession)—ampte ; nes (nest)—neste.

3. Plurals in -s :

(*a*) Nouns of more than one syllable ending in -el, -em, -en, -er, and not having the accent on the last syllable :

kêrel (fellow) kêrels
besem (broom) besems
laken (sheet) lakens
moeder (mother) moeders

(*b*) Nouns of two syllables ending in weakly accented -ing take s

toring (tower) torings
kussing (pillow) kussings
voering (lining) voerings

(*c*) Nouns in -ing formed from verbs usually have two plurals : -s : vergadering (meeting) vergaderings and -e : vergaderinge, but nouns in -ling and -eling usually take -e :

nuweling (newcomer) nuwelinge

There seems to be a tendency in Afrikaans, however, to prefer the -s in the plural ending rather than -e, especially in regard to the above nouns in -ing, -ling, and -eling (*d*) Nouns ending in an unaccented e take s:

belofte	(promise)	beloftes
gedagte	(thought)	gedagtes

(*e*) Nouns of foreign origin with the accent on the last syllable often have two plurals:

-e:	koepon	(coupon)	koeponne and -s, koepons
	hotel	(hotel)	hotels and hotelle

Sometimes they take -s only:

generaal	(general)	generaals

(*f*) Nouns ending in -aal, -aar, -aard, -ier take s if they denote persons, but e if they denote things:

	Persons		Things	
-aal:	korporaal	(corporal)	kwartaal	(quarter)
	korporaals		kwartale	
-aar:	bedelaar	(beggar)	gevaar	(danger)
	bedelaars		gevare	
-ier:	barbier	(barber)	papier	(paper)
	barbiers		papiere	

(*g*) Nouns ending in weakly accented -ee and -ie take s:

-ee:	skáduwee	(shadow)	skaduwees
-ie:	stasie	(station)	stasies

(*h*) All diminutives take s:

boompie	(small tree)	boompies	(little trees)
bokkie	(small goat)	bokkies	(little goats)

4. Plurals in -'s:

(*a*) Letters of the alphabet: a's, d's, k's,

(*b*) Nouns ending in an accented -a or -o:

pa's	(fathers);	hoera's	(hurrahs);
buro's	(bureaux);	tablo's	(tableaux)

(*c*) Foreign names in -ee, -i, -o, -u:

kafeé	(café)	kafee's
impi	(impi)	impi's
iempie		iempies
duo	(duo)	duo's
duet		duette
parvenu	(parvenu)	parvenu's
parwenu		parwenu's

5. Plurals in -ers and -ere:

A few nouns take -ers or -ere in the plural:

-ers:	kind	(child)	kinders
	lam	(lamb)	lammers
	kalf	(calf)	kalwers
-ere:	gemoed	(mind)	gemoedere
	lied	(song)	liedere

6. Irregular Plurals:

(*a*) In order to preserve the short vowel sound in the plural, a final consonant preceded by such a vowel is doubled:

dak	(roof)	dakke
hen	(hen)	henne

(*b*) A good many nouns lengthen the short vowel in the plural:

pad	(path)	paaie
vlag	(flag)	vlae
weg	(road)	weë
verdrag	(treaty)	verdrae
gebrek	(want)	gebreke
gebed	(prayer)	gebede
vat	(vat)	vate

(*c*) Additional irregular plurals:

hemp	(shirt)	hemde
jas	(raincoat)	jaste, jasse
lewe	(life)	lewes, lewens
graf	(grave)	grafte, graftes
nôi, nooi	(mistress)	nôiens, nooiens
sog	(sow)	sôe
stad	(town)	stede
skip	(ship)	skepe
wa	(waggon)	waens

(*d*) Nouns ending in -heid have -hede in the plural:

waarheid	(truth)	waarhede
swarigheid	(difficulty)	swarighede
nuwigheid	(novelty)	nuwighede
aanvalligheid	(loveliness, charms)	aanvallighede
beslistheid	(decision)	beslisthede

(*e*) A few nouns compounded with -man have -manne, -mense, or -mans in the plural:

-manne:	staatsman	(statesman)	staatsmanne
-mense:	werksman	(workman)	werksmense
-mans:	koopman	(merchant)	koopmans

but:

Engelsman	(Englishman)	Engelse
Fransman	(Frenchman)	Franse
buurman	(neighbour)	bure

(*f*) A number of nouns have more than one plural:

bad	(bath)	badde, baddens, batte
bed	(bed)	bedde, beddens
graf	(grave)	grafte, graftes, grawe
klip	(stone)	klippe, klippers
lewe	(life)	lewes, lewens
mied, miet	(stack)	miede, miedens, miete
vark	(pig)	varke, varkens
volk	(nation)	volke, volkere
vrou	(woman, wife)	vroue, vrouens, vroumense
voorskoot	(apron)	voorskote, voorskooie

(*g*) Some nouns have two plurals with different meanings:

bad	badde, baaie	(natural or hot baths)
	badde, baddens, batte	(baths to wash in)

blad	blaaie	(leaves of a book)
blad, blaar	blare	(leaves of a tree)
drif	drifte	(passions)
	driwwe	(fords)
goed	goedere	(possessions)
	goeters	(things)
hoop	verwagtinge	(expectations)
	hope	(heaps)
las	laste	(loads, difficulties)
	lasse	(joints)
letter	letters	(of the alphabet)
	lettere	(literature)
maat	maats, maters	(comrades)
	mate	(measures)
raad	raadegewings	(advice)
	rade	(councils)
rug	rugge, rugte	(backs)
	ruens	(hill-crests)
saal	saals	(saddles)
	sale	(halls)
skof	skowwe	(hump on neck of an ox)
	skofte	(work-shifts)
vorm	vorms	(moulds)
	vorme	(forms, aspects)

(*h*) A few diminutives have a double plural :

goedjie	goedjies, goetertjies	(little dears, tiny things)
kalfie	kalfies, kalwertjies	(little calves)
klippie	klippies, klippertjies	(tiny stones)
lammetjie	lammetjies, lammertjies	(little lambs)
maatjie	maatjies, matertjies	(little play-mates)

(*i*) Some nouns have a borrowed plural :

aabod	(offer)	aanbiedinge (ahnbeedinge(r))
bedrog	(deceit)	bedrieërye (be(r)dree-e(r)reye(r))
beleg	(siege)	beleëringe (be(r)ley-e(r)ringe(r))
doel	(purpose)	doeleindes (dooleyende(r)s)
eer	(honour)	eerbewyse (eyrbe(r)veyse(r))
genot	(enjoyment)	genietinge (che(r)neetinge(r))
seën	(blessing)	seëninge (sey-e(r)ninge(r))

7. A large number of nouns are only used in the plural, and have no singular :

harsings	(brains)	medisyne	(medicine)
pokkies	(small-pox)	komplemente	(compliments)

masels	(measles)	semels	(bran)
toiings	(rags)	fraiings	(tassels)
koste, onkoste	(costs)		

8. Some NOUNS have no PLURAL :

(*a*) Names of materials :

goud (gold) ; koper (copper) ; silwer (silver).

(*b*) The majority of abstract nouns :

hoogmoed (pride) ; welsprekenheid (eloquence) ; liefde (love). etc

9. NOUNS denoting MEASURE, WEIGHT, NUMBER, or VALUE, preceded by a definite numeral adjective, are used in the singular (although accompanied by plural numerals) with a plural meaning :

drie paar kouse	(three pairs of stockings)
vyf jaar gelede	(five years ago)
tien pond sterling	(ten pounds sterling)
sewe voet hoog	(seven feet high)

Vader is sestig jaar oud
(Father is sixty years of age)
Hy het 'n inkoms van duisend pond (collectively)
(He has an income of a thousand pounds)
Ek het hier drie sjielings (singly)
(I have three shillings here)
Vier pond suiker (collectively)
(Four pounds of sugar)
Vier ponde suiker (separately, one by one)
(Four pounds of sugar)
Drie jaar (three years) (one period)
Drie jare (three years taken separately).

Case (Naamval)

It has already been noted that there are no case-endings in Afrikaans. As in English, the relation is shown by the position of the noun in the sentence, and by the aid of prepositions.

[See under " se " (') and " sê " (say).]

Vir (to, for)

The preposition VIR is used :

(*a*) with the indirect object :

Gee vir Piet jou mes
(Give Peter (lit. to Peter) your knife) ;

(*b*) after transitive verbs with the direct object, if the direct object is a proper name :

Die onderwyser slaan vir Jan
(The teacher beats John) ;

(*c*) with pronouns, very extensively, even in the Accusative Case (Direct Object) :

Ek sal vir jou slaan
(I'll thrash you)
Die perd sal vir hom skop
(The horse will kick him)

Gee vir haar die regter hand
(Give her your right hand)
Sê vir my jou naam
(Tell me your name).
(See Prepositions, page 133.)

The Adjective (Die Byvoeglike Naamwoord)

Adjectives are divided into six classes:
(*a*) Adjectives of Quality.
(*b*) Adjectives of Quantity (Numeral Adjectives).
(*c*) Participles (present and past) used as Adjectives.
(*d*) Demonstrative Adjectives.
(*e*) Possessive Adjectives.
(*f*) Interrogative Adjectives.

The last three classes are really pronouns used adjectively, and they will, therefore, be dealt with under the Pronoun.

Use of Adjectives

Adjectives of Quality and of Quantity may be used
(*a*) Attributively:
'n sterk man (a strong man)
(*b*) Predicatively:
die man is sterk (the man is strong)

Some adjectives are generally used only Attributively:
(*a*) Those signifying the material of which a thing is made:
'n goue ring (a golden ring)
(*b*) Adjectives formed from proper names:
Londonse vrede (peace of London)
(*c*) Adjectives formed from adverbs of time:
Ons daelikse brood (our daily bread)
(*d*) A few others like:

voorste	(foremost)
boonste	(topmost)
binneste	(innermost)
ganse	(whole)

Some adjectives, again, are only used Predicatively:

kinds	(childish)
geheg	(attached)
bevrees	(afraid)

NOTE.—Material adjectives always end in -e and are mostly used in a figurative sense.

Inflexion of Adjectives

Only adjectives used ATTRIBUTIVELY may be inflected by adding -e to the stem.

Adjectives used PREDICATIVELY never take -e.

N.B.—Where pronunciation is omitted, it will be found given previously

N.B.—Some Nouns of quality are here given for convenient reference;

Adjectival Suffixes (Byvoeglike Naamwoorde se Agtervoegsels)

Many adjectives are original adjectives; others are formed from nouns and verbs by the addition of suffixes, as they often are in English. Thus the adjectival suffix:

-e (English en)

goue, golden;
silwere, piece of silver;
geestelike, clergyman, parson, priest.

-ig (English y) signifies "of the nature or substance of"

geestig, mental, intellectual (die *geest*, mind, spirit);
gelowig, believing, credulous (die *geloof*, belief, creed);
smerig, dirty (die *smerigheid*, dirt);
klipperig, stony (*klip*, stone);
rustig, quiet, restful (*rus*, repose).

-lik (English ly or like) signifies "characteristic of":

geestelik, spiritual, spiritlike;
gelooflik, credible;
heerlik, glorious, lordly (*heer*, master, lord);
kinderlik, childlike;
manlik, masculine, male (*man*, man);
vroulik, feminine, female (*vrou*, woman)

-s (English ish) signifies "pertaining to":

kinds, childish (*kind*, child);
aards, worldly, earthly (*aarde*, earth);
hemels, heavenly, celestial (*hemel*, heaven);
Afrikaans, African (Africa);
Engels, English (England);
Frans, French (France).

-baar (English ible) signifies "capable of" (in passive sense):

vrugbaar, fruitful, fertile (*vrug*, fruit);
genecsbaar, curable;
dankbaar, thankful, grateful;
wonderbaar, wonderful.

-saam (English some) signifies "capable of" (in active sense):

waaksaam, vigilant, watchful (*waak*, to watch);
gehoorsaam, submissive, docile;
heilsaam, wholesome, beneficial (*heil*, welfare, good);
minsaam, kind, affable (*min*, love);
duursaam, durable, lasting (*duur*, to last).

Numeral Adjectives (Telwoorde)

NUMERAL ADJECTIVES consist of:

1. CARDINAL NUMERALS (Hooftelwoorde):

(*a*) Definite (Bepaalde):

een	(one)
ag(t)[1]	(eight)
nege, neë	(nine)
duisend	(thousand)
halwe	(half)
albei	(both)

[1] **Ag, from Dutch, acht, still retains the t before uur: agtuur (eight o'clock). Ag uur (written as two words) = eight hours.**

(*b*) Indefinite (Onbepaalde):

al	(all)
min	(few)
baie	(many)
sommige	(some)
elke	(each)

2. ORDINAL NUMERALS (Rangtelwoorde):

(*a*) Definite (Bepaalde):

eerste	(first)
agste	
ag(t)ste	(eighth)
negende	
neënde	(ninth)
duisendste	(thousandth)

(*b*) Indefinite (Onbepaalde):

laaste	(last)
hoeveelste	(which in numerical order)
soveelste	(so many in numerical order)

A full list of Definite Cardinal and Ordinal Numerals will be found at the end of the Vocabularies, pages 114 and 116.

The equivalent for the English -fold is -voudig:

tienvoudig (tenfold); honderdvoudig (hundredfold)

But note—eenvoudig means simple, singular; credulous; plain; for example: dis eenvoudig gekheid (it is sheer madness)

Fractions (Breuke)

FRACTIONS are classified as:

DEFINITE CARDINAL NUMERALS:

('n)aks	[eighth (of an inch)]
vier-vyfdes	(four-fifths)
een-vyfde	(one-fifth)
vier-sewendes	(four-sevenths)

Notes on Numeral Adjectives, Fractions, and other Numeral Derivatives

The Ordinal Numerals are, like the Attributive Adjectives, not declined. They are formed from the Cardinals in the following way:

(*a*) From *two* to *nineteen* by adding de to the Cardinal.

(*b*) From *twenty* upwards by adding ste to the Cardinal. The only Ordinals not formed regularly are:

i. die *eerste*, the first (not eerde);
ii. die *derde*, the third (not driede);
iii. die *agste*, the eighth (not agde).

NOTE.—(i) Die hoeveelste is dit?
What day of the month is it?
(lit. the how-much-th is it?); die laaste, the last.

(ii) One and a half is *anderhalf*, but Afrikanders now mostly use the form een-en-'n half.

NUMERAL DERIVATIVES:

By adding various suffixes to the Cardinals we get whole series of useful expressions:

(*a*) --mal, time or times.

tweemal een, the multiplication table (lit. the twice one);
tweemal twee, twice two (lit. two times two);
eenmal, once; tweemal, twice; driemaal, thrice, three times.

But once upon a time, eens:

Ek is dit met jou *eens*, I agree with you;
Eens en vir altyd, once and for all.

(*b*) -voudig, -fold.

enkelvoudig, single;
tweevoudig, twofold;
drievoudig, threefold.

NOTE.—Enkelvoudig is the same as eenvoudig, but the latter has a more contemptuous meaning, simple (imbecile).

(*c*) -erlei, of (one, two, three, etc.) kinds.

enerlei, of the same kind;
tweërlei, of two kinds;
drieërlei, of three kinds;
velerlei, various, many kinds;
allerlei, all kinds of, all sorts.

(*d*) -ns, -ly.

eerstens, firstly; *twedens*, secondly; *derdens*, thirdly, etc.

NOTE.—*Ten eerste*, at first; *ten twede*, secondly; *ten derde* thirdly; *ten laaste*, at last; *eindelik*, lastly.

Time of the Day

The Afrikaans method of reckoning the time of the day differs from the English in two ways:

(1) The half-hours are spoken of as being half-way on toward the next hour, i.e.:
"half-past twelve" is spoken of as being "half one," *half een*,

(2) The quarters are reckoned as in English or on towards the next hour:
"quarter past twelve," *kwart oor twaalf*;
"quarter to one," *kwart voor een*.

Cardinal numbers are used to show the Years:

e.g., 45 B.C., vyf-en-veertig voor Kristus se geboorte (*or* die geboorte van Kristus);

A.D. 200 (Latin, *anno domini*) tweehonderd na Kristus se geboorte (*or* na die geboorte van Kristus).

(I.e. voor, before—na, after—the birth of Christ.)

In the year 1912 (in die jaar negentienhonderd-en-twaalf).

George the Fifth lives in the twentieth century (Georg die Vyfde leef in die twintigste eeu).

Ordinal numbers are used for the months and days of the week.

1. After the verb *to be*, thus:

It is the first of[1] May, *dis die eerste Mei*.

[1] Note that *of* is omitted in Afrikaans.

2. After " on " :

(*a*) expressing definite time, thus :
He came on Friday, hy het Vrydag die eerste gekom.

(*b*) expressing indefinite time, thus :
He comes on Tuesdays,[1] hy kom Dinsdags (-dae).
(*Hy doen dit saans,* he does it of an evening).

3. Duration of time (" how long ? ") is expressed thus :

(*a*) He worked the whole day, hy het die hele (ganse) dag gewerk (gearbei) ; *or*

(*b*) with lank :
He worked (for) one hour, hy het een uur lank gewerk.

For a list of years, months, days, etc., see VOCABULARIES, pages 31-2.

COMPARISON OF ADJECTIVES

(Vergelyking van Byvoegelike Naamwoorde)

Degrees of Comparison (Trappe van Vergelyking)

The Comparative degree (vergrotende trap) is formed by adding -er and the Superlative (oortreffende) by adding -ste to the Positive (stellende) :

Pos.		Comp.	Sup.
oud	(old)	ouer	oudste
breed	(broad)	breër	breedste
dof	(muffled)	dowwer	dofste

Adjectives ending in -r take d before the Comparative ending -er :

teer	(tender)	teerder	teerste
suur	(sour)	suurder	suurste
bitter	(bitter)	bitterder	bitterste

Adjectives in -s also add -ste for the Superlative :

fluks	(diligent)	flukser	fluksste
juis	(correct)	juister	juisste
skaars	(scarce)	skaarser	skaarsste

Adjectives in -g take -ter in the Comparative :

(*a*) if the g is the modified form of the Dutch -cht :

sag	(soft, D. zacht)	sagter	sagste ;

(*b*) if it is not then it drops out before -er :

laag	(low D. laag)	laer	laagste.

Meer (more) and mees (most) are rarely used in the comparison of adjectives, but are generally used with past participles of verbs used as adjectives :

gebroke	(broken)	meer gebroke	mees gebroke
beskadig	(damaged)	meer beskadig	mees beskadig

The following adjectives have irregular degrees of comparison :

goed	(good)	beter	beste
siek	(ill)	sieker, erger	siekste, ergste

[1] I.e. of a Tuesday.

baie	(many, much)	meer	meeste
min, weinig	(few, little)	minder	minste
nuut, nuwe	(new)	nuter, nuwer	nuutste
kwaad, kwaai	(angry)	kwater, kwaaier	kwaadste, kwaaiste
laat	(late)	later	laatste, laaste
vroeg	(early)	vroeër, eerder	vroegste, eerste
jong, jonk	(young)	jonger	jongste
lang, lank	(long)	langer	langste

With the positive is used so . . . soos :

Jan is so groot soos sy pa
(John is as tall as his father)
Pagel is so sterk soos 'n olifant
(Pagel is as strong as an elephant).

With the Comparative is used dan or as :

Katrina is mooier as (or dan) haar ma
(Catherine is prettier than her mother)
Johannesburg is grooter as (or dan) Pretoria
(Johannesburg is greater than Pretoria)

To strengthen the Superlative aller may be used :

Dit is 'n allerpragtigste roos
(This is a most beautiful rose)
'n mens kry die allerlieflikste natuurskoon in Suidafrika
(One finds the most lovely scenery in South Africa).

When comparing two nouns without using dan or as, the Superlative must be used, and NOT the Comparative, as in English :

Van die twee osse is die swartste die sterkste maar die luiste
(Of the two oxen the darker is the stronger but the lazier)
Van die twee boksers is Georg die swakste maar die slimste
(Of the two boxers George is the weaker but the smarter)
Ons dieretuin is die mooiste van die twee
(Our Zoological garden is the prettier of the two).

Some adjectives do not admit of degrees of comparison :

(*a*) Those denoting material :
'n goue ketting (a golden chain);

(*b*) Those derived from proper names and adverbs of time :
Die Heidlelbergse Kategismis (catechism of Heidelberg)
Die jaarlikse verslag (the yearly return or the annual statement) ;

(*c*) Those like -dood (dead) ; leeg (empty) ; bloed-rooi (blood-red) ; ontelbaar (innumerable) ; almagtig (almighty) ; pikswart (pitch-black) ; goudgeel (yellow as gold) ; doodmoeg (dead tired), which already denote a state of completeness.

Some prepositions as bo (above), onder (below), binne (inside), buite (outside) may be used adjectivally, and then have a Superlative :

Die boonste steen (the topmost brick)
Die onderste plank (the lowermost plank)
Die binneste vere van 'n harlosie (the innermost springs of a watch)
Die buitenste mure van Jerusalem (the outermost walls of Jerusalem).

Adverbs (Bywoorde)

Most adjectives and many participles in Afrikaans can be used also as adverbs :

Dit gaan met my goed (I am well)
Dit was baie mooi gesê (that was very prettily said)
Julle het dit heeltemal onderstebo (verkeerd) gemaak (aangepak) (You have set about it in the wrong way)

Adverbs are formed by adding -lyk, -lyks, -lings, -e, -ens, -s, -jies, -pies, -tjies, -kens, -gewyse to a noun or adjective, as :

einde	(end)	eindelik	finally
dag	(day)	daagliks, daeliks	daily
kort	(short)	kortelings	lately, shortly
ver	(far)	op vere na, op vere na nie	by far, not in the least
minste	(least)	minstens	at least
reg	(right)	regs	to the right
soet	(sweet)	soetjies	softly, gently
warm	(warm)	warmpies	warmly
	(daar warmpies insit, to be fairly rich)		
stil	(silent)	stilletjies	silently
sag	(soft)	saggies, sagkins	softly, gently
trap	(degree)	trapsgewyse	by degrees

Adverbs of time (Bywoorde van tyd) :

altoos, altyd	(always)	soms; somtyds	(sometimes)
dan	(then)	telkens	(repeatedly)
dikwils	(often)	toe	(when, then)
eer	(before, ere)	voortaan	(henceforth)
gou, gou-gou	(soon, quickly)	vanmelewe	(in olden days)
later	(later on)	vroeer	(formerly)
nog	(still)	weer	(again)
nou, nou-nou	(now, this minute)	weleer	(long ago)
selde	(seldom)	wanneer	(when)

Adverbs of place (Bywoorde van plaas) :

af	(off, down)	naby	(near)
bo	(above)	onder	(below)
daar, daarso	(there)	op, opwaarts	(upwards)
êrens, iewers	(somewhere)	tuis	(at home)
ginds, gunter	(yonder)	ver	(far)
heen	(away)	waar, waarso	(where)
hier, hierso	(here)	weg	(away)
heen en weer	(to and fro)	wyd en syd	(far and wide)

Adverbs of manner (Bywoorde van wyse) :

broekskeur	(with much difficulty)
bekoorlik	(enchantingly)
liewers(te)	(rather)
moeielik	(with difficulty)
rustig	(peacefully)
heerlik	(delicious)
hemels	(heavenly)

Modal adverbs, which express :

(*a*) Affirmation (bevestiging) :
ja (yes), seker, stellig (certainly), ongetwyfeld (undoubtedly) werklik, waarlik (really), natuurlik (naturally),

(*b*) Doubt (twyfel) :
altemit ; miskien (perhaps), straks (perhaps) ; konsius, kamma (ostensibly).

(*c*) Negation (ontkenning) :
nee (no), nie (not), nooit (never), volstrek nie, glad nie (not at all).

(*d*) A Wish ('n wens) :
tog : kom tog! (do come!)
maar : help hom maar! (do assist him!)
dan : praat dan! (do speak!).

Adverbs of Degree or Quality (Bywoorde van graad of hoeveelheid) :
Baie (very much), deur en deur (thoroughly), glad (quite), juis (exactly), minstens (at least), op sy meeste (at most), skaars (scarcely), taamlik (tolerably), verreweg (by far).

Adverbs of Causality (Bywoorde van Kausaliteit) which express :

(*a*) The Reason (rede) for an action :
daarom (therefore), hierom (for this reason), derhalwe (hence), ook (also), dus (thus).

(*b*) A Purpose (doel) :
hiertoe (for this purpose), daartoe (for that purpose).

(*c*) Cause (oorsaak) :
waardeur (by what means), daardeur, hierdeur.

(*d*) Concession (toegewing) :
egter (however), desnieteenstaande (notwithstanding)

(*e*) A Means (middel) :
waarmee (wherewith), daarmee, hiermee.

Adverbs of Number and Order (Bywoorde van Getal en Orde) : daarna (after that) ; eenmaal, eenslag (once) ; vereers (firstly) ; ten tweede, twedens (secondly) ; ten derde, derdens (thirdly) ; verder (furthermore).

Conjunctive Adverbs (Voegwoordelike Bywoorde) :

(*a*) Copulative (aaneenskakelend) :
ook (also) ; selfs (even) ; daarna (thereafter) ; daarby (in addition to that) ; as ook (as well as).

(*b*) Adversative and Disjunctive (teenstellend) :
egter (however) ; daarenteë, inteendeel (on the contrary) ; nietemin, ewenwel, nogtans (nevertheless).

(*c*) Illative (oorsaklik) :
daardeur (by that means) ; derhalwe (therefore) ; hierom, daarom (hence) ; bygevolg (consequently).

Derivative Adverbs—(Afgeleide Bywoorde) :

Adverbs are also formed from nouns, adverbs, prepositions, or their combinations :

snags	by night	stroomop	upstream
smôrens	of a morning	aanvang	in the beginning
ooit, steeds	ever	ongelukkig	unluckily
nooit	never	stroomop	upstream

dan	**then, at that time**	**eerstens, eenvoudig, eenmal**	**firstly, singly, once**
naderhand	**afterwards**	**heeltemal**	**wholly, quite**
meestendeels	**mostly, for the most part**	**alreeds**	**already**
		buitekant	**outside**
bergaf	**downhill**	**binnekant**	**inside**
reguit	**straight on**	**voorkant**	**in front**
somtyds	**sometimes (at whiles)**	**agterkant**	**behind**
		omgekeer	**vice versa**
sinds, sedert	**since**	**kortliks**	**shortly**
in alle gevalle	**in any case**	**presies**	**punctually,** ***also*** **punctual**
op hierdie manier	**in this wise**		
		ondertoe	**downwards**
gelukkig	**luckily**	**agterwaarts**	**backwards**
huiswaarts	**homewards**		

Graag makes idiomatic compounds with verbs :

graag hê, to like ; graag sit, to like to sit ;
graag weet, like to know ; graag lees, to like to read, etc.

Ek sit graag by die fenster, I like to sit by the window.

The Comparative and Superlative of graag :

Pos.	Comp.	Sup.
Graag (gladly, fain)	liewer(s) (rather)	liefs, liewerste, graagste

can be used in the same way :

Ex.—Ek sit liewer by die venster as by die kaggel ; maar ek sit darem liewerste daar buite in die tuin.
I like to sit by the window better than by the stove ; but I like best of all to be outside in the garden.

Comparison of Adverbs

The Comparative and Superlative of Adverbs are formed in the same way as those of adjectives :

Pos.		Comp.	Sup.
agter	(behind)	verder agter (further behind)	agterste
erg	(very, badly)	erger	ergste
dikwils	(often)	meer, meermale	meeste
naby	(near)	nader	naaste
selde	(seldom)	minder (less frequently)	minste
vroeg	(early)	eerder, vroeër	eerste, vroegste
wel, goed	(well)	beter	beste

Conjunction (Die Voegwoord)

Conjunctions are of two kinds. Co-ordinating (Neweskikkende Voegwoorde) link together in a sentence words or phrases of equal value. Subordinating Conjunctions (Onderskikkende Voegwoorde) link words and phrases to some other word or phrase on which they are dependent.

Co-ordinating Conjunctions are divided into:

(*a*) Copulative (aaneenskakelend):
en (and); beide . . . en (both . . . and); sowel . . . as (as well . . . as); further also the conjunctive adverbs: nog, ook, daarna, asook, etc.

(*b*) Disjunctive and Adversative (teenstellend):
maar, dog (but); of, òf . . . òf (either . . . or); nòg . . . nòg (neither . . . nor); further the conjunctive adverbs: egter tog, nogtans, etc.

(*c*) Causative (oorsaaklik):
want (for); further conjunctive adverbs: dus, derhalwe, hierom, etc.

Subordinating Conjunctions;

(*a*) Time:
voor, voordat (before); wanneer (when); toe (when); totdat (until); nadat (after); so gou as (as soon as); eer, eerdat (before).

(*b*) Purpose:
opdat, dat (in order that).

(*c*) Condition:
as (if); mits (provided that); tensy (unless); ingeval, ingeval dat (in case).

(*d*) Concession:
al (although); hoewel, alhoewel, ofskoon (although); nieteenstaande (notwithstanding, although).

(*e*) Reason:
om, omdat (because); aangesien (since); daar (since).

(*f*) Comparison:
nes, net soos (just like); soos (like); as, dan (than).

(*g*) Demonstrative:
dat (that).

(*h*) Consequence:
sodat (so that); waarom, waardeur (whence).

Prepositions (Voorsetsels)

In Afrikaans, as in English, all Prepositions govern Nouns or Pronouns in the Objective Case.

For a list of Prepositions see Vocabularies, page 133.

The following prepositions, however, require particular attention:

1. Aan may be used in two senses:
(*a*) to: Ek sê aan (vir) my vrou (I say to my wife);
(*b*) at: Die kinders sit almal aan tafel (the children are all sitting at table).

2. Agter is used for rest at a place or motion, but never for time:
Ek sit agter my pa in die kerk (In church I sit behind my father).
Die poliesman hardloop agter die dief aan (The policeman runs after the thief).

NA.—To express time, na must be used : na die vakansie (after the holidays), but *never* : agter die vakansie. Na hy dit gedoen het, stap hy bedaard weg (After he had done that he walked away calmly).

NA is also used of motion towards, and is then usually followed by toe (towards) :

Dogtertjie, kom na my toe!
(Little girl, come to me!)

Môreoggend gaan ek dorp-toe, huis-toe, ens.
(To-morrow morning I am going to the village home, etc.)
Die meisies loop heirnatoe, die jongetjies daarnatoe
(The girls walk this way, the boys that way).

3. Bo is usually used with op and in (upon and in) :

Sannie staan bo-op die platdak
(Susan stands on top of the flat roof)
Jan sit bo-in die boom
(John sits high up in the tree).

4. DEUR may mean :

(*a*) through : Ek steek my arm deur die mou (I put my arm through the sleeve) ;
(*b*) by means of, through the instrumentality of : Hy het die prys deur jou vriendelikheid gekry (He obtained the prize through your kindness).

5. OM may mean :

(*a*) at (of time) : om drie-uur (at three o'clock), om die ander dag (every second day) ;
(*b*) round : Die hond loop om die huis (The dog walks round the house) ;
(*c*) for the sake of : Hy het dit om jou gedoen (He did it for your sake) ;
(*d*) on account of : Ek huil om jou (I weep on account of you).

6. SAAM MET : The following examples will illustrate the use :

(*a*) Jan, gaan jy saam met my stad-toe ? (John, are you going with me to town ?) ;
(*b*) Ja, ek sal met jou saamgaan (Yes, I'll go with you) ;
(*c*) Neem hierdie brief, saam met die boek, na Mnr. B. toe (Take this letter, together with the book, to Mr. B.) ;
(*d*) Saam may also be used alone : Pa gaan Durban toe en ek gaan saam (Father is going to Durban, and I am going with him).

7. TEENOOR may mean :

(*a*) over against : Hy stel sy eis teenoor myne (He puts in his claim over against mine) ;
(*b*) towards : Die generaal was baie vriendelik teenoor sy soldate (The general was very kind towards his soldiers).

8. TOT may mean :

(*a*) To : Die Engel sê *tot* Lot (The Angel said to Lot). This usage is mostly found in biblical expressions. In ordinary Afrikaans we rather use *vir* (*b*) until: Wag tot (of totdat) hy 'n antwoord stuur (Wait until he sends a reply). Ons werk van die more tot die aand (We work from morning till night).

9. VAN may express:
(*a*) possession (of): Die hoed van Jan (John's hat); De steweltjies van Sannie (Sannie's little boots); Die wiel van die wa (The wheel of the waggon).
(*b*) motion (from): 'n brief van Jan (A letter from John); Kom jy van Pretoria af? (Do you come from Pretoria?); Van Maandag tot Saterdag (From Monday to Saturday).

10. VIR is a preposition used very extensively, and with a variety of meanings:
(*a*) for: Hier is 'n present vir jou (Here is a present for you); Dit is jou kos vir die dag (This is your food for the day); Vir twee jaar het ek hom nooit gesien nie (For, or during, two years I never saw him).
(*b*) to: Vir my lyk die saak maar ernstig (To me the matter appears to be rather serious); Hy sê vir my ek moet gou maak (He says to me that I must hurry up).
(*c*) Vir is also used with the Indirect Object where in English we would not use a preposition: Gee vir hom 'n stukkie brood (Give him a piece of bread); Se vir haar sy moet kom (tell her to come).
(*d*) It is also used with the names of persons as Indirect Object: Ek sal vir jou slaan (I'll beat you); Die perd het vir Gert geskop (The horse kicked Gert). (*See also* VIR *supra*.)

11. UIT may mean:
(*a*) out: Is jou baas tuis? Nee, hy is vandag uit (Is your master at home? No, he is out to-day);
(*b*) out of, from: Hy het dit uit afguns gedoen (He did it out of envy); Hy loop uit die kamer (He walks out of the room).
(*c*) from (motion): Waar kom jy vandaan? Ek kom uit die skool (Where do you come from? I come from school).

12. It will be observed that many of these words given as prepositions may also be used as adverbs, and that many adverbs may also be used as prepositions:
(*a*) Agter: Hy loop agter (He walks behind)—*adverb*. Hy loop agter my (He walks behind me)—*preposition*;
as also
(*b*) onder: Piet werk onder (Piet works below); Gert sit onder 'n boom (Gert sits beneath a tree).
(*c*) om: As die rivier vol is, loop ek om (If the river is full, I shall walk round); Hy reis om die wereld (He travels round the world).
(*d*) voor: Piet, kom sit hier voor! (Piet, come and sit in front here!); Die dief moet voor die magistraat kom (The thief must appear before the magistrate).

CONVERSATIONAL PHRASES AND SENTENCES

Greetings and Polite Expressions

(Begroetings en Beleefde Uitdrukkings)

English.	Afrikaans.	Pronunciation.
Good morning, Mr. A.	goeienmôre, meneer (Mnr.) A. *or* môre meneer A.	choo'i-e(r)n-maw-re(r), me(r)neyr A. mawre(r) me(r)neyr A. (=ah)
good day, sir	dag, meneer	da(h)ch, me(r)neyr
good night, miss	nag, juffrou	na(h)ch, yu(r)f'fro
good evening, Mrs. A.	goeienaand, mevrou A.	choo'i-e(r)nahnt, me(r)fro A.
good-bye, farewell	tot siens, vaarwel	tot seens, fahrve(r)l
how do you do ?	hoe gaan dit ?	hoo chah(r)n dit ?
how are you ?	hoe gaan dit met U?	hoo chah(r)n dit me(r)t êû ?
are you quite well ?	is U heeltemal vris ?	iss êû heylte(r)-mahl friss ?
quite well, thank you	ja, heeltemal gesond, dankie	ya(h), heylte(r)-mahl che(r)-so(r)nt, da(h)nkee
how is Mr. F. ?	hoe gaan dit met meneer F. ?	hoo chah(r)n dit me(r)t me(r)neyr F. ?
I am so pleased to meet you	bly om (jou) U te ontmoet	bley o(r)m (yoh) êû te(r) o(r)ntmoot
the pleasure is mine	die genoeë (plesier) is myne	dee che(r)nohe(r) (ple(r)seer) iss meyne(r)
the pleasure is mutual	die plesier is wedersyds	dee ple(r)seer iss veede(r)rseyts
I hope we may meet again	ek hoop ons sal weer ontmoet	e(r)k hohp o(r)ns sa(h)l veyr o(r)nt-moot
pleased to make your acquaintance	bly met U (jou) kennis te maak	bley me(r)t êû (yoh) ke(r)nne(r)s te(r) mahk

English.	Afrikaans.	Pronunciation.
this is a pleasure!	dit is 'n genot!	dit iss i(h)n che(r)-not!
I must go now	ek moet nou loop	e(r)k moot no lohp
will you excuse me?	sal U (jy) my asseblief verskoon?	sa(h)l yey mey ə(h)sse(r)bleef fe(r)rskohn?
must you go yet?	moet U (jy) dan nou al gaan?	moot êû (yey) da(h)n no a(h)l chahn?
I'm afraid I can't stay any longer	ek is jammer maar ek kan nie langer bly nie	e(r)k iss ya(h)mme(r)r mahr e(r)k ka(h)n nee la(h)nge(r)r bley nee
thank you, thanks	dankie	da(h)nkee
no, thanks	nee, dankie	ney, da(h)nkee
please (if you——)	asseblief	a(h)sse(r)bleef
I thank you	dankie; ek dank U (jou)	da(h)nkee; e(r)k da(h)nk êû (yoh)
many thanks	baie dankie	bah'i-e(r) da(h)nkee
much obliged	seer verplig	seyr ferplich
I am very much obliged to you	ek bly U (jou) seer (baie) dankbaar	e(r)k bley êû (yoh) seyr (bah'i-e(r)) da(h)nkbahr
excuse (pardon) me, sir	ekskuus (pardon), meneer	e(r)kskêûs (pa(h)r-do(r)n), me(r)neyr
I beg (your) pardon	ekskuus	e(r)kskêûs
I'm sorry, miss	dit spyt my, juffrou	dit speyt mey yu(r)f'fro
I'm so (or very) sorry	ek is baie jammer	e(r)k iss bah'i-e(r) ya(h)me(r)r
it is nothing	dis niks	dis nix
it doesn't matter	dit maak niks	dit mahk niks
there is no harm done	dit het niks gemaak nie (daar is g'n skade veroorsaak nie)	dit he(r)t niks che(r)-mahk nee (dahr iss ch'n skahde(r) ferohrsahk nee)
pray don't mention	ag, sê tog maar niks	a(h)ch sai(r) toch mahr niks
I must apologise	ek moet my verskoon	e(r)k moot mey fer-skohn

English.	Afrikaans.	Pronunciation.
make my apologies	my verskoning maak	mey ferskohning mahk
permit me to apologise	laat my toe dat ek U (jou) om verskoning vra	laht mey too da(h)t e(r)k eû (yoh) om ferskohning frah
no apology is needed	g'n ferskoning is nodig nie	ch'n ferskohning iss noh(r)dich nee
don't apologise	maak g'n ekskuus nie	mahk ch'n e(r)k-skeûs nee
it was my fault	dit was my skuld	dit va(h)s mey skult
not at all	glad nie	chla(h)t nee
can I be of any assistance to you?	kan ek U (jou) op enige manier help?	ka(h)n e(r)k eû (yoh) op eyniche(r) ma(h)neer he(r)lp
you are very kind	dis baie goed van U (jou)	dis bah'i-e(r) choot fa(h)n (yoh) eû
may I ask?	mag ek vra?	ma(h)ch e(r)k frah?
have the kindness (goodness)	wees so goed	veys soh choot
allow me	vergun my; gee my die eer; laat my toe	ferchun mey; chey mey dee eyr; laht mey too
with pleasure	met plesier	me(r)t ple(r)seer
yes, sir	ja, meneer	yah, me(r)neyr
yes, miss	ja, juffrou	yah, yu(r)f'fro
yes, madam	mevrou	me(r)fro

Useful and Necessary Idiomatic Expressions and Phrases

(Nuttige en Nodige Idiomatiese Uitdrukkings en Spreekwyse)
[nuttich-e(r) e(r)n nohdiche(r) ee-dee-o(h)-mahtee-se(r) uitdrukkinge(r) e(r)n spreyk-veyse(r)]

Does anyone here speak English?	is daar iemand hier wat kan Engels praat?	iss dahr ee-ma(h)nt heer va(h)t ka(h)n e(r)nge(r)ls praht?
yes, madam	ja, mevrou	yah, me(r)fro
is Afrikaans also spoken here?	praat hulle Afrikaans ook?	praht hul'le(r) a(h)-freekahns ohk?
oh yes, sir	o ja, meneer	o ya(h) me(r)neyr

English.	Afrikaans.	Pronunciation.
do you speak English and Afrikaans?	praat U (jy) Engels en Afrikaans?	praht e͡u (yey, same as Eng. yea) e(r)ng-e(r)ls e(r)n a(h)freekahns?
I am bi-lingual, sir	ek is tweetálig, meneer	e(r)k iss tveytahlich, me(r)neyr
I should like to speak to you	ek wil graag met U (jou) praat	e(r)k vil chrahch me(r)t e͡u (yoh) praht
I do not speak Afrikaans	ek praat nie Afrikaans nie	e(r)k praht nee a(h)-freekahns nee
Is there anyone here who *can* speak Afrikaans?	is daar iemand hier wat *kan* Afrikaans praat?	iss dahr eema(h)nt heer va(h)t ka(h)n ahfree-kahns praht?
I speak Afrikaans a little	ek praat Afrikaans so 'n bietjie	e(r)k praht ahfree-kahns soh i(h)n beetyee
what can I do for you?	wat kan ek vir U (jou) doen?	va(h)t ka(h)n e(r)k fir e͡u (yoh) doon?
please take a seat	gaan sit maar asse-blief	chahn sit mahr a(h)sse(r)-bleef
you are very kind	dis baie goed van U (jou)	diss bah'i-e(r) choot fa(h)n e͡u (yoh)
can you read Afrikaans?	kan U (jy) Afrikaans lees?	ka(h)n e͡u (yey) a(h)-freekahns leys?
you read very well	U (jy) lees baie goed	e͡u (yey) leys bah'i-e(r) choot.
how long have you learnt?	hoe lank leer U (jy) al?	hoo la(h)nk leyr e͡u (yey) a(h)l?
a short time only	nie lank nie, maar net 'n kort tydjie	nee la(h)nk nee, mahr ne(r)t i(h)n ko(r)rt teytyee
who taught you?	wie het vir U (jou) onderwys gegee?	vee he(r)t fir e͡u (yoh) onderveys che(r)chey?
I do not find the pronunciation difficult	ek vind die uitspraak nie baie swaar (moeilik) nie	e(r)k fint dee uit-sprahk nee bah'i-e(r) svahr (moo'i-lik) nee

English.	Afrikaans.	Pronunciation.
you have a good accent	U (jy) het 'n goeie uitspraak	eû (yey) he(r)t i(h)n choo'i-e(r) uit-sprahk
what did you say?	wat het U (jy) gesê?	va(h)t he(r)t eû (yey) che(r)sai(r)?
I have nothing to say against it	ek het niks daarteen te sê nie	e(r)k he(r)t niks dahrteyn te(r) sai(r) nee
what do you want?	wat wil U (jy) hê?	va(h)t vil eû (jy) hai(r)?
what did you ask?	wat het U (jy) gevra?	va(h)t he(r)t eû (yey) che(r)frah?
speak louder	praat harder	praht ha(h)rde(r)r
what do you mean?	wat meen (bedoel) U (jy)?	va(h)t meyn (be(r)-dool) eû (yey)?
what do you say?	wat sê U (jy)?	va(h)t sai(r) eû (yey)?
what does it signify?	wat beduie dit? wat gee dit te kenne?	va(h)t be(r)dui-e(r) dit? va(h)t chey dit te(r) ke(r)n-ne(r)?
it is all the same to me	dis vir my net die selfde (net eners)	dis fir mey ne(r)t dee se(r)lfde(r) (ne(r)t eyne(r)rs)
never mind	dit maak nie saak nie	dit mahk nee sahk nee
I believe (think) so	ek dink so	e(r)k dink so(h)
I believe (think) not	ek dink nie so nie	e(r)k dink nee so(h) nee
I have no objection to it	ek het daar niks op teen nie	e(r)k he(r)t dahr niks op teyn nee
I beg your pardon?	ekskuus? pardon?	e(r)kskeûs pa(h)rdon
what is the matter?	wat makeer?	va(h)t ma(h)keyr?
nothing	niks nie	niks nee
what is it about?	waaroor praat hulle omtrent wat is dit?	vahrohr praht hul-le(r)?; o(r)m-tre(r)nt va(h)t iss dit?
it does not matter	dit maak nie saak nie	dit mahk nee sahk nee

English.	Afrikaans.	Pronunciation.
I understand	ek verstaan goed; ek begryp wel	e(r)k fe(r)rstahn choot; e(r)k be(r)-chreyp ve(r)l
it is all a mistake	die hele ding is 'n fout	dee heyle(r) ding iss i(h)n fo't
what is to be done?	wat nou gedaan?	va(h)t no che(r)-dahn?
I haven't a notion	ek het g'n idee nie	e(r)k he(r)t ch'n eedee nee
that is of no consequence	dit beteken niks	dit be(r)teykc(r)n niks
that depends	dit hang af	dit ha(h)ng a(h)f
do you understand?	verstaan U (jy)?	ferstahn eû (yey)?
I don't understand	ek verstaan nie	e(r)k ferstahn nee
carry this	dra dit (hierdie)	drah dit (heerdee)
take this away	neem dit weg	neym dit ve(r)ch
come along, make haste!	saamgaan? komaan, gou maak!	sahmchahn? ko(r)-mahn cho'mahk!
take care!	pasop!	pa(h)sop!
look out!	oppas!	oppa(h)s!
listen!	luister (hier)!	luiste(r)r (heer)!
come in!	kom in! kom binne!	ko(r)m in! ko(r)m binne(r)!
come here!	kom hierso' kom hiernatoe!	ko(r)m heerso! ko(r)m heerna(h)-too!
go away!	gaan weg!	chahn ve(r)ch!
this way	hierheen	heerheyn
in this way	op hierdie manier	op heerdee má(h)n'-neer
that way (direction)	soontoe	sohntoo
too soon, too late	te vroeg, te laat	te(r) frooch, te(r) laht
very well (sir)	goed (meneer)	choot (me(r)neyr)
not very well	nie al te vris nie	nee a(h)l te(r) fris nee
what do you want	wat wil U (jy) hê?	va(h)t vil eû (yey) hai(r)
of course	natuurlik	na(h)teûrlik
on the contrary	inteendeel	inteyndey!

English.	Afrikaans.	Pronunciation.
once for all	eens vir altyd	eyns fir a(h)lteyt
between ourselves	tussen ons	tusse(r)rn o(r)ns
after all	tog, per slot van rekening	to(r)ch, per clo(h)t fa(h)n reyke(r)n-ing
the other day	die ander dag	dee a(h)nde(r)r da(h)ch
at the end of a year	aan die end van 'n jaar	ahn dee ent fa(h)n i(h)n yahr
everybody knows it	almal weet dit	a(h)l'mal weyt dit
that is of no consequence	dit beteken nie baie nie	dit be(r) teyke(r)n nee bah'i-e(r) nee
I remember it	ek onthou dit	e(r)k ontho dit
ever so little	nog somin	no(h)ch soo-minn
all at once	skielik	skeelik
nowhere	nerens (niewers) nie	nai(r)e(r)ns (nee-ve(r)rs) nee
no great thing	niks besonders nie	niks be(r)sonde(r)rs nee
sooner or later	vroeër of later	froo'e(r)r of lahte(r)r
leave me alone	laat vir my met rus, laat my staan	laht fir mey me(r)t rus, laht mey stahn
are you joking?	korswil jy?	ko(h)rsvill yey?
you are right	U (jy) het reg	êu (yey) he(r)t re(r)ch
without a doubt, beyond a question	sonder twyfel, buiten sprake	sonde(r)r tveyfe(r)l, buite(r)n sprahk-ke(r)
I give it up	ek gee dit op	e(r)k chey dit op
so much the more	des temeer	de(r)s te(r)meyr
for want of time	by gebreke aan tyd	bey che(r)breyke(r) ahn teyt
with all my heart	van ganser harte	fa(h)n cha(h)nse(r) ha(h)rte(r)
do your best	doen U (jou) bes	doon êu (yoh) be(r)ss
are you going anywhere?	gaan U (jy) uit (êrens heen)?	chahn êu (yey) uit, (ai(r)'ns heyn)
I am going to town	ek gaan na die stad toe	e(r)k chahn na(h) dee sta(h)t too

English.	Afrikaans.	Pronunciation.
from top to bottom	van bo tot onder	fa(h)n boh tot onde(r)r
upstairs	op die boonste verdieping	op dee bohnste(r) ferdeeping
downstairs	ondertoe, die trappe af	onde(r)rtoo, dee tra(h)pe(r) a(h)f
I am in a hurry	ek is haastig	e(r)k iss hahstich
where have you come from?	waar kom U (jy) vandaan?	va(h)r ko(r)m eû (yey) fa(h)ndahn?
don't go away	moenie weggaan nie	moonee ve(r)ch-chahn nee
don't stir	moenie roer nie	moonee roor nee
I shall go home	ek sal huistoe gaan	e(r)k sa(h)l huistoo chahn
on horseback	te perd	te(r) pe(r)rt
he has come back	hy het (is) teruggekom	hey he(r)t (iss) te(r)-ruch-che(r)kom
nor I either	ek ook nie	e(r)k ohk nee
in some way or other	op een of ander manier	op eyn of a(h)nder ma(h)neer
that is just like you	dis 'net soos jy is (lyk)	dis net sohs yey iss (leyk)
give him that from me	gee vir hom dit van my af	chey fir ho(r)m dit fa(h)n mey a(h)f
he is a friend of mine	hy is 'n vriend van my	hey iss i(h)n freent fa(h)n mey
will you kindly?	sal U (jy) asseblief?	sa(h)l eû (yey) a(h)s-e(r)bleef?
in the meantime	intussen	intusse(r)n
first of all	in die eerste plek	in dee eyrste(r) ple(r)k
that is what vexes me	dit is wat vir my kwaadmaak	dit iss va(h)t fir mey kvahtmahk
he has just come in	hy het nou nou ingekom (nou net) kom	hey het no no (no net) inche(r)kom
he came a little while ago	hy het netnou gekom	hey he(r)t netno che(r)kom
he pretends that	hy gee voor dat	hey gey fohr da(h)t
don't imagine	moenie jou verbeel nie	moonee yoh ferbeyl nee

English.	Afrikaans.	Pronunciation.
within everybody's reach	binne iedereen se bereik	binne(r) eyde(r)reyn se(r) be(r)reyk
what good is it?	wat baat dit?	va(h)t baht dit?
what's the good?	wat help dit?	va(h)t he(r)lp dit?
as for me	wat my betref	va(h)t mey be(r)-tre(r)f
in a good temper	in 'n goeie luim (humeur)	in i(h)n choo'-e(r) luim (heûmu(r)r)
unknown to me	dis my onbekend	dis mey onbe(r)kent
at the latest	op sy laaste	op sey lahste(r)
where was I?	waar was ek?	vahr va(h)s e(r)k?
you speak at random	U (jy) praat so-maar-so, sonder eers te dink	eû (yey) praht soh-mahr-soh son-de(r)r eyrs te(r) dink
I did it in a hurry	ek het dit haastig gedoen	e(r)k he(r)t dit hah-stich che(r)doon
he may say what he likes	hy kan sê wat hy wil	hey ka(h)n sai(r) va(h)t hey vill
he began to laugh	hy begin toe te lag	hey be(r)chin too te(r) la(h)ch
	hy het toe begin lag	hey he(r)t too be(r)-chin la(h)ch
I cannot see any longer	ek kan nou nie meer sien nie	e(r)k ka(h)n no nee meyr seen nee
three are enough for me	drie is genoeg vir my	dree iss che(r)nooch fir mey
it only depends upon you	dit hang alleen van U (jou) af	dit ha(h)ng a(h)l-leyn fa(h)n eû (yoh) a(h)f
one is as good as another	die een is so goed as die ander	dee eyn iss soh choot a(h)s dee a(h)nde(r)r
I can do without it	ek kan daar sonder klaarkom	e(r)k ka(h)n dahr sonder klahrkom
will you give me...?	gee asseblief...fer my?	chey a(h)sse(r)bleef ...fir mey?
he will do just the same	hy sal net (presies) dieselfde doen	hey sa(h)l ne(r)t (pre(r)sees) dee-se(r)lfde(r) doon

English.	Afrikaans.	Pronunciation.
everything considered	alles in aanmerking geneem	a(h)lle(r)s in a(h)n-me(r)rking che(r)-neym
that is too much	dit is te veel	dit iss te(r) feyl
I am sure of what I say	ek is seker van wat ek praat	e(r)k iss seyke(r)r fa(h)n va(h)t e(r)k praht
I have been told	hulle het vir my gesê	hulle(r) he(r)t fir mey che(r)sai(r)
I have come to tell you	ek het vir U (jou) kom sê; ek het gekom om vir U (jou) te sê	e(r)k he(r)t fir eû (yo) kom sai(r); e(r)k he(r)t che(r)-kom om fir eû (yo) te(r) sai(r)
I don't think much of it	ek dink nie veel daarvan nie	e(r)k dink nee feyl dahrfa(h)n nee
no sooner said than done	so gesê so gedaan	soh che(r)sai(r) soh che(r)dahn
I can bear it no longer	ek kan dit nie langer uithou nie	e(r)k ka(h)n dit nee la(h)nge(r)r uitho nee
I like being here	ek hou daarvan om hier te wees	e(r)k ho dahrfa(h)n om heer te(r) veys
as much as I can	soveel as ek kan	soh feyl a(h)s e(r)k ka(h)n
that comes to the same thing	dit kom op dieselfde neer	dit kom op dee-se(r)lfde(r) neyr
it is not my fault	dis nie my skuld nie	dis nee mey skult nee
I value it very much	ek waardeer dit baie	e(r)k vahrdeyr dit bah'i-e(r)
I am used to it	ek is gewend (gewoond) daaraan	e(r)k iss che(r)-ve(r)nt (cher-vohnt) dahrahn
	ek is daaraan gewend	e(r)k iss dahrahn che(r)ve(r)nt
	ek is daaraan gewoond	e(r)k iss dahrahn che(r)vohnt
I am not able to do it	ek kan dit nie doen nie	e(r)k ka(h)n dit nee doon nee

English.	Afrikaans.	Pronunciation.
who is it calls me?	wie roep vir my daar?	vee roop fir mey dahr?
there is a change in the weather	daar is 'n verandering in die weer	dahr iss i(h)n fer-a(h)ndering in dee veyr
it snows	dit kapok	dit ka(h)pok
it freezes	dit vries, ys toe	dit frees, eys too
it is very dirty	dit is baie vuil	dit iss bah'i-e(r) fuil
it is slippery	dit is glad, glyerig	dit iss chla(h)t, chleye(r)rich
I nearly fell	ek het amper (byna) geval	e(r)k he(r)t a(h)m-pe(r)r che(r)fa(h)l
do you think it will rain?	dink U (jy) dit sal reën?	dink eû (yey) dit sa(h)l rey(r)n?
I am afraid so	ja, ek dink so	yah e(r)k dink soh
it is very windy	dis baie winderig	dis bah'i-e(r) vin-derich
how cold it is!	is dit nie koud nie?	iss dit nee ko(h)t nee?
it is very cold, warm	dit is baie koud, warm	dit iss bah'i-e(r) ko(h)t, va(h)rm
we must have a fire	ons moet ('n) vuur maak	ons moot (i(h)n) feûr mahk
it is dark	dit is donker	dit iss donke(r)r
it will soon be dark	dit sal nou gou donker wees	dit sa(h)l no cho donke(r)r veys
it is a fine day	dis 'n mooi dag	dis i(h)n moh'i dahch
between ourselves	onder ons gesê	onder ons che(r)-sai(r)
that depends	dit hang af	dit ha(h)ng a(h)f
are you going anywhere?	gaan U (jy) erens heen (natoe)?	cha(h)n eû (yey) ai(r)e(r)ns heyn na(h)too?
she is always well dressed	sy is maar altyd goed aangetrek	sey iss mahr a(h)l-teyt choot ahn-che(r)tre(r)k
I am going home now	ek gaan nou huistoe	e(r)k chahn no huis-too

Expressions of Surprise, Sorrow, Joy, Anger, etc.
(Uitdrukkinge van Verbasing, Smart, Vreugde, Toorn, Ens.)

English.	Afrikaans.	Pronunciation.
What?	wat?	va(h)t?
you surprise me	U (jy) verbaas vir my	êû (yey) ferbahs fir mey
is it possible?	is dit moontlik?	iss dit mohntlik?
that is impossible	dit is onmoontlik	dit iss ontmohntlik
indeed!	regtig? inderdaad!	re(r)chte(r)ch, in-de(r)rdaht!
that cannot be	dit kannie wees nie	dit ka(h)nnee weys nee
my fault	my skuld	mey skult
oh! it's nothing	O! dis niks nie	o! dis niksnee
don't mention it	ag, laat tog maar staan	ach, laht toch mahr stahn
I am sorry for it	ek het daar spyt van	e(r)k he(r)t dahr speyt fa(h)n
I am quite vexed about it	ek is net kwaad daaroor	e(r)k iss nett kvaht dahrohr
what a pity!	hoe jammer tog!	hoo yahme(r)r toch!
it is a sad thing	dit is 'n treurige geval	dit iss i(h)n tru(r)-riche(r) che(r)fahl
I am very glad	ik is baie bly	e(r)k iss bah'i-e(r) bley
how happy I am!	hoe gelukkig is ek tog!	hoo che(r)lukkich iss e(r)k toch!
how delightful	o, hoe heerlik!	o, hoo heyrlik!
what a shame!	wat vir 'n skande!	vaht fir i(h)n ska(h)nde(r)!
how could you do it?	hoe kon U (jy) dit doen?	hoo konn êû (yey) dit doon?
he is very angry	hy is baie kwaad	hey iss bah'i-e(r) kvaht
you are very much to blame	U (jy) is baie te blameer	êû (yey) is bah'i-e(r) te(r) blahmeyr
I am ashamed of you	ek skaam my vir U (jou)	e(r)k skahm mey fir êû (yoh)
you are very wrong	U (jy) is baie ver-keerd	êû (yey) iss bah'i-e(r) ferkeyrt

English.	Afrikaans.	Pronunciation.
for shame!	skande!	ska(h)nde(r)!
how vexing!	hoe ergerlik!	hoo e(r)rgerlik!
help!	help!	help!
be quiet, don't answer	bly stil	bley still

Making Enquiries (Inligting Vra)

Can I see Mr. H.?	kan ek meneer H. te siene kry?	ka(h)n e(r)k me(r)n-eyr H. te(r) see-ne(r) krey?
when does he return?	wanneer kom hy terug?	va(h)nneyr kom hey te(r)rûch?
please give him my card	gee vir hom asse-blief my kaartjie	chey fir ho(h)m a(h)sse(r)bleef mey kahrtyee
I will call again to-morrow between 10 and 11 a.m.	ek sal weer môre tussen 10 en 11 v.m.[1] kom	e(r)k sa(h)l veyr mawre(r) tus-se(r)n 10 e(r)n 11 v.m.[1] kom
where is...?	waar is...?	vahr iss...?
which is the way to...?	watter is die pad na...toe?	va(h)tte(r)r iss dee pa(h)t na(h)...too
how can I get to...?	how kom 'n mens by...?	hoo kom i(h)n me(r)ns bey...?
is there a convey-ance?	is daar 'n rytuig ('n geleendheid)?	iss dahr i(h)n rey-tuich [i(h)n che(r)-leyn theyt]
do you hear me?	hoor U (jy) vir my?	hohr eû (yey) fir mey?
would you kindly...?	sal U (jy) asseblief ...?	sa(h)l eû (yey) a(h)s-se(r)bleef...?
do you understand?	verstaan U (jy)?	ferstahn eû (yey)?
what is that?	wat is dit?	va(h)t iss dit?
do you know...?	[2]ken U (jy)...? weet U (jy)...?	ke(r)n eû (yey)...? veyt eû (jy)...?
what do you mean?	wat meen U (jy)?	va(h)t meyn eû (yey)?

[1] v.m. = voor middag (fohr middach).

[2] Ken, to be acquainted with (someone, something). Weet, to know (a fact).

English.	Afrikaans.	Pronunciation.
what does that mean?	wat meen dit?	va(h)t meyn dit?
what is that for?	wat is dit voor?	va(h)t iss dit fohr?
are you sure?	is U (jy) seker?	iss eû (yey) seyke(r)r?
who is that?	wie is daardie?	vee iss dahrdee?
who is there?	wie is daar?	vee iss dahr?
is that Mr....?	is dit Mnr.... daardie?	iss dit me(r)neyr... dahrdee?
where can I buy an English newspaper?	waar kan ek 'n Engelse koerant (nuusblad) koop?	vahr ka(h)n e(r)k i(h)n E(r)ng-e(r)l-se(r) koora(h)nt [neû(r)sbla(h)t] kohp

Notices (Kennisgewings)

Admission free	toegang vry	toocha(h)ng frey
apartments	kamers	ka(h)me(r)rs
apartments to let	kamers te huur	ka(h)me(r)rs te(r) heûr
bedroom to let	slaapkamer te huur	slahpkahme(r)r te(r) heûr
bedroom for single gentleman	slaapkamer vir een heer alleen	slahpkahmer fir eyn heyr a(h)l-leyn
danger	gevaar	che(r)fahr
dogs not admitted	honde word nie toegelaat nie	honde(r) vort nee tooche(r)laht nee
entrance, exit	ingang, uitgang	incha(h)ng, uit-cha(h)ng
fire alarm	brandklok (-fluit)	bra(h)ntklok (-fluit)
forbidden	verbode	ferbohde(r)
for information	vir informasie	fir informahsee
for (hiring) apartments, apply to...	vir kamers (om te huur) doen aansoek by...	fir kahme(r)rs [om te(r) heûr] doon ahnsook bey...
free library	vry biblioteek	frey biblee-oh-teyk
furnished house to let	gemeubileerde huis te huur	che(r)mu(r)be(r)-leyrde(r) huis te(r) heûr

English.	Afrikaans.	Pronunciation.
furnished rooms	gemeubileerde kamers	che(r)mu(r)be(r)-leyrde(r) ka(h)-me(r)rs
just published	nou net uitgegee	no nett uitche(r)-chey
keep off the grass	bly van die gras af (weg)	bley fa(h)n dee chra(h)s a(h)f (vech)
knock, ring	klop, lui	klop, lui
no admittance	geen. toegang nie toegang verbode	cheyn toocha(h)ng nee, toocha(h)ng ferbohde(r)
no smoking allowed	rook is verbied	rohk iss ferbeet
no thoroughfare	geen deurweg! g'n deurweg nie	cheyn du(r)rvech, ch'n du(r)rvech nee
please do not touch	versoek nie aanteraak nie	fersook nee ahnte(r) rahk nee
please wipe your feet	vee asseblief U (jou) voete af	fey a(h)s-se(r)-bleef eû (yoh) foote(r) a(h)f
	versoek U (jou) voete aftevee	fersook U (yoh) fohte(r) a(h)fte(r) fey
private	privaat	preefaht
public notice	publieke kennisgewing	publeeke(r) ke(r)n-niss che(r)ving
pull, push	trek, druk	tre(r)k, dru(r)k
refreshments	verversinge	firfersinge(r)
to (be) let	om te verhuur	om te(r) ferheûr
unfurnished bedroom to let	ongemeubileerde slaapkamer te huur	onche(r)mu(r)be(r)-leyrde(r) slahp-kahme(r)r te(r) heûr
warning, caution	waarskuing	vahrskeûing
you are requested not to smoke	U (julle) word versoek om nie te rook nie	eû [yulle(r)] vorrt fersook om nee te(r) rohk nee

The Custom-House (Die Doeane-kantoor)

English.	Afrikaans.	Pronunciation.
Come to the custom-house	kom na die doeane-kantoor toe	kom na(h) dee doo-hahne(r)-kan(h)n-tohr too
the custom-house officer	die doeane-amptenaar	dee dooahne(r)-a(h)mpte(r)nahr
open your bag	maak oop U (jou) sak	mahk ohp ëû (yoh) sa(h)k
unlock this box	sluit oop hierdie kis	sluitohpheerdeekiss
will you examine this trunk?	ondersoek asseblief hierdie koffer?	onde(r)rsook a(h)sse(r)bleef heerdee ko(r)f'fe(r)r?
here are the keys	hier is die sleutels	heer iss dee slu(r)te(r)ls
have you anything to declare?	het U (jy) eenig iets om aantegee?	he(r)t ëû eynich eyts om ahnte(r)chey?
not that I know of	niks, wat ek van weet nie	niks, va(h)t e(r)k fa(h)n veyt nee
no, nothing but wearing apparel	nee niks anders dan klerasie nie	ney niks a(h)nde(r)rs da(h)n kleyrahsee nee
have you any tobacco or cigars?	het jy tabak of seroete?	he(r)t yey ta(h)ba(h)k of se(r)roote(r)?
I have a few cigars	ek het so 'n paar seroete	e(r)k he(r)t soh i(h)n pahr se(r)roote(r)
is that all?	is dit al?	iss dit a(h)l?
those are free	die (dit, daardie) is vry	dee (dit, dahrdee) iss frey
I have nothing liable to duty	ek het niks wat kan belas word nie	e(r)k he(r)t niks va(h)t ka(h)n be(r)la(h)s vort nee
what is the duty?	wat is die belasting?	va(h)t iss dee be(r)la(h)sting?
is my luggage passed?	is my goed nou afgedaan?	iss mey choot no a(h)fche(r)dahn?
can I remove it?	kan ek dit nou wegneem?	ka(h)n e(r)k dit no ve(r)chneym?

The Railway (Die Spoorweg)

English.	Afrikaans.	Pronunciation.
To the station	na die stasie-toe	na(h) dee sta(h)see-too
we want a porter	ons wil 'n portier hê	ons will i(h)n porteer hai(r)
here is my luggage	hier is my bagasie	heer iss mey ba(h)-chah' see
I wish to register it	ek wil dit graag registreer	e(r)k will dit chrahch re(r)-che(r)streyr
take it to the cloak room	neem dit na die bagasiekamer-toe	neym dit na(h) dee ba(h)chah'see-kahmer-too
go and get my luggage	gaan haal my bagasie	cha(h)n hahl mey ba(h)chah'see
have you the ticket ?	het U (jy) die kaartjie ?	he(r)t eû (yey) dee kahrtyee ?
yes, here it is	ja, hier is dit	ya(h) heer iss dit
what luggage have you ?	watter bagasie het U (jy) ?	wa(h)t'ter ba(h)-chah'see he(r)t eû (yey) ?
it is overweight	dis oor die gewig	dis ohr dee che(r)r-vich
cross the line by the bridge	gaan oor die brug	cha(h)n ohr dee bruch
by the subway	by die onderaardse deurweg (deur-gang, duikweg) longs	bey dee onde(r)-rahrdse(r) du(r)r-ve(r)ch [du(r)rch-cha(h)ng, duik-ve(r)ch] la(h)ngs
where is the railway station ?	waar is die stasie ?	va(h)r iss dee stah-see ?
where is the refreshment room ?	waar is die verversings kamer ?	va(h)r iss dee firfers-ingskahmer ?
the ladies' waiting-room	die dames wag-kamer	dee dahme(r)s va(h)chkahmer
where is the booking office ?	waar is die bespreek-plek ?	va(h)r iss dee be(r)-spreyk ple(r)k ?

English.	Afrikaans.	Pronunciation.
where is the enquiry office ?	waar is die informasieburo ?	va(h)r iss dee informahseeburo ?
where is the train for... ?	waar is die trein wat na...toe gaan ?	va(h)r iss dee treyn va(h)t na(h)...too chahn ?
where is the lavatory ?	waar is die waskamer ?	va(h)r iss dee va(h)s-kahmer ?
are you going by the express ?	gaan U (jÿ) met die sneltrein ?	chahn êu (yey) me(r)t dee sne(r)l-treyn ?
show me a time-table	wys vir my 'n tyd-tafel	veys fir mey i(h)n teyt-ta(h)fe(r)l
when does the train start ?	wanneer vertrek die trein ?	va(h)nneyr fer-tre(r)k dee treyn ?
can I book through to Johannesburg ?	kan ek 'm deurgaan-kaartjie na Johannesburg-toe kry ?	ka(h)n e(r)k i(h)n du(r)rchahnkahrtyee na(h) Yoh'-hahnne(r)s-burch-too krey ?
I want a first-class single ticket to Bloemfontein	ek wil 'n eersteklas eenpersoons-kaartjie na Bloemfontein-toe hê	e(r)k vill i(h)n eyr-ste(r)klahss eyn-persohnskahrtyee nah Blohmfon-teyn-too hai(r)
second return, Port Elizabeth	'n retoerkaartjie, twedeklas, na Port Elizabeth-toe	i(h)n tveyde(r)-kla(h)s re(r)toor-kahrtyee nah Port E(r)liza(h)-be(r)t-too
for how long is it valid ?	vir hoelank is dit geldig ?	fir hoo lahnk iss dit che(r)ldich ?
	hoelank is dit van krag ?	hoo lahnk iss dit fa(h)n kra(h)ch ?
two third singles	twee derdeklas een-persoons kaart-jies	tvey de(r)rde(r)-klahs eynper-sohnskahrtyees
what is the fare to Buluwayo ?	wat is die passa-siersgeld na Buluwayo-toe ?	va(h)t iss dee pa(h)s-se(r)seersche(r)lt na(h) Buluveyho-too ?

English.	Afrikaans.	Pronunciation.
what class, sir?	watter klas, meneer?	va(h)t'te(r)r kla(h)s, me(r)neyr?
how much is it?	hoeveel is dit?	hoo feyl iss dit?
we want sleeping places	ons wil slaapplek hê	ons vill slahpple(r)k hai(r)
a through carriage	'n deurgaande wa	i(h)n du(r)rchahnde(r) va(h)
a through train	'n deurgaande trein	i(h)n du(r)rchahnde(r) treyn
through passengers	deurgaande passasiers	du(r)rchahnde(r) pa(h)ssa(h)seers
through traffic	deurgaande verkeer	du(r)rchahnde(r) ferkeyr
platform tickets	platform-kaartjie	pla(h)tformkahrtyee
we want a carriage for ladies	ons wil 'n wa (spoorwa) vir dames hê	ons vill i(h)n va(h) [spohrva(h)] fir da(h)me(r)s hai(r)
we want a smoking compartment	ons wil 'n rookkoepee hê	ons vill i(h)n rohkkoopee hai(r)
no smoking	rook is verbied	rohk iss ferbeet
the communication cord	die kommunikasielyn (koord)	dee kommunika(h)seeleyn (kohrt)
the dining-car	die eetsalon (-wa)	dee eytsa(h)lon (-va(h))
this is the train for...	dit is die trein ver... (na...toe)	dit iss dee treyn fir ...(na(h)...too)
do we take (engage) places for meals?	moet ons by etenstye plekke bespreek?	moot ons bey eyte(r)nsteye(r) ple(r)kke(r) be(r)spreyk?
where must I change for...?	waar moet ek vir... oorklim?	vahr moot e(r)k fir ...ohrklim?
you will travel via	U (jy) reis oor...	eû (yey) reys ohr...
is this seat engaged?	is hierdie plek geneem?	iss heerdee ple(r)k che(r)neym?
there is no room	daar is g'n plek nie	dahr iss ch'n ple(r)k nee
the train is just going to start	die trein vertrek nou nou	dee treyn fertre(r)k no no

English.	Afrikaans.	Pronunciation
call the guard	roep die kondukteur	roop dee konduk-tu(r)r
open the door	maak oop die deur	mahk ohp dee du(r)r
close the window	maak toe die venster	mahk too dee fe(r)n-ste(r)r
here is the station	hier is die stasit	heer iss dee sta(h)-see
do we stop here?	hou die trein hier stil?	hoh dee treyn heer stil?
do we get out here?	klim ons hier af?	klim ons heer a(h)f?
do we change for...?	klim ons oor vir...?	klim ons ohr fir...?
show your tickets	toon julle kaartjies	tohn yulle(r) kahrt-yees
how long do we stop here?	hoe lank vertoef ons hier?	hoo la(h)nk fertoof ons heer?
five minutes	vyf minute	feyf min'neûte(r)
all change (here)!	almal moet hier oorstap (oorklim)	a(h)lma(h)l moot heer ohrsta(h)p (ohrklim)
change for...	na...oorklim	na(h)...ohrklim
tickets, please!	kaartjies aseblief!	kahrtyees a(h)s-se(r)bleef!
give up your tickets	gee op julle kaartjies	chey op yulle(r) kahrtyees
my luggage is lost	my bagasie is verlore	mey ba(h)chahsee iss ferlohre(r)
I shall claim for it	ek sal dit opeis	e(r)k sa(h)l dit opeys
I left it in the train	ek het dit in die trein laatstaan	e(r)k he(r)t dit in dee treyn laht-stahn
what train did you travel by?	met watter trein het jy gereis (gekom)?	me(r)t va(h)tte(r)r treyn he(r)t yey che(r)kom she(r)-reys (che(r)kom)?
the train due here at 2.10	met die trein wat om 2.10 hier aankom	me(r)t dee treyn va(h)t om 2.10 heer ahnkom
I have missed my train	ek het my trein misgeloop	e(r)k he(r)t mey treyn missche(r)-lohp

English.	Afrikaans.	Pronunciation.
when is the next?	wanneer volg daar weer 'n ander?	va(h)nneyr fo(r)lch dahr veyr i(h)n a(h)nde(r)r?

The Steamboat (Die Stoomboot)

Is this the boat for ...?	is dit die boot vir ...?	iss dit dee boht fir ...?
when do we start?	wanneer vertrek ons?	va(h)nneyr fer-tre(r)k ons?
what time are we due at...?	hoe laat kom ons by...aan?	hoo laht kom ons bey...ahn?
wait for me	wag ver my	va(h)ch fir mey
time is up	die tyd is om	dee teyt iss om
when shall we arrive?	wanneer kom ons aan?	va(h)nneyr kom ons ahn?
where is our luggage?	waar is onse bagasie?	vahr iss onse(r) bah-chahsee?
where is my berth?	waar is my bed?	wahr iss mey bett?
let us go down into the cabin	kom ons gaan onder na ons kajuit (kabin) toe	kom ons chahn on-der na(h) ons ka(h)bin [ka(h)-yuit] too
I want a cabin to myself	ek wil 'n kajuit (kabin) alleen hê	e(r)k vill i(h)n kah-yuit [ka(h)bin] ahlleyn hai(r)
is the sea smooth?	is die see stil?	iss dee sey stil?
there is a rough sea	die see is onstuimig	dee sey iss onstui-mich
it is blowing a gale	daar waai 'n sterk wind	dahr wah'i i(h)n ster(r)k vint
I feel sick	ek voel (is) siek	e(r)k fool (iss) seek
can you bring me some tea?	kan U (jy) vir my 'n bietjie tee bring?	ka(h)n eü (yey) fir mey i(h)n beet-yee tey bring?
call the stewardess	roep asseblief die hofmeesteres	roop a(h)sse(r)bleef dee ho(r)fmey-ste(r)re(r)s
look for my things	soek asseblief na my goed	sook a(h)sse(r)bleef na(h) mey choot

English.	Afrikaans.	Pronunciation.
there is another trunk	daar is nog 'n ander koffer	dahr iss noch i(h)n a(h)nder kofie(r)r
passengers are requested to keep clear of the gangway	passasiers word versoek om van die loopplank af wegtestaan	pa(h)sse(r)seers vort fersook om fa(h)n dee lohppla(h)nk a(h)f ve(r)ch te(r) stahn
how much does the boatman want?	hoeveel wil die skipper (roeier) hê?	hoofeyl vill dee skipper (roo'ie(r)) hai(r)?

Aviation (Lug (skeep) vaart)

There are many aeroplanes in the Union of South Africa	daar is baie lugskepe in die Unie van Suidafrika	dahr iss bah'i-e(r) luchskeype(r) in dee éunee fa(h)n suita(h)freeka(h)
the air-force is part and parcel of the defence-force	die lugmag is part en deel van die verdedigingsmag	dee luchma(h)ch iss pa(h)rt e(r)n deyl fa(h)n dee ferdeydichingsma(h)ch
it is controlled by the Honourable the Minister of Defence	dit word beheer deur (die) s'n Hoog Edele die Minister can Verdediging	dit vort be(r)heyr du(r)r (dee) s'n (say, sin) hohch eyde(r)le(r) dee minister fa(h)n ferdeydiching
there are quite a number of aerodromes in the Union	daar is heeltemal 'n groot aantal lugbane in die Unie	dahr iss heylte(r)mahl i(h)n chroht ahnta(h)l luchbahne(r) in dee éunı
have you an aerodrome in Johannesburg?	is daar 'n lugbaan in Johannesburg?	iss dahr i(h)n luchbahn in Yoha(h)ne(r)sburch?
yes, the Baragwanath aerodrome	ja, dee ba(h)ra(h)gvahna(h) luchbahn	ya(h), dee Baraguanath lugbaan
there is an aerodrome near Pretoria	daar is 'n lugbaan naby Pretoria	dahr iss i(h)n luchbahn nah'bey Preytoreea(h)

English.	Afrikaans.	Pronunciation.
many aeroplanes are housed there	baie lugskepe is daar onder dak	bah'i-e(r) luchskey-pe(r) iss dahr on-der da(h)k
Pretoria is the seat of the Northern Aircraft	Pretoria is die setel van die lugskepe in die Norde	Pre(r)toreea(h) iss dee seyte(r)l fa(h)n dee luch-skeype(r) in dee nohrde(r)
the air-force officers are stationed at Roberts Heights	die lugmag offisiere is gehuisves op Robertshoogte	dee luchma(h)ch of-fiseere(r) iss che(r) huisfe(r)s op Robe(r)rts-hohchte(r)
Captain...is considered the best aviator in the Union	Kaptein ... word beskou vir die beste vlieër in die Unie	ka(h)pteyn... vort be(r)sko fir dee be(r)ste(r) flee-e(r) in dee eûnee
have you ever been up in an aeroplane ?	het (u) jy al ooit in 'n lugskip gevlieg ?	he(r)t (eû) yey a(h)l oh'it in i(h)n luch-skip che(r) fleech ?
which do you prefer,	watter een hou U (jy) die meeste van,	va(h)tte(r)r eyn ho eû (yey) dee mey-ste(r) fa(h)n,
a mono-, bi-, or tri-plane ?	'n een-, twee-, of driedekker ?	i(h)n eyn-, tvee-, of dreede(r)k-ke(r)r ?
I have no knowledge of any of them	ek het g'n kennis van enige van hulle nie	e(r)k he(r)t ch'n ke(r)nne(r)s fa(h)n eyne(r)-che(r) fa(h)n hul-le(r) nee
the pilot is at the steering-wheel	die stuurman hou die stuurrat	dee steûrma(h)n ho dee steûrra(h)t
the fan makes many revolutions per minute	die waaier maak baie rewolusies per minute	dee vah'i-e(r)r mahk bah'i-e(r) re(r)-volusees pe(r)r me(r)neût

English.	Afrikaans.	Pronunciation.
it is pleasant to fly from Johannesburg to Pretoria and back	dit is (dis) aangenaam om van Johannesburg na Pretoria-toe te vlieg en weer terug	dit iss (dis) ahnche(r) nahm om fa(h)n Yohha(h)nne(r)sburch na(h) Pre(r) toreea-too te(r) cha(h)n e(r)n veyr te(r)ruch
some people get squeamish (seasick) when flying in an aeroplane	party mense word mislik (seesiek) wanneer hulle in 'n vliegmasjien is	pa(h)rtey mense(r) vort misslik (seyseek) va(h)nneyr hulle(r) in i(h)n fleechma(h)syeen iss
I like it very much	ek hou daar baie van	e(r)k ho dahr bah'-i-e(r) fa(h)n
the landing makes me feel queer sometimes	die afkom na die aarde-toe wat my partykeer naar maak voel	diss dee a(h)fkom na(h) dee ahrde(r)-too vaht mey pa(h)rteykeyr nahr mahk fool
the ascent is nothing	die opgaan is niksnie	dee opchahn iss niksnee
the mechanics at the aerodromes are always busy	die masjieniste by die vliegbane is maar altyd besig	dee ma(h)sheeniste(r) bey dee fleechbahne(r) iss mahr a(h)lteyt beysich
the engine, the wings, the body, the tail, the shaft, the fuel-pipe, the rudder, the sparking-plug, the crank, the crank-case, in fact the whole frame and body and every particle of machinery and fit-	die masjien, die vleuels, die bak, die stert, die as, die brandstofpyp, die roer, die vonkontstekingsprop, die slinger, die slingerdoos, ja, feitlik die hele raam en bak en elke kleinste deeltjie van al die	dee ma(h)sheen, dee flu(r)e(r)ls, dee ba(h)k, dee stert, dee a(h)s, dee bra(h)ntstofpeyp, dee roor, dee fonkontsteykingsprop, dee sling-e(r)r, dee sling e(r)rdohs, ya(h), feyte(r)lik dee heyle(r) rahm

English.	Afrikaans.	Pronunciation.
tings require the most careful examination daily	masjienerie en toebehore vra daeliks die sorgvuldigste ondersoek	e(r)n ba(h)k e(r)n e(r)lke(r) kleynste(r) deylt-yee fa(h)n a(h)l dee ma(h)sheene(r)-rey e(r)n toobe(r)-hohre(r), fra(h)-da(h)le(r)ks dee sorchfuldichste(r) ondersook

Arrival (Aankoms)

call a cab	loop haal 'n rytuig	lohp hahl i(h)n rey-tuich
open, closed	oop, toe	ohp, too
what is the fare for the journey (by the hour), cab-man?	wat vra jy vir die rit (per uur), keb-man?	va(h)t fra(h)'yey fir dee rit (per eûr) ke(r)pma(h)n?
put my luggage in the cab	ist· my bagasie in die keb	sit mey ba(h)cha(h) see in dee ke(r)p
drive me to...	bring my na...toe	bring mey na(h)... too
drive quickly	ry vinnig, ja aan	rey finnich, ya(h) ahn
drive slower	ry stadiger (lang-samer)	rey sta(h)diche(r)r [la(h)ngsahm-e(r)r]
stop! go on!	hou stil! gaan aan!	ho still! chahn ahn!
wait!	wag 'n bietjie!	va(h)ch i(h)n beet-yee!
I wish to get out	ek wil afklim	e(r)k wil a(h)fklim

The Omnibus and Tram (Die Omnibus en Trem)

The omnibus station	die omnibus stasie	dee omnibus sta(h)-see
show me your tariff (official charges)	wys vir my U (jou) tarief (offisiele vragpryse)	veys fir mey eû (yoh) ta(h)reef (offis-see-eyle(r) fra(h)chpreyse(r))

English.	Afrikaans.	Pronunciation.
is there a bus or tram to...?	is daar 'n bus of trem na...toe?	iss dahr i(h)n buss of tre(r)m na(h) ...too?
what is the fare to...?	wat kos dit na... toe?	va(h)t koss dit na(h) ...toe?
is there room for two inside?	is daar plek vir twee binnekant?	iss dahr ple(r)k fir tvey binne(r)-ka(h)nt?
room for three outside	plek vir drie buite-op	ple(r)k fir dree buite(r)op
where can I get a bus to...?	waar kan ek 'n bus na...toe kry?	va(h)r ka(h)n e(r)k i(h)n buss krey na(h)...too?
where does it start from?	waar begin dit vandaan af?	va(h)r be(r)chin dit fa(h)ndahn a(h)f?
does this car go to ...?	gaan hierdie trem na...toe?	chahn heerdee tre(r)m na(h)... too?
no, the next one	nee, die volgende een	ney, dee folche(r)n-de(r) eyn
we shall take a bus	ons sal 'n bus neem	ons sa(h)l i(h)n buss neym
a motor bus	'n moter bus	i(h)n moter buss
an electric tram	'n elektriese trem	i(h)n e(r)lektreesee tre(r)m
a horse, steam, tram	'n perde, stoom, trem	i(h)n pe(r)rde(r), stohm trem
conductor	kondukteur	konduktu(r)r
do you go to...?	gaan U (jy) na... toe?	chahn êû (yey) na(h)...too?
do you pass...?	gaan U (jy) verby ...?	chahn êû (yey) fer-bey...?
put me down at...	sit my by...af	sit mey bey... a(h)f
fares, please	kaartjies asseblief'	kahrtyees a(h)s-se(r)bleef
give me a ticket	gee vir mey 'n kaartjie	chey fir mey i(h)n kahrtyee
full!	vol!	fol!
full! inside	vol binnekant	fol binne(r)ka(h)nt

English.	Afrikaans.	Pronunciation.
outside only	buitekant-op alleen	buite(r)ka(h)nt-op a(h)lleyn
cars stop here	trems hou hier stil	tre(r)ms ho heer still

Hotel and Rooms (Hotel en kamers)

Is there a good hotel here?	is daar 'n goeie hotel hier?	iss dahr i(h)n choo'-e(r) hote(r)l heer?
which is the best hotel?	watter een is die beste hotel?	vahtte(r)r eyn iss dee be(r)ste(r) hote(r)l?
I want a bedroom and sitting-room	ek wil 'n slaapkamer en sitkamer hê	e(r)k will i(h)n slahpkahmer e(r)n *eyn* sitkahmer hai(r)
let me see the rooms	laat ek die kamers sien asseblief	laht e(r)k dee kahmers seen a(h)sse(r)bleef
what is the charge for this room?	wat is die prys van hierdie kamer?	va(h)t iss dee preys fir heerdee ka(h)mer?
five shillings a day	vyf s(j)ielings per dag	feyf s(y)ilings per da(h)ch
does that include everything?	sluit dit alles in?	sluit dit a(h)lle(r)s in?
that is too dear	dit is te deur	dit iss te(r) dẽur
I want a cheaper one	ek wil 'n goedkoper een hê	e(r)k will i(h)n chootkohper eyn hai(r)
have you a double-bedded room?	het U (jy) 'n kamer met 'n dubbelde kooi?	he(r)t ẽu (yey) i(h)n ka(h)mer me(r)t i(h)n dubbe(r)lde(r) koh'i
can you recommend me a boarding-house?	kan U (jy) vir my 'n koshuis (losieshuis) aanbeveel?	ka(h)n ẽu (yey) fir mey i(h)n koshuis (lohseeshuis) ahnbe(r)feyl?
may I see your rooms?	kan ek U (jou) kamers sien?	ka(h)n e(r)k ẽu (yoh) ka(h)mers seen?

English.	Afrikaans.	Pronunciation.
what rooms have you to let?	watter kamers het U (jy) om te verhuur?	va(h)tter ka(h)mers he(r)t eû (yey) om te(r) ferheûr?
what rooms do you want?	watter kamers wil U (yey) hê?	va(h)ter ka(h)mers will eû (yey) hai(r)?
we will take these rooms	ons sal hierdie kamers neem	ons sa(h)l heerdee ka(h)mers neym
how long do you want them for?	vir hoelank wil U (jy) dit hê?	fir hoola(h)nk vill eû (yey) dit hai(r)?
we shall stay a week	ons bly vir 'n week	ons bley fir i(h)n veyk
you must stay four days	U (jy) moet vier dae bly	eû (yey) moet feer da(h)e(r) bley
are the beds well aired?	het die beddes goed lug gekry?	he(r)t dee be(r)dde(r)s choot luch che(r)krey?
what is my number?	wat is my nommer?	va(h)t iss mey nommer?
go up by the lift	gaan met die hystoestel (lift) op	chahn me(r)t dee heystooste(r)l op
show this gentleman No. 8	wys vir nierdie heer nommer ag	veys fir heerdee heyr nommer a(h)ch
second floor, please	twede verdieping, asseblief	tveyde(r) ferdeeping, a(h)sse(r)bleef
what number, sir?	watter nommer, meneer?	va(h)tte(r)r nommer, me(r)neyr?
send the chambermaid to me	stuur die kamermeisie hier na my-toe	steûr dee kahmermeysee heer na(h) may-too
ring for the waiter	lui vir die tafelbediende	lui fir dee ta(h)fe(r)lbe(r)deen-de(r)
let me have my boots—a pair of slippers	bring vir my my skoene—'n paar slippers	bring fir mey mey skohne(r) i(h)n pahr slippers
let us have supper soon	gee asseblief gou vir ons sopper (aandete)	gey a(h)sse(r)bleef cho fir ons sopper (ahnteyte(r))

English.	Afrikaans.	Pronunciation.
are our rooms ready?	is onse kamers klaar?	iss onse(r) kah-me(r)rs klahr?
give me the key of my room	gee vir my die sleutel van my kamer	chey fir mey dee slu(r)te(r)l fa(h)n mey ka(h)me(r)
has anyone asked for me?	het iemand na my gevra?	he(r)t eemant na(h) mey che(r)frah?
if someone calls for me	as iemand na my vra	a(h)s eemant na(h) mey frah
call me at seven	roep my om sewe uur	roop mey om sey-ve(r) êur
we will take coffee at eight	ons sal om ag(t)uur koffie drink	ons sa(h)l om ach(t)-êur koffee drink
are there any letters for me?	is daar miskien briewe vir my?	iss dahr miskeen breeve(r) fir mey?
where is the w.c.?	waar is die gemak-huisie?	vahr iss dee che(r)-mahk huisee?
can I have a warm bath?	kan ek 'n warm bad kry?	ka(h)n e(r)k i(h)n va(h)rm ba(h)t krey?
I should like a cold bath	ek wil graag 'n kou bad hê	e(r)k vill chrahch i(h)n ko(h) ba(h)t hai(r)
the bathroom is on this floor	die badkamer is op hierdie landing	dee ba(h)tkahmer iss op heerdee la(h)nding
at the end of the corridor	op die end van die gang	op dee e(r)nt fa(h)n dee cha(h)ng
a Turkish bath	'n Turkse bad	i(h)n turkse(r) ba(h)t
a swimming bath	'n swembad	i(h)n sve(r)mba(h)t
bring me some warm water	bring vir my 'n bietjie warm water	bring fir mey i(h)n beetyee va(h)rm va(h)te(r)r
put it down	sit dit neer	sit dit neyr
give me a candle, please	gee vir my 'n kers asseblief	chey fir mey i(h)n kers a(h)sse(r)-bleef
there are no matches here	daar is g'n vuur-houtjies hier nie	dahr iss ch'n fêur-hohtyees heer nee

English.	Afrikaans.	Pronunciation.
we leave early to-morrow morning	ons vertrek môre-oggend vroeg	ons fertre(r)k mawre(r) och'-che(r)nt frooch
I want another blanket	ek wil nog 'n kombers hê	e(r)k vill noch i(h)n kombe(r)rs hai(r)
give me a brush down	borsel my asseblief af	borse(r)l mey a(h)s-se(r)bleef a(h)f
cut my hair	sny my hare	sney mey hahre(r)
a shampoo	'n hoofwassing en wrywing	i(h)n hohfva(h)sing e(r)n vreyving
I want a shave	ek wil my laat skeer	e(r)k vill mey laht skeyr
my bill, please	my rekening, asse-blief	mey reyke(r)ning a(h)sse(r)bleef
there is a mistake in my bill	daar is 'n fout in my rekening	dahr iss i(h)n foht in mey re(r)ke(r)n-ing
I think you will find it's correct	ek dink U (jy) sal sien dat dit reg is	e(r)k dink êû (yey) sa(h)l seen da(h)t dit re(r)ch iss
I did not dine here on Tuesday	Dinsdag het ek nie hier geëet nie	dinsda(h)ch he(r)t e(r)k nee heer che(r)eyt nee
you have charged a day too much	U (jy) het vir een dag teveel gevra	êû (yey) he(r)t fir eyn da(h)ch te(r)-feyl che(r)fra(h)
this is an over-charge	dit is te hoog gere-ken	dit iss te(r)hohch che(r)reyke(r)n
you have over-charged me	U (jy) het vir my oorvra	êû (yey) he(r)t fir mey ohrfra(h)

Correspondence (Briewewisseling)

I must write a letter	ek moet 'n brief skryf	e(r)k moot i(h)n breef skreyf
I have some letters to write	ek het nog enige briewe om te skrywe	e(r)k he(r)t noch eyniche(r) bree-ve(r) om te(r) skreyve(r)
I want some paper	ek het papier nodig	e(r)k he(r)t pa(h)-peer nohdich

English.	Afrikaans.	Pronunciation.
have you any thin note-paper?	het U (jy) misskien dun skryfpapier?	he(r)t êû (yey) misskeen dun skreyfpa(h)peer?
have you any ink?	het (u) jy ink hier?	he(r)t (êû) yey ink heer
will you give me some?	sal U (jy) vir my 'n bietjie gee?	sa(h)l êû (yey) fir mey i(h)n beetyee chey
can you lend me a pen?	kan U (jy) vir my 'n pen leen?	ka(h)n êû (yey) fir mey i(h)n pe(r)n leyn?
please give me some note-paper	gee vir my asseblief 'n bietjie skryfpapier	chey fir mey a(h)sse(r)bleef i(h)n beetyee skreyfpa(h)peer
one sheet will do	een vel sal genoegwees	eyn fe(r)l sa(h)l che(r)nooch veys
I will take a quire	ek sal 'n boek daarvan neem	e(r)k sa(h)l i(h)n book da(h)rfa(h)n neym
I want an envelope, also a post-card	ek wil 'n konvert, en ook 'n poskaart hê	e(r)k vill i(h)n konfert, e(r)n ohk i(h)n posskahrt hai(r)
how much a packet?	hoeveel kos dit vir 'n pakkie?	hoofeyl koss dit fir i(h)n pa(h)kee?
a packet of envelopes	'n pakkie konverte	i(h)n pa(h)kkee konfe(r)rte(r)
can you let me have a few picture post-cards?	kan U (jy) vir my 'n paar prentposkarte laat kry?	ka(h)n êû (yey) fir mey i(h)n pahr prentposskahrte(r) laht krey?
I use a fountain-pen	ek gebruik 'n vulpen	e(r)k che(r)bruik i(h)n fulpen
could you re-fill my pen?	sal U (jy) asseblief my vulpen weer vlomaak?	sa(h)l êû (yey) a(h)sse(r)bleef mey fulpen veyr fo(h)lmahk?

English.	Afrikaans.	Pronunciation.
I have a note to enclose	ek het 'n briefie om intesluit	e(r)k he(r)t i(h)n breefeeominte(r)-sluit
lend me a sheet of paper	leen vir my 'n vel papier	leyn fir mey i(h)n fel pa(h)peer
I like a hard pen	ek hou van 'n stywe pen	e(r)k ho fa(h)n i(h)n steyve(r) pen
do you like a hard pen?	hou U (jy) van 'n stywe pen?	ho êû (yey) fa(h)n i(h)n steyve(r) pen?
what is the day of the month?	die hoeveelste is dit van dag, watter datum is dit vandag?	dee hoofeylste(r) iss dit fa(h)nda(h)ch va(h)ter dahtum iss dit fa(h)n-da(h)ch?
to-day (this) is the first	vandag (dit) is die eerste	fa(h)nda(h)ch (dit) iss dee eyrste(r)
seal your letter	laktoe U (jou) brief	la(h)k too êû (yoh) breef
there is no wax	daar is g'n lak nie	da(h)r iss ch'n la(h)k nee
I have a letter to answer	ek het 'n brief wat ek moet antwoord	e(r)k he(r)t i(h)n breef va(h)t e(r)k moot a(h)ntvohrt
take this letter to the post	neem hierdie brief (na die) pos-toe	neym heerdee breef (na(h) dee) poss-too
pay the postage	betaal die posgeld	be(r)ta(h)l dee poss-chelt
please deliver this by hand	lewer dit asseblief persoonlik af	leyver dit a(h)s-se(r)bleef pe(r)r-sohnlik a(h)f
newspaper wrapper	koerantomslag	koora(h)ntom-sla(h)ch
shall I wait for an answer?	moet ek vir 'n ant-woord wag?	moot e(r)k fir i(h)n a(h)ntvohrt va(h)ch?
yes, wait for an answer	ja, wag op 'n ant-woord	ya(h), va(h)ch op i(h)n a(h)nt-vohrt

Beginning and Ending Letters (Die begin en afsluit van Briewe)

English.	Afrikaans.	Pronunciation.
Dear Sir	weledele heer	ve(r)leyde(r)le(r) heyr
dear Mr. Murray	geagte meneer Murray	che(r)a(h)chte(r) heyr M.
dear Miss Louisa	liewe juffrou L.	leeve(r) yuffro L.
my beloved sister	my beminde suster	mey be(r)minde(r) suster
my dear papa	my liewe vader (pa)	mey leeve(r) fa(h)der (pa(h))
dearest mother	liefste moeder (ma)	leefste(r) mooder (ma(h))
dear cousin	liewe (m.) neef liewe (f.) niggie	leeve(r) neyf leeve(r) nich'chee
the proprietor	die eienaar	dee eye(r)nahr
the landlord	die huisbaas	dee huisbahs
the manager	die bestuurder	dee be(r)steûrde(r)r
the secretary	die sekretaris	dee se(r)kre(r)ta(h)ris
the postmaster	die posmeester	dee posmeyster
the station master	die stasiemeester	dee sta(h)seemeyster
yours obediently	U dienswillige dienaar	eû deensvilliche(r) deenahr
your obedient servant	Uedeler Dienswillige Dienaar	eûeydle(r)r deensvilliche(r)deenahr
yours truly	die uwe	dee eûve(r)
yours faithfully	U dienswillige dienaar	eû deensvilliche(r) deenahr
yours sincerely	U opregte	eû opre(r)chte(r)
your most (very) sincerely	U allerbeste	eû a(h)lle(r)rbeste(r)
yours affectionately	liefhebbende die uwe	leefhe(r)bbe(r)nde(r) dee eûve(r)
your affectionate friend	U liefhebbende vriend	eû leefhe(r)bbe(r)nde(r) freent
ever your devoted daughter	altyd U toegeneë dogter	a(h)lteyt eû tooche(r)neye(r) dochter

English.	Afrikaans.	Pronunciation.
to the Governor	aan die Goewerneur	ahn dee choover-nu(r)r
His Excellency . . .	Syn Eksellensie...	seynekse(r)lensee...
your Excellency's obedient servant	van U Eksellensie die Onderdanige Dienaar	fa(h)n e͡u ekse(r)-lensee dee onder-dahniche(r) dee-nahr
to a President	aan 'n President	ahn i(h)n pre(r)see-de(r)nt
His Honour President...	die Hoogedele Heer President...	dee hohch eyde(r)-le(r) heyr pre(r)-seede(r)nt ...
your obedient servant	UHEds. Onderdanige Dienaar	e͡u-heds. onderdah-niche(r) deenahr
to a Member of Parliament or Cabinet Minister	aan 'n Lid van die Parlement of Minister	ahn i(h)n lit fa(h)n dee pa(h)rle(r)-ment of minister
to a Chief Justice	aan 'n Hoofregter	a(h)n i(h)n hoh-fre(r)chte(r)r
His Honour the Chief Justice	die HoogEdel Gestrenge Heer, die Hoofregter	dee hohcheyde(r)l che(r)strenge(r) heyr, dee hoh-fre(r)chte(r)r
to a Judge	aan 'n Regter	ahn i(h)n re(r)chte(r)r
the Honourable Mr. Justice...	die HoogEdel Gestrenge Heer...	dee hohcheyde(r)-le(r) che(r)-stre(r)nge(r) heyr ...
to a Consul	aan 'n Konsul	ahn i(h)n konsul
...Esq., Consul-General for ...	Die Weledel Gestrenge Heer..., Konsul-Generaal vir...	dee ve(r)leyde(r)l che(r)stre(r)nge(r) heyr..., Konsul-che(r)ne(r)-rahl fir...
Sir	Weledel Gestrenge Heer	ve(r)leyde(r)le(r) che(r)stre(r)nge(r) heyr
to a Clergyman	aan 'n Predikant	ahn i(h)n pre(r)dee-ka(h)nt

English.	Afrikaans.	Pronunciation.
dear sir	Weleerwaarde Heer	ve(r)leyrvahrde(r) heyr
The Superintendent-General of Education	Die Superintendent Generaal van Onderwys	dee superintendent-che(r)ne(r)rahl fa(h)n onderweys
to a Doctor of Literature or Laws	aan 'n Doktor indie Letterkunde of die Regsgeleerdheid	ahn i(h)n dokter in dee letterkunde(r) of dee re(r)chs-che(r)leyrtheyt
..., Esq., Litt.D. (LL.D.)	Die Weled. SeerGel. Heer..., Litt.D. (LL.D.)	dee ve(r)leyd, seyr-che(r)l, heyr... Litt.D. (LL.D.)
Sir,	Weledel Seergeleerde Heer	ve(r)leyde(r)l seyr-che(r)leyrde(r) heyr,
to a Professor at a College or University	aan 'n Professor aan 'n Uniwersiteit of Kollege	ahn i(h)n professor ahn i(h)n eûnee-verseeteyt of kol-leesj
Professor ...	Die Hooggeleerde Heer Professor...	dee hohch'che(r)-leyrde(r) heyr professor...
to a Town Council	aan 'n Stadsraad	ahn i(h)n sta(h)ts-raht
His Worship the Mayor and Members of the Town Council of...	Die Edelagbare Here, Burgemeester en Lede van die Stadsraad van...	dee eyde(r)la(h)ch-bahre(r) heyre(r), burche(r)meys-te(r)r e(r)n ley-de(r) fa(h)n dee sta(h)tsraht fa(h)n...
Gentlemen	Edelagbare Here	eyde(r)lahchbah-re(r) Heyre
to a man of station or of means	aan iemand uit aansienlike stand	ahn eemant uit ahn-seenlike(r) sta(h)nt
..., Esq.	Die weledele Heer...	dee ve(r)leyde(r)-le(r) heyr...
Dear Sir	Weledele Heer	ve(r)leyde(r)le(r) heyr

English.	Afrikaans.	Pronunciation.
to anyone addressed as Mr.	aan enigeen wat geadreseer word as Mr.	ahn eynicheyn va(h)t che(r)a(h)-dre(r)seyr vort a(h)s Mr.
Mr....	Die Heer...	dee heyr
Dear Sir	meneer	me(r)neyr
yours truly	die uwe	dee êûve(r)

NOTES ON THE ABOVE

If one is on intimate terms, or equal social standing, with the one he corresponds with, Waarde Heer may be substituted for either *Die Heer* or *Weledele Heer*.

A married lady is addressed as *Mevrou*, while an unmarried lady is addressed as *Mejuffrou*, and a girl under the age of 16 as *Jongejuffrou*. A widow is addressed as *Mevrou* die *Weduwe*.

Ladies do not have the titles of their husbands added to any form of address: Mrs. Professor Hoernle is simply Mevrou Hoernle, unless of course she is herself a Professor.

Surnames are not included in terms of address: " Dear Mr. Butler " should be rendered *Meneer*, or *Waarde Heer*, but not *Waarde Heer Butler*.

In addressing ladies, " Dear Miss Young " is best rendered *Mejuffrou*, but may also be expressed *Liewe Juffrou Young*. Likewise, " Dear Mrs. Ingram " is best put *Mevrou* only, but may also be rendered *Liewe Mevrou Ingram*.

Though *Mevrou* is the Afrikaans term used for married ladies, the English Mrs. is without exception applied to both the " upper " classes and lower ranks, in this Sub-Continent.

Post, Telegraph, and Telephone (Pos, Telegraaf en Telefoon)

Where is the Post Office?	waar is die Poskantoor?	va(h)r iss dee posska(h)ntohr?
post this letter at once	pos hierdie brief dadelik	poss heerdee breef da(h)de(r)lik
pay the postage on it	betaal die posgeld daarop	be(r)tahl dee possche(r)lt dahrop
what is the postage on this letter?	wat is die posgeld vir (op) die brief?	va(h)t iss dee possche(r)lt fir (op) dee breef?
were you in time for the post?	was (u) jy nog in tyd vir die pos?	va(h)s (êû) yey noch in teyt fir dee poss?
maximum weight	maksimum gewig	ma(h)kseemum che(r)vich

English.	Afrikaans.	Pronunciation.
is this letter over weight?	is hierdie brief oor die gewig?	iss heerdee breef ohr dee che(r)vich?
yes, it wants another stamp	ja, dit vra nog 'n seël	ya(h) dit fra(h) noch i(h)n seye(r)l
what name, sir?	wat is die naam, meneer?	va(h)t iss dee nahm, me(r)neyr?
and the address?	en die adres?	e(r)n dee a(h)dress?
write your name and address here	skryf U (jou) naam en adres hier	skreyf ēū (yoh) nahm e(r)n a(h)-dre(r)ss heer
I wish to register this letter	ek wil graag hierdie brief registreer	e(r)k vill chrahch heerbreef rechi-streyr
office of origin	kantoor van afsend-ing	ka(h)ntohr fa(h)n a(h)fse(r)nding
signature	handtekening	ha(h)nt'tykee(r)n-ing
to register a letter	'n brief registreet	i(h)n breef re(r)-che(r)streyr
a registered letter	'n geregistree de brief	i(h)n che(r)re(r)-cheestreyrde(r) breef
by to-day's post	met vandaag se pos	me(r)t fa(h)ndahch se(r) poss
by return of post	per kerende pos	per keyre(r)nde(r) poss
is there a foreign parcel-post?	is daar 'n buite-landse pakkies-pos (pakketpos)?	iss dahr i(h)n bui-te(r) la(h)ntse(r) pa(h)kkeesposs (pa(h)ke(r)t-poss)?
the latest delivery is at	die laaste aflewer-ing van briewe is om...	dee lahste(r) a(h)f-leyvering fa(h)n breever iss om...
printed matter	drukwerk	dru(r)kverk
have you any letters for the post?	het U (jy) enige briewe vir die pos?	he(r)t ēū (jy) eyni-che(r) breeve(r) fir dee poss?
is it time for the post?	is dit tyd vir die pos?	iss dit teyt fir dee poss?

English.	Afrikaans.	Pronunciation.
you are too late for the post	U (jy) is te laat vir die pos	êû (yey) iss te(r) laht fir dee poss
am I in time for the mail?	is ek nog in tyd vir die mail?	iss e(r)k noch in teyt fir dee mail?
the mail has gone	die mail is al weg	dee mail iss a(h)l ve(r)ch
the next mail goes at 7 p.m.	die volgende mail (train) vertrek hiervandaan om 7 n.m.	dee folche(r)nde(r) mail (train) fertre(r)k heerfa(h)n dahn om 7 n.m,
when is the next collection?	wanneer is die volgende kolleksie (insameling) van briewe?	va(h)nneyer iss dee folche(r)nde(r) kolle(r)ksee (insa(h)me(r)ling) fa(h)n breeve(r)?
when is the next delivery?	wanneer (hoe laat) word briewe weer afgelewer?	va(h)nneyer (hoo la(h)t) vort breeve(r) veyr a(h)fche(r)leyve(r)r?
there is another delivery to-night	daar is vanaand nog weer 'n aflewering	dahr iss fa(h)nahnt noch veyr i(h)n a(h)fleyve(r)ring
is your letter ready for the post?	is U (jou) brief klaar vir die pos?	iss êû (yoh) breef klahr fir dee poss?
will you post this letter for me?	sal U (jy) asseblief hierdie brief vir my pos?	sa(h)l êû (yey) a(h)sse(r)bleef heerdee breef fir mey poss?
when does the office close?	wanneer (hoe laat) sluit die kantoor?	va(h)nneyr (hoo la(h)t) sluit dee ka(h)ntohr?
office-hours	kantoor ure	ka(h)ntohr êûre(r)
customs declaration	doeane deklarasie	dooahne(r) de(r)kler-ra(h)see
value of contents	waarde van inhoud	va(h)rde(r) fa(h)n inhoht
office of origin	kantoor van afsending	ka(h)ntohr fa(h)n a(h)fse(r)nding
stamp of office of origin	seël van kantoor van afsending	seye(r)l fa(h)n ka(h)ntohr fa(h)n a(h)fse(r)nding

English.	Afrikaans.	Pronunciation.
place of destination	plaas van bestemming	plahs fa(h)n be(r)ste(r)m'ing
name and address of sender	naam en adres van afsender	nahm e(r)n a(h)dre(r)ss fa(h)n a(h)fse(r)nde(r)
will this letter go tonight?	sal die brief nog vanaand weggaan?	sa(h)l dee breef noch fa(h)nahnt ve(r)chchahn?
have you any letters for Mr....?	is hier briewe vir meneer...?	iss heer breeve(r) fir me(r)neyr...?
when does the mail leave for England?	wanneer vertrek die mailboot vir Engeland?	va(h)neyr fertre(r)k dee mailboht fir e(r)ngla(h)nt?
is the London mail in yet?	het die Londonse mail al ingekom?	he(r)t dee Londonse(r) mail a(h)l inche(r)kom?
I want a money (postal) order for ...	ek wil 'n poswissel hê, van bedrag...	e(r)k vill i(h)n posvisse(r)l hai(r) fa(h)n be(r)dra(h)ch...
payable at the G.P.O.	betaalbaar aan die Hoofposkantoor	be(r)ta(h)lbahr ahn dee hohfposka(h)ntohr
Telegraph Office	telegraafkantoor	te(r)le(r)chrahfka(h)ntohr
telegrams	telegramme	te(r)le(r)chra(h)mme(r)
where is the telegraph-office?	waar is die telegraaf-kantoor?	vahr iss dee te(r)le(r)chrahfka(h)ntohr?
I want to send a telegram	ek wil 'n telegram stuur	e(r)k vill i(h)n te(r)le(r)chrahm stêûr
what is the charge?	wat sal dit kos?	va(h)t sa(h)l dit kos?
the first twelve words	die eerste twaálf woorde	dee eyrste(r) tvahlf vohrde(r)
every additional word	elke bykomende (ekstra) woord	e(r)lke(r) beykohme(r)nde(r) vohrt (e(r)kstra(h))

English.	Afrikaans.	Pronunciation.
Telephone Office	telefoonkantoor	te(r)le(r)fohn-ka(h)ntohr
are you on the telephone?	is U (jy) op die telefoon?	iss êû (yey) op dee te(r)l le(r)fohn?
what is your number?	wat is U (jou) nommer?	va(h)t iss êû (yoh) nomme(r)r?
who is speaking, please?	wie praat daar, asseblief?	vee praht dahr a(h)sse(r)bleef?
ring up Mr....	bel meneer...op	be(r)l me(r)neyr... op
is that Mr....?	is dit meneer...?	iss dit me(r)neyr...?
speaking	ja, dis ek wat praat	ya(h) dis e(r)k va(h)t praht
are you there?	is U (jy) daar?	iss êû (yey) dahr?
who is speaking?	wie praat daar?	vee praht dahr?
wrong number, sorry	verkeerde nommer, ek is jammer	ferkeyrde(r) nommer, e(r)k iss ya(h)me(r)r
I want No....	ek wil No.... hê	e(r)k vill No.... hai(r)
you are through	U (jy) is deur (aan die beurt)	êû (yey) iss du(r)r [ahn dee bu(r)rt]
I don't (can't) hear you	ek kan niks hoor nie	e(r)k ka(h)n niks hohr nee
no reply from...	g'n (geen) antwoord van...nie	ch'n (cheyn) a(h)nt-vohrt fa(h)n... nee
I can't get No....	ek kan No.... nie kry nie	e(r)k ka(h)n No.... nee krey nee
your call is cancelled	U (jou) bestelling (aanroep) is gekanseleer	êû (yoh) be(r)ste(r)-ling (ahnroop) iss che(r)ka(h)nse(r)-leyr
the charge for your call is...	die koste van U (jou) (oproep) gesprek is...	dee koste(r) fa(h)n êû (yoh) cher-spre(r)k (oproop) iss...
ring off!	bel af!	be(r)l a(h)f!

Breakfast (Ontbyt, Brekfis, Môre-ete)

English.	Afrikaans.	Pronunciation.
Is breakfast ready?	is die ontbyt (brekfis) klaar?	iss de ontbeyt (bre(r)kfis) klahr?
breakfast is ready	die môre-ete is nou klaar	dee mawre(r)-eyte(r) iss no klahr
is the tea made?	is die teẹ al gemaak?	iss dee tey a(h)l che(r)mahk?
do you drink tea or coffee?	drink U (jy) tee of koffie?	drink êû (yey) tey of koffee?
coffee with (without) milk	koffie met (sonder) melk	koffee me(r)t (sonder) me(r)lk
a cup of coffee	'n koppie koffie	i(h)n koppe koffee
do you take milk and sugar?	neem U (jy) melk en suiker?	neym êû (yey) me(r)lk e(r)n suike(r)r?
no sugar, thank you	g'n suiker nie, dankie	ch'n suike(r)r nie, da(h)nkee
take some more sugar	neem nog 'n bietjie suiker	neym noch i(h)n beetyee suike(r)r
this cream is sour	hierdie room is suur	heerdee rohm iss sêûr
will you take an egg?	sal U (jy) 'n eier neem?	sa(h)l êû (yey) i(h)n eye(r)r neym?
these eggs are hard	die eiers is hard	dee eye(r)rs iss ha(h)rt
a little more fish	nog 'n stukkie vis, asseblief	noch i(h)n stukkee fiss, a(h)sse(r)bleef
this is excellent	dit is uitstekend	dit iss uitsteyke(r)nt
but this butter is not fresh	maar die botter is nie vars nie	mahr dee botter iss nee fa(h)rs nee
give me some fresh butter	gee vir my 'n stukkie (bietjie) vars botter	chey fir mey i(h)n stukkee (beetyee) fa(h)rs botter
bring some more	bring nog 'n bietjie	bring noch i(h)n beetyee
pass me the salt	gee asseblief vir my die sout aan	chey a(h)sse(r)bleef fir mey dee sout ahn

English.	Afrikaans.	Pronunciation.
take some more...	neem nog 'n bietjie (stukkie) ...	neym noch i(h)n beetyee (stukkee)
is the coffee strong enough?	is die koffie sterk genoeg?	iss dee koffee ste(r)rk che(r)nooch?
we want more cups	ons wil nog 'n paar koppies vol hê	ons vill noch i(h)n pahr koppees fol hai(r)
cold meat	kou vlees	ko fleys
some hot rolls	'n paar vars bolletjies	i(h)n pahr fa(h)rs bolle(r)tyees
a piece of toast	'n stuk roosterbrood	i(h)n stuk rohste(r)r broht
a rasher of bacon	'n dun syndjie spek	i(h)n dun sneytyee spe(r)k
nothing more, thank you	niks meer nie, dankie	niks meyr nee, da(h)nkee
you can take away the things	jy kan nou maar die skottelgoed wegneem	yey ka(h)n no mahr dee skotte(r)l-choot ve(r)ch-neym
we will take breakfast in our room	ons sal in onse kamer brekfis	ons sa(h)l in onse(r) kahmer bre(r)kfiss

Dinner (Middagmaal)

Where is there a good restaurant?	waar is 'n goeie eetsaal?	va(h)r iss i(h)nchoo' ie(r) eytsahl?
call the waiter	roep die tafelbediende	roop dee ta(h)fe(r)l-be(r)deende(r)
show me the bill-of-fare	laat ek die spyskaart sien	la(h)t e(r)k dee speyskahrt seen
what have you ready?	wat is daar wat klaar is?	va(h)t iss dahr va(h)t klahr iss?
will you have soup?	sal U sop neem?	sa(h)l êû sop neym?
what time is dinner?	wanneer is dit julle etenstyd?	va(h)nneyr iss dit yulle(r) eyte(r)n-steyt?
we shall dine at six o'clock	dinee is om ses uur	deeney iss om se(r)s êûr
are you hungry, thirsty?	is U honger, dors?	iss êû hohnge(r)r, dorss?

English.	Afrikaans.	Pronunciation.
I am very thir ty	ek is baie dors	e(r)k iss bah'i-e(r) dors
reserve this table for me	hou (reserveer) die tafel vir my	ho (reyse(r)rfeyr) dee ta(h)fe(r)l fir mey
that table is reserved	daardie tafel is al bespreek	da(h)rdee ta(h)fe(r)l iss a(h)l be(r)-spreyk
we expect a friend	ons verwag 'n vriend	ons ferva(h)ch i(h)n freent
have you a large table?	het jy 'n groot tafel?	he(r)t yey i(h)n chroht ta(h)fe(r)l?
here is a table for two	hier is 'n tafel vir twee	heer iss i(h)n ta(h)-fe(r)l fir tvey
we are a party of four	ons is vier	ons iss feer
this way, madam	hier langs, juffrou	heer la(h)ngs, yuf-fro
take my coat	neem my jas	neym mey ya(h)s
the dinner is at a fixed price	die dinee is teen 'n vaste prys	dee deeney iss teyn teyn i(h)n fa(h)s-che(r)ste(r)lde(r) preys
what is the price?	wat is die prys?	va(h)t iss dee preys?
is wine included?	is die wyn saamgere-ken? sluit dit die wyn in?	iss dee veyn sahm-che(r)reyke(r)n? sluit dit dee veyn in?
we charge *à la carte*	die pryse is na die kaart	dee preyse(r) iss na(h) dee kahrt
a serviette, please	'n servet, asseblief	i(h)n se(r)rfe(r)t, a(h)sse(r)bleef
this is not clean	dit is nie skoon nie	dit iss nee skohn nee
we are in a hurry	ons is hastig	ons iss hahste(r)ch
what have you in soup?	wat het jy vir sop?	va(h)t he(r)t yey fir so(r)p?
clear soup	vleissoussop	fleys-sohs-so(r)p
pea soup	ertjiesop	e(r)rtyeeso(r)p
vegetables soup	groentesop	chroonte(r)so(r)p
broth	meelsop	meylso(r)p

English.	Afrikaans.	Pronunciation.
what shall I help you to ?	met wat kan ek U dien ?	me(r)t va(h)t ka(h)n e(r)k êü deen ?
will you have some fish ?	sal U vis neem ?	sa(h)l êü fiss neym ?
what fish have you ?	watter soort vis het jy ?	va(h)te(r)r sohrt fiss he(r)t yey ?
see, here is the menu	hier is die spyskaart	heer iss dee speys speyskahrt
we have salmon with sauce Hollandaise	ons het geelbek vis met 'n Hollandse sous	ons he(r)t cheyl-be(r)k fis me(r)t i(h)n Holla(h)n-tse(r) sous
fried soles	gebakte tongvis	che(r)ba(h)kte(r) tongfiss
eels and grated cheese	paling en geraspede kaas	pa(h)ling e(r)n che(r)ra(h)spe(r)-de(r)kahs
fresh herrings	vars harders	fa(h)rs ha(h)rde(r)rs
have you any roast beef ?	het jy gebraaide beesvleis ?	he(r)t yey che(r)-brah'ide(r) beys-fleys ?
— — — boiled mutton ?	gekookte skaap-vleis ?	che(r)kohkte(r) skahpfleys ?
roast lamb	lammerbraad	la(h)m'me(r)r-braht
pork	varkvleis	fa(h)rkfleys
cutlets (chops)	karbonaadjies	ka(h)rbonahtyees
bring me a glass of water	bring vir my 'n glas water	bring fir mey i(h)n chla(h)s va(h)-te(r)r
bring me something to drink	bring vir my iets om te drink	bring fir mey eets om te(r) drink
this wine is flat	die wyn is laf (smaakloos)	dee weyn iss la(h)f (smahklohs)
what do you drink ?	wat drink U dan ?	va(h)t drink êü da(h)n ?
bring me the wine list	bring vir my die wynkaart	bring fir mey dee weynkahrt
here is the list	hier is die lys	heer iss dee leys
what wine will you have ?	watter soort wyn wil U hê ?	va(h)tte(r)r sohrt veyn vill êü hai(r)

English.	Afrikaans.	Pronunciation.
I will have a bottle	ek wil 'n bottel vol hê	e(r)k vill i(h)n botte(r)l fol hai(r)
a half-bottle of dinner wine	'n halwe bottel tafelwyn	i(h)n ha(h)lve(r) botte(r)l tahfe(r)l veyn
champagne	sjampanje	sha(h)mpa(h)nye(r)
hock	rynwyn	reynveyn
whisky	wiskie	viskey
brandy	brandewyn	bra(h)nde(r)veyn
another, please	nog een, asseblief	noch eyn, a(h)sse(r)bleef
I do not like this wine	ek hou nie van die wyn nie	e(r)k ho nee fa(h)n dee veyn nee
some ice, please	'n stukkie ys asseblief	i(h)n stukkee eys a(h)sse(r)bleef
help yourself	help U self	he(r)lp êû se(r)lf
make yuurself at home	maak uself tuis	mahk êûse(r)lf tuis
bring me a salad	bring vir my slaai	bring fir mey slah'i
some mixed fruit	deurmekaargemaakte vrugte	du(r)rme(r)ka(h)rche(r)mahkte(r) fruchte(r)
potatoes	ertappels	ai(r)ta(h)pe(r)ls
—, boiled	—, opgekook	—, op che(r)kohk
—, mashed	—, fyngemaak	—, feynche(r)mahk
—, chips, fried in butter	—, ertappelsnippers, in botter gebraai	—, ai(r)ta(h)ppe(r)lsnippe(r)rs, in botte(r)r che(r)brah'i
green peas and beans	groen (dop) erte en groenboontjies	chroon (dop) ai(r)rte(r) en chroon bohntyees
Brussels sprouts	Brusselse spruitjies	brusse(r)lse(r) spruityees
spinach and broccoli	spinasie en spruitkool	speenahsee e(r)n spruitkohl
remove the plates	neem af (weg) die borde	neym vech (a(h)f) dee borde(r)

English.	Afrikaans.	Pronunciation.
bring me some roast turkey	bring vir my 'n stukkie gebraaide kalkoenvleis	bring fir mey i(h)n stukkee che(r)-brah'ide(r) ka(h)l-koonfleys
— roast chicken	— gebraaide hoender	— che(r)brah'ide(r) hoonde(r)r
— boiled fowl	— gekookte hoender	— che(r)kohkte(r) hoonde(r)r
what sweet dishes have you?	watter soort soetkos het julle?	va(h)tte(r)r sohrt sootkos he(r)t yulle(r)?
we have (sweet) omelettes with ham	ons het (soet) ommelette met ham	ons he(r)t (soot) omme(r)le(r)tte(r) me(r)t ha(h)m
omelettes with herbs	ommelette met kruie	omme(r)le(r)tte(r) me(r)t kruie(r)
— with rum	— met rum	— me(r)t rum
give me a clean fork, knife, spoon	gee vir my 'n skoon vurk, mes, lepel	chey fir mey i(h)n skohn furk, me(r)s, leype(r)l
will you take some more?	sal U nog iets meer neem?	sa(h)l eû noch eets meyr neym?
please pass the salt, pepper, vinegar, oil, mustard	gee vir my asseblief die sout, peper, asyn, olie, mosterd aan	chey fir mey a(h)s-se(r)bleef dee sout peyper, a(h)seyn, ohlee, moste(r)rt ahn
I am very thirsty	ek is baie dors	e(r)k iss bah'i-e(r) dors
may I trouble you for a glass of water?	kan ek vir U (jou) vir 'n glas water lastig val?	ka(h)n e(r)k fir eu (yoh) fir i(h)n chla(h)s va(h)-te(r)r la(h)ste(r)ch fa(h)l
some blanc-mange	blamans	bla(h)mahns
fruit-tart	vrugtetert	fruchte(r)te(r)rt
rice and prunes	rys en gedroogde pruime	reys e(r)n che(r)-drohchte(r) pruime(r)
vanilla ice	vanille ys	fa(h)neelle(r)·eys

English.	Afrikaans.	Pronunciation.
what dessert have you?	wat het julle vir dessert?	va(h)t he(r)t yulle(r) fir de(r)sse(r)rt?
we have only stewed fruits	ons het maar net gestoofde vrugte	ons he(r)t mahr ne(r)t che(r)stohf-te(r) fruchte(r)
peaches, apples	perskes, appels	pe(r)rske(r)s, a(h)p-pe(r)ls
some black coffee, please	'n bietjie swart koffie, asseblief	i(h)n beetyee sva(h)rt koffee a(h)sse(r)bleef
some cigarettes	'n paar sigarette	i(h)n pahr sichahr-e(r)tte(r)
do you smoke a pipe?	rook U (jy) ('n) pyp?	rohk eû (yey) (i(h)n) peyp?
I prefer a cigar	ek hou meer van 'n sigaar, seroet	e(r)k ho meyr fa(h)n i(h)n seechahr, se(r)root
what liqueurs have you?	watter soort likeure (soetsopies) hou julle aan?	va(h)te(r)r sohrt leeku(r)re(r) ho yulle(r) ahn?
waiter, come here	bediende, kom hier	be(r)deende(r) kom heer
give (get) me the bill	gee (loop haal) vir my die rekening	chey (lohp hahl) fir mey dee reyke(r)-ning
pay for me	betaal vir my part	be(r)tahl fir mey pahrt
you can keep the change	jy kan die kleingeld vir jou hou	yey ka(h)n dee kleynche(r)lt fir yo ho

Tea (Tee)

Afternoon tea	agtermiddagtee	a(h)chte(r)rmid-da(h)chtey
will you come to tea?	sal U 'n koppie te by my kom geniet (gebruik)?	sa(h)l eû i(h)n kop-pee tee bey mey kom che(r)neet (che(r)bruik)?
tea is quite ready	die tee is klaar	dee tey iss klahr
pour out the tea	skink (in) die tee	skink (in) dee tey

English.	Afrikaans.	Pronunciation.
tea for two	tee vir twee	tey fir tvey
do you like strong tea?	hou U van sterk tee?	ho êû fahn ste(r)rk tey?
not too strong	nie te sterk nie	nee te(r) ste(r)rk nee
I like it rather weak	(ek hou van) taamlik flou (tee)	[e(r)k ho fa(h)n] tahmlik flo (tey)
do you take cream?	sal U room neem?	sa(h)l êû rohm neym
ring, if you please	lui, asseblief	lui, a(h)sse(r)bleef
a little more milk	nog 'n bietjie melk	noch i(h)n beetyee me(r)lk
more bread	nog brood	noch broht
some bread and butter	'n bietjie brood en botter	i(h)n beetyee broht en botte(r)r
some (little) cakes	'n weinig (klein) koekies	i(h)n veynich (kleyn) kookees
will you take some cake?	sal U koek neem?	sa(h)l êû kook neym?
a small piece	'n klein stukkie	i(h)n kleyn stukkee
make more toast	braai nog brood; maak nog roosterbrood	brah'i noch broht mahk noch rohste(r)rbroht
this is excellent tea	dis baie lekker tee	dis bah'i-e(r) le(r)kke(r)r tey
is your tea sweet enough?	is U tee soet genoeg?	iss êû tey soot che(r)nooch?
another cup of tea	nog 'n koppie tee	noch i(h)n koppee tey
I should like rather less sugar	ek sal liewer 'n bietjie minder suiker neem	e(r)k sa(h)l leeve(r)r i(h)n beetyee minde(r)r suike(r)r neym

Supper (Aandete)

English.	Afrikaans.	Pronunciation.
Come and have some supper	kom eet saam vanaand	kom eyt sahm fa(h)nahnt
this is a capital place	dit is 'n agtermekaar plek hierdie (die)	dit iss i(h)n achte(r)r me(r)kahr ple(r)k dee (heerdee)

English.	Afrikaans.	Pronunciation.
it is all ready	dis alles klaar	dis a(h)lle(r)s klahr
it will not be long	dit sal nie meer lank wees nie	dit sa(h)l nee meyr la(h)nk veys nee
thank you, I will only have a cup of coffee—of tea	dankie, ek sal maar net 'n koppie koffie—tee neem	da(h)nkee e(r)k sa(h)l mahr ne(r)t i(h)n koppee kof-fee-tey-neym
a glass of beer	'n glas bier	i(h)n chla(h)s beer
a fruit drink	'n vrugtedrankie	i(h)n freuchte(r)-dra(h)nkee
I should like a drink and a smoke	ek wil graag iets te drinke hê en dan rook	e(r)k vill chrahch eetste(r)drinke(r) hai(r) e(r)n da(h)n rohk
no thanks, I must get (be getting) home	nee dankie, ek moet nou huis-toe gaan	ney da(h)nkee, e(r)k moot no huis-too chahn
let me call you a taxi	laat ek vir jou 'n taksie roep	laht e(r)k fir yoh i(h)n ta(h)ksee roop
my carriage is waiting	my rytuig wag	mey reytuich va(h)ch
I can go by train	ek kan met die trein gaan	e(r)k ka(h)n me(r)t dee treyn chahn
mine does not go well	myne loop nie goed nie	meyne(r) lohp nee choot nee
it keeps very good time	dit hou goed tyd	dit ho choot teyt
you are an hour late	U (jy) is 'n uur laat	eû (yey) iss i(h)n eûr laht
we have plenty of time	ons het baie tyd	ons he(r)t bah'i-e(r) teyt
let us be early	laat ons vroeg wees	laht ons frooch veys
he came in good time	hy het in goeie tyd gekom	hey he(r)t in choh'i-e(r) teyt che(r)-kom
at nine a.m. (9 a.m.)	om nege uur voormiddag (9 v.m.)	om neyge(r) eûr fohrmidda(h)ch (9 v.m.)
ten-thirty (10-30)	tien uur dertig	teen eûr de(r)rtich

English.	Afrikaans.	Pronunciation.
four-forty-five p.m. (4-45 p.m.)	vier uur vyf-en-veertig (4.45 n.m.)	feer eûr feyf-e(r)n-feyrtich (4.45 n.m.)

Times and Seasons : Weather (Tye- en Jaargetye : Die weer

A short time since	'n kort tydjie gelede	i(h)n kort teytye) che(r)leyde(r)
it is scarcely two days ago	dis skaars twee dae gelede	dis skahrs tvey dahe(r) che(r)ley-de(r)
it is at least a month ago	dit is ten minste 'n maand gelede	dit iss te(r)n min-ste(r) i(h)n mahnt che(r)leyde(r)
a few days ago	'n paar dae gelede	i(h)n pahr dahe(r) che(r)leyde(r)
that was two or three days ago	dit was twee of drie dae gelede	dit va(h)s tvey of dree dahe(r) che(r)leyde(r)
at about this time	omtrent hierdie (die) tyd	omtre(r)nt heerdee (dee) teyt
this day week	vandag oor ag(t) dae	fa(h)n da(h)ch ohr a(h)ch(t) da(h)e(r)
next year	ander jaar	a(h)nde(r)r yahr
in a month's time	in 'n maand se tyd	in i(h)n mahnt se(r) teyt
on the first of the month	die eerste van aan-staande maand	dee eyrste(r) fa(h)n ahnstahnde(r) mahnt
at the end of this month	die einde van die (hierdie) maand	dee einde(r) fa(h)n dee (heerdee) mahnt
since the 19th of December	sedert die 19de Desember	seyde(r)rt dee 19de Deysembe(r)r
until the 25th of March	tot die 25ste Maart	tot dee 25ste Mahrt
the middle of January	die middel van Januarie	dee midde(r)l fa(h)n Ya(h)nuahree
in the course of a week	in die loop van ag(t) dae	in dee loph fa(h)n ach(t) dahe(r)
from time to time	van tyd tot tyd	fa(h)n teyt tot teyt

English.	Afrikaans.	Pronunciation.
from day to day	van dag tot dag	fa(h)n da(h)ch tot da(h)ch
before long	binne kort	binne(r) kort
every day	elke dag	e(r)lke(r) da(h)ch
it was only last week	dit was maar net laaste week	dit va(h)s mahr ne(r)t lahste(r) veyk
the twentieth century	die twintigste eeu	dee tvintichste(r) ee'u
during the season	gedurende die seisoen	che(r)deûre(r)nde(r) dee seysoon
in season	tydig	teydich
out of season	ontydig	onteydich
how long does the season last?	hoe lank duur die seisoen?	hoo la(h)nk deûr dee seysoon?
about three months	omtrent drie maande	omtre(r)nt dree mahnde(r)
how the time flies!	hoe vlieg die tyd, tog!	hoo fleech dee teyt toch!
it is like a spring day	die net soos 'n lente dag	dis ne(r)t sohs i(h)n le(r)nte(r) da(h)ch
the height of the summer	somer op sy hoog ste	sohme(r)r op sey hohchste(r)
it's just like summer	dis net soos in die somer	dis ne(r)t sohs in dee sohme(r)r
the days are closing in	die dae neem af (word korter)	dee da(h)e(r) neym a(h)f (vort korte(r)r)
winter will soon be here	nou gou het ons weer winter (winter is op hande)	no cho he(r)t ons veyr vinte(r)r (vinte(r)r iss op ha(h)nde(r))
it is so cold	dit is so koud	dit iss soh kout
it is as cold as winter	dit is so koud as in die winter	dit iss soh kout a(h)s in dee vinte(r)r
in the depth of winter	in die middel van die winter	in dee midde(r)l fa(h)n dee vinte(r)r
what kind of weather is it?	wat vir weer het ons?	va(h)t fir veyr he(r)t ons?

English.	Afrikaans.	Pronunciation.
It is beautiful weather	dis mooi weer	dis moo'i veyr
it is very warm	dis baie warm	dis bah'i-e(r) va(h)rm
it is windy	dis winderig	dis winder(r)rich
it is quite calm	dit is heeltemal stil	dit is heylte(r)mahl stil
the sky is overcast	die lug is bewolk; dis toegetrek	dee luch iss be(r)-volk; dis too-che(r)tre(h)k
I am afraid it will rain	ek vrees dit gaan reën	e(r)k freys dit chahn reye(r)n
it will not last long	dit sal nie lank duur nie	dit sa(h)l nee la(h)nk deûr nee
the sun is coming out again	die son kom al weer uit	dee son kom a(h)l veyr uit
I do hope it will be fine	ek hoop dit sal dit sal mooi weer wees	e(r)k hohp dit sa(h)l moo'i veyr veys
if it doesn't rain I shall go out	as dit nie reën nie sal ek uitgaan	a(h)s dit nee rey-e(r)n nee sa(h)l e(r)k uitchahn
it is frosty	dis wit van die ryp	dis vitt fa(h)n dee reyp
it is getting very cold	dit word baie koud	dit vort bah'i-e(r) ko(h)t
I am so cold	ek is so koud	e(r)k iss so(h) ko(h)t
I am shivering with the cold	ek bewe van die koue	e(r)k beyve(r) fa(h)n dee koue(r)
it rains; it hails	dit reën, dit hael	dit reye(r)nt, dit hahe(r)l
has it been snowing?	het dit kapok? het dit gesneeu?	he(r)t dit ka(h)-ko(r)k? he(r)t dit che(r)snee'w?
it snows fast	dit kapok sterk	dit ka(h)po(r)k 'ste(r)rk
the weather is very changeable	die weer is baie veranderlik	dee veyr iss bah'i-e(r) fera(h)n-de(r)r lik

English.	Afrikaans.	Pronunciation.
what a change in the weather !	watter 'n verandering in die weer!	va(h)tte(r)r i(h)n fera(h)nde(r)ring in dee veyr!
how high the wind is!	hoe sterk is die wind!	hoo ste(r)rk is dee vint!
it is going to rain	dit gaan reën	dit chahn reye(r)n
we shall have a storm	ons gaan 'n storm kry	ons chahn i(h)n storr'm krey
the wind is in the East	die wind kom van die Ooste (kant)	dee vint ko(r)m fa(h)n dee ohste(r) (ka(h)nt)
the dust is terrible	die stof is verskriklik	dee sto(r)f iss ferskrikle(r)k
we were covered with dust	ons was vol stof; ons was toe van die stof	ons va(h)s fo(r)l sto(r)f; ons wa(h)s too fa(h)n dee sto(r)f
what dreadful weather!	wat is die weer nie vreeslik ontsettend nie!	va(h)t iss dee veyr nee freyslik ontse(r)tte(r)nt nee!
how it pours!	dit stortreën	dit sto(r)rt reye(r)n
I am wet through	ek is deur en deur nat	e(r)k iss du(r)r e(r)n du(r)r na(h)t
would you like an umbrella?	wil U (jy) 'n sambreel hê?	vill êû (yey) i(h)n sa(h)mbreyl hai(r)?
look at the rainbow	kyk die reenboog	keyk dee reynbohch
oh, how hot it is!	o, (ag) hoe warm is dit tog!	o, (a(h)ch) hoo va(h)r'm iss dit toch!
it thunders	dit donder	dit donde(r)r
I heard the thunder	ek het die donderweer gehoor	e(r)k he(r)t dee donde(r)r-veyrche(r)t hohr
it lightens	dit weerlig, dit blits	dit veyrlich, dit blits
did you see the lightning?	het U (jy) die weerlig gesien?	he(r)t êû (yey) dee veyrlich che(r)seen?
there is a new moon	dis nuwe maan	dis nu(r)ve(r) mahn
it is full moon	dis vol maan	dis fo(r)l mahn

Health (Gesondheid)

English.	Afrikaans.	Pronunciation.
How are you?	hoe gaan dit mey U (jou)?	hoo chahn dit me(r)t êû (yoh)?
are you quite well?	is U (jy) heeltemal vris?	iss êû (yey) heylte(r)mahl friss?
pretty well, thanks	taamlik vris, dankie	tahmlik friss, da(h)nkee
quite well	heeltemal vris	heylte(r)ma(h)l friss
I am ill	ek is siek	e(r)k iss seek
I am not very well	ek is nie heeltemal vris nie	e(r)k iss nee heylte(r)mahl friss nee
I don't feel well	ek voel nie vris nie	e(r)k fool nee friss nee
I have caught a chill	ek het 'n kou gevat	e(r)k he(r)t i(h)n ko che(r)fa(h)t
I have rheumatism	ek het rumatiek	e(r)k he(r)t rêûmahteek
I have a headache	ek het hoofpyn	e(r)k he(r)t hohfpeyn
— — — sore throat	— — seerkeel	— — seyrkeyl
— — — stomach-ache	— — maagpyn	— — mahchpeyn
I have a cold	ek is verkoue	e(r)k iss ferko'e(r)
how much is the doctor's fee for a visit?	hoeveel vra die dokter vir 'n besoek?	hoofeyl fra(h) dee dokte(r)r fir i(h)n be(r)sook?
send for a doctor	laat 'n dokter kom	laht i(h)n dokte(r)r ko(r)m
I want to see a...	ek wil 'n...sien	e(r)k vill i(h)n... seen
she has a bad cough	sy het 'n slegte (lelike) hoes	sey he(r)t i(h)n sle(r)chte(r) (leyle'r)ke(r)) hoos
she is hoarse	sy is hees	sey iss heys
where is there a chemist's shop?	waar is hier 'n apteek?	vahr iss heer i(h)n a(h)pteyk?
how do you feel?	hoe voel U (jy)?	hoo fool êû (yey)?
I feel better	ek voel beter	e(r)k fool beyte(r)r

English.	Afrikaans.	Pronunciation.
I hope you will soon be better	e(r)k hoop U (jy) sal gou beter wees	e(r)k hohp e͡u (yey) sa(h)l cho bey-te(r)r veys
do you sleep well?	slaap U (jy) good?	slahp e͡u (yey) choot
when must I call again?	wanneer moet ek weer kom?	va(h)nneyr moot e(r)k veyr ko(r)m
will you give me a prescription?	sal U vir my 'n voorskrif gee as-seblief?	sa(h)l e͡u fir mey i(h)n fohrskrif chey?
have this prescrip-tion made up	laat hierdie voor-skrif opmaak	laht heerdee fohr-skrif opmahk
see me again on Wednesday	kom sien my Woens-dag weer	ko(r)m seen mey Voonsda(h)ch veyr
one tablespoonful three times a day	een eetlepel vol drie maal op 'n dag	eyn eytleype(r)l fo(r)l dree mahl op i(h)n da(h)ch
to be taken after each meal	na ieder maaltyd te neem	na(h) eede(r)r mahl-teyt te(r) neym
shake the bottle	voor die gebruik skud die bottel	fohr dee che(r)bruik skut dee botte(r)l
Poison, not to be taken	gif: moet dit nie inneem nie	chif: moot dit nee inneym nee
for outward applica-tion only	alleen om uitwendig aantesmeer	a(h)lleyn o(r)m uit-ve(r)ndich ahn-te(r)smeyr

In Town (In Die Stad)

English.	Afrikaans.	Pronunciation.
Where can I get an omnibus?	waar kan ek 'n om-nibus kry?	vahr ka(h)n e(r)k i(h)n omneebuss krey?
go quickly	gaan gou	chahn cho
go slowly	gaan stadig	chahn stahde(r)ch
let us go	kom ons loop (ry)	ko(r)m ons lohp (rey)
please direct me to...	wys vir my die pad na...asseblief	veys fir mey dee pat na(h)...a(h)sse(r)-bleef

English.	Afrikaans.	Pronunciation.
which omnibus (tram) must I take for... ?	watter omnibus (trem) moet ek neem ver... (na ...toe) ?	va(h)tte(r)r omnee-bus (trem) moot e(r)k neym fir... (na(h)...too) ?
where shall we go ?	waar sal ons heen-gaan ?	vahr sa(h)l ons heynshahn ?
which is the way to ... ?	watter is die pad na ...toe ?	va(h)tte(r)r iss dee pa(h)t na(h)...too
where does this road lead ?	waar loop die pad na-toe ?	vahr lohp dee pa(h)t na(h)-too ?
to the right	regs	re(r)chs
to the left	links	links
go up the street	gaan die straat op	chahn dee straht op
is it far from here ?	is dit ver hiervan-daan ?	iss dit fe(r)r heer-fa(h)ndahn ?
how far is it too... ?	hoe ver is dit na... ...toe ?	hoo fe(r)r iss dit na(h)...too ?
about a mile	omtrent 'n myl	o(r)mtre(r)nt i(h)n meyl
straight before you	reg voor jou (U) uit, (reguit)	re(r)ch fohr (êü) yoh uit (re(r)chuit)
show me the way	wys vir my die pad	veys fir mey dee pa(h)t
turn to the right	draai regs	drah'i re(r)chs
keep to the left	hou links	ho links
take the first to the left, and the second to the right	neem die eerste straat aan die linkerkant, en die tweede aan die regterkant	neym dee eyrste(r) straht ahn dee linke(r)rka(h)nt, e(r)n dee tveyde(r) ahn dee re(r)chte(r)-ka(h)nt
cross the street	gaan die straat oor	chahn dee straht ohr
in what street ?	in watter straat ?	in va(h)tte(r)r straht ?
is this the way to...?	is dit die pad na... toe ?	iss dit dee pa(h)t na(h)...too ?
is the road easy to find ?	is die pad maklik om te kry ?	iss dee pa(h)t ma(h)klik o(r)m te(r) krey ?

English.	Afrikaans.	Pronunciation.
do you know Mr....?	ken U (jy) vir Mnr. ...?	ke(r)n êû (yey) fir me(r)neyr... ?
I don't know any one of that name	ek ken niemand van die naam nie	e(r)k ke(r)n neem-a(h)nt fa(h)n dee nahm nee
I know him very well	ek ken hom baie good	e(r)k ke(r)n ho(r)m ba(h)'i-e(r) choot
he is a friend of mine	hy is 'n vriend van my	hey iss i(h)n freent fa(h)n mey
where does he live?	waar woon hy?	va(h)r vohn hey?
close by	naby	nahbey
can you direct me to his house?	kan U (jy) vir my die pad na sy huis toe wys?	ka(h)n êû (yey) fir mey dee pa(h)t na(h) sey huis-too veys?
is Mr.... (Mrs....) at home?	is Mnr.... (Mev....) tuis?	iss me(r)neyr... (Me(r)fro)... tuis?
can I see Mr....?	kan ek met Mnr.... praat?	ka(h)n e(r)k me(r)t me(r)neyr praht?
he is out just now	hy is op die oomblik nie hier nie (uit)	hey iss op dee ohm blik nee heer nee (uit)
he is engaged	hy is besig	hey iss beysich
does he expect you?	verwag he vir U (jou)?	ferva(h)ch hey fir êû (yoh)?
have you an appointment (with him)?	het U (jy) met hom 'n afspraak gemaak?	he(r)t êû (yey) me(r)t ho(r)m i(h)n a(h)fsprahk che(r)mahk?
when does he return?	wanneer kom hy terug?	va(h)nneyr ko(r)m hey te(r)ruch?
when could I see him?	wanneer kan ek hom te siene kry?	va(h)nneyr ka(h)n e(r)k ho(r)m te(r) seyne(r) krey?
I will call on Monday	ek sal Maandag kom	e(r)k sa(h)l Mahn-da(h)ch ko(r)m
could you call again?	kan U (jy) weer kom?	ka(h)n êû (yey) veyr kom?
I expect him every minute	ek verwag hom elke minuut	e(r)k fe(r)rva(h)ch hom elke(r) minêût

English.	Afrikaans.	Pronunciation.
have you your card ?	het U (jy) 'n kahrtyee ?	he(r)t êû (yey) i(h)n kahrtyee ?
what name shall I say ?	wie moet ek sê is hier ?	vee moot e(r)k sai(r) iss heer ?
Mrs....is not at home	Mevrou....is nie tuis nie	me(r)fro... iss nee tuis nee
she is away from home	sy is op reis	sey iss op reys
how is Mrs.... ?	hoe gaan dit met mevrou... ?	hoo chahn dit me(r)t me(r)fro... ?
give my compliments to...	gee my groete aan...	chey mey chroote(r) ahn...
so pleased to see you	so bly om U (jou) te sien	soh bley o(r)m êû (yoh) te(r) seen
I must go	ek moet loop (gaan)	e(r)k moot lohp (chahn)
must you go already?	moet U (jy) dan nou al gaan ?	moot êû (yey) da(h)n no a(h)l chahn ?
I wish you good morning	ek wens U (jou) goeiemôre	e(r)k ve(r)ns êû (yoh) choo'i-mawre(r)
good-bye	vaarwel	fahrve(r)l

Changing Money (Geld Wissel)

Where can I get money changed ?	waar kan ek kleingeld kry ?	vahr ka(h)n e(r)k kleynche(r)lt krey ?
where is the bank ?	waar is die bank ?	va(h)r iss dee ba(h)nk ?
I want change for a £5 note	ek wil 'n vyf pond noot klein gemaak hê	e(r)k vill i(h)n feyf pont noht kleynche(r)mahk hai(r)
will you cash this cheque for me ?	sal U (jy) die tjek vir my klein maak (wissel) ?	sa(h)l êû (yey) dee tye(r)k fir mey kleyn mahk (visse(r)l) ?
this cheque needs endorsing	hierdie tjek moet geendosseer word	heerdee tye(r)k moot che(r)e(r)ndosseyr vort

English.	Afrikaans.	Pronunciation.
how will you take it?	hoe wil U (jy) dit hê?	hoo vill e͡u (yey) dit hai(r)?
what is the exchange on it?	hoeveel is die wisselkoers daarop?	hoofeyl iss dee visse(r)lkoors da(h)rop?
please give me gold and silver, not paper money	gee vir my asseblief goud en silwer, nie paper geld nie	chey fir mey a(h)sse(r)bleef chout e(r)n silve(r)r, nee pa(h)peer che(r)lt nee
I will take it in gold	ek sal dit in goudgeld neem	e(r)k sa(h)l dit in chout che(r)lt neym
a bank-note	'n banknoot	i(h)n ba(h)nknoht
a sovereign	'n goue pond	i(h)n choue(r) pont
will you change me these sovereigns?	sal U (jy) vir my die goue ponde klein maak, asseblief?	sa(h)l e͡u (yey) fir mey dee choue(r) ponde(r) kleyn mahk, a(h)sse(r)bleef?
will you have the kindness to change this gold for me?	sal U (jy) so goed wees om die goud vir my klein te maak?	sa(h)l e͡u (yey) soh choot veys o(r)m dee chout fir mey kleyn te mahk?
can you oblige me with some small change?	kan U (jy) vir my 'n bietjie kleingeld laat kry?	ka(h)n e͡u (yey) fir mey i(h)n beetyee kleynche(r)lt laht krey?
a bill of exchange	'n wissel	i(h)n visse(r)l
it is payable at sight	dis betaalbaar op sig	dis be(r)tahlbahr op sich
give me the amount in...	gee vir my die bedrag in...	chey fir mey dee be(r)dra(h)chin... chout
have you an agent in...?	het U 'n agent in...?	he(r)t e͡u i(h)n a(h)che(r)nt in...?

Shopping (In 'n Winkel)

show me...	wys vir my...	veys fir mey...
how much?	hoe veel?	hoo feyl?

English.	Afrikaans.	Pronunciation.
what is the price?	wat is die prys?	va(h)t iss dee preys?
that is too much	dit is te veel	dit iss te(r) feyl
I wish to buy...	ek wil graag...koop	e(r)k vill chrahch... kohp
I will take this	ek sal hierdie neem	e(r)k sa(h)l heerdee neym
I should like to see some (silk) ribbons	ek sal graag (sy) lint wil sien	e(r)k sa(h)l chra(h)ch (sey) lint vill seen
this colour is too dark, too light	kie kleur is te donker, te lig	dee klu(r)r iss te(r) donke(r)r, te(r) lich
have you any narrower?	het U vat nouer is?	he(r)t êû va(h)t no-e(r)r iss?
what is this a yard?	wat kos die by die jaart (el)?	va(h)t kos dee bey dee yahrt (e(r)l)?
it is faded	dis verbleek	dis ferbleyk
not so fine	nie so vyn nie	nee soh feyn nee
this will do	hierdie sal goed wees	heerdee sa(h)l choot veys
show me some gloves	wys vir my die habdskoene	veys fir mey dee ha(h)ntskoone(r)
what are they a pair?	wat kos dit vir 'n paar?	va(h)t kos dit fir i(h)n pahr?
I want some calico	ek wil katoen (linne) hê	e(r)k vill ka(h)toon (linne(r)) hai(r)
a skein of silk	'n string sy	i(h)n string sey
a packet of mixed pins	'n pakkie spelde klein en groot, deur mekaar	i(h)n pa(h)kee spe(r)lde(r) kleyn e(r)n chroht, du(r)r me(r)kahr
how much does that come to?	wat maak dit tesame?	va(h)t mahk dit te(r)sahme(r)?
are you being attended to?	word U bedien?	vort êû be(r)deen?
to make to order	volgens bestelling maak	fo(r)lche(r)ns be(r)ste(r)l-ling mahk
do you keep...?	het U (jy)...?	he(r)t êû (yey)...?

English.	Afrikaans.	Pronunciation.
we have none in stock	ons het nie daarvan in voorraad nie	ons he(r)t nee dahrfahn in fohrraht nee
we can get you some	ons kan vir U (jou) daarvan kry	ons ka(h)n fir êû (yoh) dahrfahn krey
what price, madam?	van watter prys, Mevrou (Juffrou)?	fa(h)n va(h)tte(r)r preys me(r)fro (yu(r)fro)
about four shillings a yard	omtrent vier sjielings die jaart	o(r)mtre(r)nt feer sheele(r)ngs dee ye(r)rt
may we get it for you?	sal ons dit vir U (jou) kry?	ka(h)n ons dit fir êû (yoh) krey?
a better material	'n beter materiaal	i(h)n beyter ma(h)-teyr(h)ee-ahl
have you a different pattern?	het (U) 'n ander patroon?	he(r)t yey (êû) i(h)n a(h)nde(r)r pe(r)-trohn?
can you recommend it?	kan U (jy) dit aanbeveel?	ka(h)n êû (yey) dit ahnbe(r)feyl?
we can recommend this	ons kan hierdie aanbeveel	ons ka(h)n heerdee ahnbe(r)feyl
we guarantee this quality	ons waarborg hierdie kwaliteit	ons vahrborch heerdee kva(h)leeteyt
will it wash?	kan dit gewas word?	ka(h)n dit che(r)-va(h)s vort?
it will wash well	dit sal goed was	dit sa(h)l choot va(h)s
show me some others	wys vir my nog ander	veys fir mey noch a(h)nde(r)r
try on these	pas die aan	pa(h)ss dee ahn
I will take them with me	ek sal dit saam neem	e(r)k sa(h)l dit sahm-neym
can I send them for you?	kan ek dit vir U (jou) stuur?	ka(h)n e(r)k dit fir êû (yoh) steur?
send them to...	stuur dit na...toe	steûr dit na(h)...too
can you send them to me at once?	kan U (jy) dit dadelik vir my stuur?	ka(h)n êû (yey) dit dahde(r)lik fir mey steûr?

English.	Afrikaans.	Pronunciation.
what name, please?	watter naam, asseblief?	va(h)tte(r)r nahm, a(h)sse(r)bleef?
to what address?	na watter adres?	na(h) va(h)tte(r)r a(h)dre(r)ss?
I will pay on delivery	ek sal op ontvangs (by aflewering) betaal	e(r)k sa(h)l op ontfa(h)ngst (bey a(h)fleyve(r)ring) be(r)tahl
clearance sale	uitverkoop	uitferkohp
offer for sale	te koop aanbied	te(r) kohp ahnbeet
all at one price	almal (alles) teen een prys	a(h)lma(h)l teyn eyn preys a(h)lle(r)s).
fixed prices	vaste pryse	fa(h)ste(r) preyse(r)
reduced prices	verminderde prys	eferminde(r)rde(r) preyse(r)
you pay at the desk	betaal aan die kassier	be(r)tahl ahn dee ka(h)sseer

The Dressmaker (Die Naaister, Kleremaakster)

Here is the dressmaker	hier is die naaister	heer iss dee nah'iste(r)r
ask her to wait	sê sy moet wag	sai(r) sey moot va(h)ch
show her in	laat vir haar inkom	laht fir hahr inko(r)m
have you brought my dress?	het jy my dabbert gebring?	he(r)t yey mey ta(h)bbe(r)rt che(r)bring?
here it is	hier is dit	heer iss dit
will you try it on?	sal U dit aanpas?	sa(h)l eû dit ahnpa(h)s?
the sleeves are not wide enough	die moue is nie wyd genoeg nie	dee mohe(r) iss nee veyt che(r)nooch nee
the skirt is too narrow	die rok is te nou	dee ro(r)k iss te(r) no
add another breadth	las nog 'n baan in	la(h)ss noch i(h)n bahn in

English.	Afrikaans.	Pronunciation.
it is too short-waisted	die lyfie is te kort	dee leyfee iss te(r) kort
it is too long-waisted	die lyfie is te lank	dee leyfee iss te(r) lank
it is not a good fit	dit pas nie goed nie	dit pa(h)ss nee choot nee
this is the latest style	dit is die nuutste mode	dit iss dee neutste(r) mohde(r)
the style doesn't suit me	die mode staan my nie aan nie	dee mohde(r) stahn mey nee ahn nee
it is very fashionable	dis danig modies	dis da(h)nich moh-dees
it fits you very well	dit pas U baie good	dit pa(h)ss êû bah'i-e(r) choot
it suits you splendidly	U lyk baie mooi daarin	êû leyk bah'i-e(r) moh'i dahrin
make all these alterations	maak al die veranderinge	mahk a(h)l dee fer-a(h)nderinge
what trimming will you put on?	watter soort opmaksel sit jy aan?	va(h)tte(r)r sohrt opma(h)kse(r)l sit yey ahn?
pale blue ribbon	ligblou lint	lichblo lint
when can you let me have it?	wanneer kan jy dit vir my laat kry?	ba(h)nneyr ka(h)n yey dit fir mey laht krey?
you shall have it on Saturday	U sal dit Saterdag kry	êû sa(h)l dit Sahte(r)da(h)ch krey
without fail	seker	seyke(r)r
don't disappoint me	stel my nie te leur nie; laat vir my nie in die steek nie	ste(r)l mey nee te(r) lu(r)r nee; laht fir mey nee in dee steyk nee

The Shoemaker (Die Skoenmaker)

I wish to see some shoes	ek wil graag die skoene sien	e(r)k vill chra(h)ch dee skoone(r) seen
ladies, gentlemen's and children's	dames, here en kinder	da(h)me(r)s, heyre(r) e(r)n kinde(r)r

English.	Afrikaans.	Pronunciation.
here is a shoe-horn	hier is 'n horing	heer iss i(h)n hoh-ring
are they comfort-able?	is hulle gemaklik?	iss hulle(r) che(r)-ma(h)klik?
the soles are rather thick	die sole is 'n weinig (bietjie) dik	dee sohle(r) iss i(h)n veynich (beetyee) dik
they are too large	hulle is te groot	hulle(r) iss te(r) chroot
they are too tight	hulle is te nou	hulle(r) iss te(r) no
I cannot get my foot in	ek kan my voet nie inkry nie	e(r)k ka(h)n mey foot nee inkrey nee
the heels are too high	die hakke is te hoog	dee ha(h)kke(r) iss te(r) hohch
they hurt my heel, toes, instep	hulle maak my hakke, tone, en die grootboeg van my voete seer	hulle(r) mahk mey hahke(r), tohne(r), e(r)n dee chroht-booch fa(h)n mey foote(r) seyr
I cannot walk in them	ek kan met hulle nie loop nie	e(r)k ka(h)n me(r)t hulle(r) nee lohp nee
I want some boot-laces	ek wil 'n paar skoen-riempies (veters) hê	e(r)k vill i(h)n pahr skoonreempees (feete(r)rs) hai(r)
take my measure-ment	neem my maat	neym mey maht
these shoes want soling and heeling	hierdie skoene moet halfsole en hakke aankry	heerdee skohne(r) moot ha(h)lf-soh-le(r) e(r)n hah-ke(r) ahnkrey
send my boots to be mended	stuur my skoene om te laat heelmaak	steûr mey skohne(r) om te(r) laht heyl-mahk
when will they be done?	wanneer sal dit klaar wees?	va(h)nneyr sa(h)l dit klahr veys?
I must have them as soon as possible	ek moet hulle so gou as moontlik hê	e(r)k moot hulle(r) soh cho a(h)s mohntlik hai(r)

English.	Afrikaans.	Pronunciation.
boots and shoes for boys and girls	stewels en skoene vir jongetjies en meisies	steyve(r)ls e(r)n skoone(r) fir yonge(r)yees e(r)n meyssees
top boots for men and women	kapstewels vir mans en vrouens	ka(h)psteyve(r)ls fir ma(h)ns e(r)n fro-e(r)ns
boot and shoe store	skoenewinkel	skoone(r)vinke(r)l
boot polish (all makes)	skoenwaks (al die soorte)	skoonva(h)ks (a(h)l dee sohrte(r))

The Laundress (Die Wasvrou)

English.	Afrikaans.	Pronunciation.
I want these things (this linen) washed	ek wil hierdie goed (die linne) gewas hê	e(r)k vill heerdee choot (dee linne(r) che(r)va(h)s hai(r)
when can I have it back?	wanneer kan ek dit terug kry?	va(h)nneyr ka(h)n e(r)k dit te(r)ruch krey?
please return this linen on Friday	bring asseblief hierdie wasgoed Vrydag terug	bring a(h)sse(r)bleef heerdee va(h)schoot freyda(h)ch te(r)ruch
you must bring back this list	jy moet hierdie lys terug bring	yey moot heerdee leys te(r)ruch bring
this is too limp (not stiff enough)	hierdie is nie styf genoeg nie	heerdee iss nee steyf che(r)nooch nee
you don't put enough starch in	jy sit daar nie genoeg stysel in nie	yey sit dahr nee che(r)nooch steyse(r)l in nee
I miss a collar	daar is 'n boordjie kort	dahr iss i(h)n bohrtyee korrt
see how badly that is done	kyk maar hoe sleg dit gewas is	keyk mahr hoo sle(r)ch dit che(r)va(h)s iss
badly starched	sleg gestywe	sle(r)ch che(r)steyve(r)
badly ironed	sleg gestryk	sle(r)ch che(r)streyk

English.	Afrikaans.	Pronunciation.
you must take it back	jy moet dit terug neem	yey moot dit te(r)-ruch neym
you have scorched this dress	jy het die rok ge-skroei	yey he(r)t dee ro(r)k che(r)sku(r)r
you put too much blue in my linen	jy het te veel blousel in my linne gesit (jou blousel was te sterk)	yey he(r)t te(r) feyl blose(r)l in mey linne(r) che(r)sit (yoh blose(r)l va(h)s te(r) ste(r)rk)
this is not my hand-kerchief	dis nie my sakdoek die ne ; hierdie is nie my sakdoek nie	diss nee mey sa(h)k-dook dee nee ; heerdee iss nee mey sa(h)kdook nee
have you your bill ?	het jy jou rekening ?	he(r)t yey yoh rey-ke(r)ning ?
deduct the amount of the lost collar	trek die bedrag van die boordjie wat vermis is af	tre(r)k dee be(r)-dra(h)ch fa(h)n dee bohrtyee va(h)t fermiss iss a(h)f
the dress you so badly scorched cost me £5	die rok wat jy so lelik geskroei het kos vir my vyf pond	dee ro(r)k va(h)t yey soh leylik che(r)skroo'i he(r)t koss fir mey feyf pont
I will pay tor it	ek sal vir dit betaal	e(r)k sa(h)l fir dit be(r)ta(h)l
I charge 3s. a dozen for washing and ironing	ek vra drie sjielings vir 'n dosyn—was en stryk	e(r)k fra(h) dree sheelings fir i(h)n do(h)seyn — va(h)s e(r)n streyk
have you washing to be done ?	het U wasgoed wat U wil laat doen ?	he(r)t e͡ü va(h)schoot va(h)t e͡ü vill laht doon ?

Amusements (Vermaaklikhede)

English.	Afrikaans.	Pronunciation.
Shall we go to the theatre?	sal ons na die teater-toe gaan?	sa(h)l ons na(h) dee teya(h)te(r)r-too cha(h)n?
what is on (what is the play) at...?	wat word opgevòer?	va(h)t vort op-che(r)foor?
where can we book seats?	waar kan ons sit-plekke bestel?	vahr ka(h)n ons sit-ple(r)kke(r) be(r)-ste(r)l?
is the box-office open?	is die sitplek bureau al oop?	iss dee sitple(r)k beûroh a(h)l ohp?
I should like to see a plan	ek wil graag 'n plan sien	e(r)k vill chrahch i(h)n pla(h)n seen
these seats are reserved	hierdie sitplekke is al bespreek	heerdee sitple(r)k-ke(r) iss a(h)l be(r)spreyk
let us take a box	laat ons 'n loge neem	laht ons i(h)n loh'-she(r) neym
we will take four seats	ons sal vier sit-plekke neem	ons sa(h)l feer sit-ple(r)kke(r) neym
where are our seats?	waar is onse sit-plase?	vahr iss onse(r) sit-plahse(r)?
where is the cloak-room?	waar is die kleed-kamer?	vahr iss dee kleyt-kahme(r)r?
there is no charge	daar is niks te be-taal nie	dahr iss niks te(r) be(r)tahl nee
children half-price	kinders half-prys	kinde(r)rs ha(h)lf-preys
give me a programme	gee vir my 'n pro-gram	chey fir mey i(h)n prohchra(h)m
who is the conductor?	wie is die geleier?	vee iss dee che(r)-leye(r)r?
how well the band plays!	hoe mooi speel die orkes!	hoo moo'i speyl dee orkess
would you like some refreshments?	wil U (jy) iets ge-niet?	vill eû (yey) eets che(r)neet?

English.	Afrikaans.	Pronunciation.
shall we go to the buffet?	sal ons na die buffet (die drinkplek)—toe gaan?	sa(h)l ons na(h) dee buffe(r)t (dee drinkple(r)k) — too chahn?
is there a good museum?	is hier 'n goeie museum?	iss heer i(h)n choo'ie(r) mêûseem?
are tickets required?	moet 'n mens kaartjes hê?	moot i(h)n me(r)ns kahrtyees hai(r)?
how much will it cost?	hoeveel sal dit kos?	hoofeyl sa(h)l dit koss?
it will take all day	dit sal die hele dag duur	dit sa(h)l dee heyle(r) da(h)ch dêûr
then we must take some sandwiches with us	dan moet ons 'n bietjie (weinig) toebroodjies saam neem	da(h)n moot ons i(h)n beetyee (veynich) toobrohtyees sahm neym
can we go by coach?	kan ons met 'n passasierswa gaan?	ka(h)n ons me(r)t i(h)n pa(h)ssa(h)seersva(h) chahn?
the coach leaves at ten	die passasierswa vertrek om tienuur gaan	dee pa(h)ssa(h)seersva(h) fertre(r)k o(r)m teenêûr
when does the coach go to...?	wanneer vertrek die passasierswa na...toe?	va(h)nneyr fertre(r)k (chahn) dee pa(h)ssa(h)seersva(h) na(h) ...too?
we should like some refreshments	ons wil graag 'n bietjie verversinge hê	ons vill chrahch i(h)n beetyee ferfer(r)rsinge(r)-hai(r)
we return from...at three o'clock	ons kom van...terug om drie-uur	ons ko(r)m fa(h)n... te(r)ruch om dree-êûr
every Wednesday	elke Woensdag	e(r)lke(r) Voonsda(h)ch
can you put us up some refreshments?	kan U (jy) vir ons iets te ete saamgee?	ka(h)n êû (yey) fir ons eets te(r) eyte(r) sahmchey?

English.	Afrikaans.	Pronunciation.
is there a good place for lunch?	is daar 'n goeie eet-saal (restourant)?	iss dahr i(h)n choo'-i-e(r) eytsahl (re(r)stoo-ra(h)ng)
when does the performance begin?	wanneer begin die voorstelling?	va(h)nneyr be(r)-chin dee fohrs-te(r)lling?
what time do the doors open?	hoe laat maak hulle deure oop?	hoo laht mahkhul-le(r) du(r)r-re(r) ohp?
an interval of fifteen minutes	'n pouse van vyftien minute	i(h)n po(h)se(r) fa(h)n feyfteen minnêute(r)
are the sports worth seeing?	is die sports dit werd dat 'n mens daarna gaan kyk?	iss dee sports dit vert da(h)t i(h)n me(r)ns dahrnah chahn keyk?
the races take place to-morrow	die reisies word môre gehou	dee reysees vort mawre(r) che(r)ho
will you take part in the tournament	gaan U (jy) in die toernooi deel-neem?	cha(h)n êû (yey) in dee toornoh'i deylneym?
an agricultural (horticultural) show	'n landbou (tuin-bou) tentoonstel-ling	i(h)n la(h)ntbou (tuinbou) te(r)n-tohnste(r)lling
are you going to the carnival?	gaan U (jy) na die karneval-toe?	chahn êû (yey) na (h) dee kahrne(r)-fa(h)l-too?
which is the best place to see it?	van watter plek kan 'n mens dit die beste sien?	fa(h)n va(h)tte(r)r ple(r)k ka(h)n i(h)n me(r)ns dit dee be(r)ste(r) seen?
there will be a battle of flowers	daar sal 'n geveg met blomme wees; 'n bloms-lag sal gelewer word	dahr sa(h)l i(h)n che(r)fe(r)ch me(r)t blomme(r) veys; i(h)n blomsla(h)ch sa(h)l che(r)ley-ve(r)r vort

English.	Afrikaans.	Pronunciation.
when does it take place?	wanneer vind dit plaas?	va(h)nneyr fint dit plahs?
the day after to-morrow	oormôre	ohrmawre(r)

Cycling (Ry met 'n Fiets)

English.	Afrikaans.	Pronunciation.
I want to hire a bicycle	ek wil 'n fiets huur	e(r)k vill i(h)n feets he͡ur
I want my own machine	ek wil my eie rywiel hê	e(r)k vill mey eye(r) reyveel hai(r)
is it ready?	is dit klaar?	iss dit klahr?
fitted with all accessories	met al die toebehoorsels	me(r)t a(h)l dee toobe(r)hohrse(r)ls
what are your terms?	wat is U (jou) voorwaardes?	va(h)t iss e͡u (yoh) fohrvahrde(r)s?
by the hour; by the day	by die uur; by die dag	bey dee e͡ur; bey dee da(h)ch
where can I put my bicycle?	waar kan ek my fiets sit?	vahr ka(h)n e(r)k mey feets sit?
have you a cycle shelter?	het U (jy) 'n plek waar ek my fiets kan bêre?	he(r)t e͡u (yey) i(h)n ple(r)k vahr e(r)k mey feets ka(h)n bai(r)e(r)?
tighten this nut	draai vas hierdie moertjie	drah'i fa(h)s heerdee moortyee
loosen the chain	maak los die ketting	mahk loss de ke(r)tting
I have broken...	ek het...gebreek	e(r)k he(r)t...che(r)breyk
are you ready?	is U (jy) klaar?	iss e͡u (yey) klahr?
my tyre is punctured	my buiteband is geprik	mey buite(r)ba(h)nt iss che(r)prik
the chain is off	die ketting is af	dee ke(r)tting iss a(h)f
I must pump up my tyres	ek moet my buitebande oppomp	e(r)k moot mey buite(r)ba(h)nde(r) oppomp
ring your bell	lui U (jou) klokkie	lui e͡u (yoh) klokkee
stop! look out!	hou stil! pas op!	ho still! pa(h)s op!

English.	Afrikaans.	Pronunciation.
don't go so fast	moenie so vinnig gann nie	moonee soh finnich chahn nee
make haste!	maak gou!	mahk cho!
we must light up	ons moet lamp aansteek	ons moot la(h)mp ahnsteyk
turn to the right, left	draai regs, links	drah'i re(r)chs, links
keep straight on	hou reguit	ho re(r)chuit
we will start at...	ons sal...begin	ons sa(h)l...be(r)-chin
have you a road guide?	het U (hy) 'n kaart (reisgids)?	he(r)t êû (yey) i(h)n (reyschits)?
yes, sir; which do you require?	ja, meneer; watter een het U (jy) noodig?	ya(h), me(r)neyr; wa(h)tte(r)r eyn he(r)t êû (yey) nohdich
the one for Johannesburg and neighbourhood	die van Johannesburg en buurte	dee fa(h)n Yohahn-ne(r)sburch e(r)n bêûrte(r)
I want my machine cleaned	ek wil my rywiel laat skoonmaak	e(r)k vill mey rey-veel laht skohn-mahk
where can I get my bicycle mended?	waar kan ek my fiets heelgemaak kry?	vahr ka(h)n e(r)k mey feets heyl-che(r)mahk krey?
can you repair this for me?	kan jy dit vir my regmaak?	ka(h)n yey dit fir mey re(r)chmahk
how long will it take?	hoe lank sal dit neem?	hoo la(h)nk sa(h)l dit neym?
at what time will it be ready?	hoe laat sal dit klaar wees?	hoo laht sa(h)l dit klahr veys?
I am a member of the Cyclists' Touring Club	ek is lid van die Fietserse Reis-Klub	e(r)k iss lit fa(h)n dee feetse(r)rse(r) reys-klup
here is my membership card	hieı is my kaart van lidmaatskap	heer iss mey kahrt fa(h)n litmaht-skahp
how far are we from .. ?	hoe ver is ons van ...af?	hoo fe(r)r isssons fa(h)n...a(h)f?

English.	Afrikaans.	Pronunciation.
why don't you come?	hoekom kom jy nie?	hooko(r)m ko(r)m yey nee?
are the roads good?	is die paaie goed?	iss dee pah'i-e(r) choot?
what are the roads like?	hoe is die paaie?	hoo iss dee pah'i-e(r)
the roads are in good condition	die paaie is in 'n goeie kondiesie (toestand)	dee pah'i-e(r) iss in i(h)n choo'i-e(r) kondeesee (too-sta(h)nt)
they are dusty	hulle is stowwerig	hulle(r) iss sto(r)v-ve(r)rich
this is a bad road	dis 'n slegte pad hierdie	dis i(h)n sle(r)ch-te(r) pa(h)t heer-dee
to cyclists	aan fietsers	ahn feetse(r)rs
this hill is dangerous	hierdie hoogte is gevaarlik	heerdee hohchte(r) iss che(r)fahrlik
ride with caution	ry versigtig	rey fersichtich
where is the nearest cycle-shop?	waar is die naaste fiets-winkel?	vahr iss dee nah-ste(r) feets-vin-ke(r)l?
is it time to light up?	is dit tyd om lampe op-te-steek?	iss dit teyt om la(h)mpe(r) op te(r) steyk?
lighting-up time (is at) eight o'clock	lamp opsteek-tyd is ag(t)-uur	lamp opsteyk-teyt iss a(h)ch(t)-êur
we must light up	ons moet lampe aansteek	ons moot la(h)m-pe(r) ahnsteyk
can you mend a puncture for me?	kan jy 'n prikgaatjie vir my heelmaak?	ka(h)n yey vir mey i(h)n prikchaht-yee heylmahk?
please fill my lamp	maak asseblief my lamp vol	mahk a(h)sse(r)-bleef mey la(h)mp fo(r)l
it wants a new wick	dit vra 'n nuwe pit	dit frah i(h)n neu-ve(r) pit
may I borrow your pump?	leen vir my jou pomp asseblief	leyn fir mey yoh pomp a(h)sse(r)-bleef

English.	Afrikaans.	Pronunciation.
can you lend me a spanner?	kan jy vir my 'n skroefhammer leen?	ka(h)n yey fir mey i(h)n skroofha(h)-mer leyn?
accommodation for cyclists	akkomodasie vir fietsryers	a(h)kkommodahsee fir feet-sreye(r)rs
could you oblige me with a match?	gee vir my asseblief 'n vuurhoutjie?	chey fir mey a(h)s-se(r)bleef i(h)n feũrhoutyee
can you put us up for the night?	kan ons hier nag-verblyf kry?	ka(h)n ons heer na(h)chferbleyf krey?

Motoring (Met 'n Moter ry)

Will you please re-pair... ?	sal jy asseblief...reg maak?	sa(h)l yey a(h)sse(r)-bleef...re(r)ch-mahk?
have you examined my speed-chang-ing gear	het jy my gangwis-sel ondersoek?	he(r)t yey mey cha(h)ngwisse(r)l onde(r)rsook?
replace my brake	sit vir my 'n ander briek in	sit fir me i(h)n a(h)nde(r)r breek in
the clutch is out of order	die koppeling (klou) is uit order uit	dee koppe(r)ling iss uit orde(r)r uit
I want a carburettor	ek wil 'n vergasser hê	e(r)k vill i(h)n fer-cha(h)sse(r)r hai(r)
the back-spring is broken	die agterveer is gebreek	dee a(h)chte(r)rfeyr iss che(r)breyk
change it	sit 'n ander een in	sit i(h)n a(h)nde(r)r eyn in
I have lost my horn (hooter)	ek het my blaashor-ing (toeter) ver-loor	e(r)k he(r)t mey blahshohring (toote(r)r) ferlohr
a pinion is wanted for the small axle	daar is 'n boutjie noodig vir die (klein) assie	dahr iss i(h)n bout-yee nohdich fir dee (kleyn) a(h)s-see

English.	Afrikaans.	Pronunciation.
have you an accumulator four volts?	het jy 'n akkumulator vier wolts?	he(r)t yey i(h)n a(h)kkeûmeû-la(h)tor feer vo(r)lts?
you must fix the radiator to the frame	jy moet die straal-verspreier aan die raam vasmaak (sit)	yey moot deestrahl-ferspreye(r)r ahn dee rahm fa(h)ss-(mahk) sit
can you put me a new tyre on?	kan jy vir my 'n nuwe buiteband aansit?	ka(h)n yey fir mey i(h)n neûve(r) buite(r)ba(h)nt ahn sit?
give me some petrol	gee vir my 'n bietjie petrol	chey fir mey i(h)n beetyee petrol
a motoring map on cloth	'n moter aanwysers-kaart op linne	i(h)n moter ahn-veyse(r)rskahrt op linne(r)
is there a motor garage in this town?	is hier 'n moterhuis in die dorp?	iss heer i(h)n moter-huis in dee dorp?
to motorists	aan moterryers	ahn moter-reye(r)rs
drive slowly through this town (village)	ry stadig deur hierdie dorp	rey stahdich du(r)r heerdee dorp
speed not to exceed ...miles	snelheid onder die ...myl; hou binne...myl per uur	sne(r)lheyt onde(r)r dee...meyl; ho binne(r)... meyl per eûr
danger: cross-roads	gevaar: kruispaaie	che(r)fahr: krui-spah'i-e(r)
what is the power of this motor?	hoeveel pêrdekrag is hierdie moter?	hoofeyl pai(r)rde(r)-kra(h)ch iss heer-dee moter?
is it a good hill-climber?	is sy klimvermoë goed?	iss sey klimfer-mohe(r) choot?
it is forty horse-power	dit is veertig perde-krag	dit iss feyrtich pai(r) de(r) kra(h)ch

English.	Afrikaans.	Pronunciation.
I want my accumulator charged	ek wil graag my akkumulator volgemaak hê	e(r)k vill chrahch mey a(h)kkeu͡-meu͡la(h)tor fo(r)lche(r)mahk hai(r)
I want an experienced driver	ek wil 'n drywer hê met ondervinding	e(r)k vill i(h)n dreyver hai(r) met onderfinding
are you an experienced driver?	het jy as 'n drywer baie ondervinding verkry?	he(r)t yey a(h)s i(h)n dreyve(r)r bah'i-e(r) onderfinding ferkrey?
what experience have you had?	watter ondervinding het jy gehad?	wa(h)tte(r)r onderfinding he(r)t yey che(r)ha(h)t?

Photography (Fotografie)

English.	Afrikaans.	Pronunciation.
Have you brought your camera?	het jy jou kamera saamgebring?	he(r)t yey yoh ka(h)merah sahmche(r)bring?
this is my camera	hierdie is my kamera	heerdee iss mey ka(h)me(r)ra(h)
must permission be obtained to photograph?	moet verlof verkry word om af te neem?	moot ferlo(r)f ferkrey vort o(r)m a(h)fte(r)neym?
I wish to take the interior	ek wil graag die binnekant afneem	e(r)k vill chra(h)ch dee binne(r)-ka(h)nt a(h)f-neym
what exposure must I give?	hoe lank moet ek dit belig?	hoola(h)nk moot e(r)k dit be(r)lich?
the light is too strong	die lig is te sterk	dee lich iss te(r) ste(r)k
this is a bad light	dis 'n slegte lig die	dis i(h)n sle(r)chte(r) lich dee
it is out of focus	dis uit fokus uit	dis uit fohkuss uit
the lens is broken	die lens is gebreek	dee le(r)ns iss che(r)-breyk

English.	Afrikaans.	Pronunciation.
what size of plate do you use?	hoe groot is die plate wat jy gebruik?	hoo chroht iss dee plahte(r) va(h)t yey che(r)bruik?
I only use quarter plate	ek gebruik maar net kwart plate	e(r)k che(r)bruik mahr ne(r)t kvahrtplahte(r)
this plate is spoilt	hierdie plaat is bederwe	heerdee plaht iss be(r)de(r)rve(r)
have you a dark room?	het jy 'n donker-kamer?	he(r)t yey i(h)n donke(r)rkah-me(r)r?
I want to develop some plates	ek wil graag 'n paar plate ontwikkel	e(r)k vill chrahch i(h)n pahr plah-te(r) ontvik-ke(r)l
I am going to print more copies	ek gaan nog meer afdrukke maak	e(r)k chahn noch meyr a(h)fdruk-ke(r) mahk
this was spoilt in printing	hierdie is met die afdruk daarvan bederwe geraak	heerdee iss me(r)t dee a(h)fdruk dahrfa(h)n be(r)-dai(r)ve(r) che(r)-rahk
that is due to over-exposure	dit is die gevolge van oorbeligting	dit iss dee che(r)-folge(r) fa(h)n ohrbe(r)lichting
what a beautiful photograph!	wat vir 'n pragtige portret!	va(h)t fir i(h)n pra(h)chtiche(r) portre(r)t!
it is a perfect picture	dis 'n volmaakte prent	dis i(h)n fo(r)lmahk-te(r) pre(r)nt
the grouping is very good	die groepering is baie goed	dee chroopeyring iss bah'i-e(r) choot
I have secured some fine views	ek het 'n paar pragtige gesigte verkry	e(r)k he(r)t i(h)n pahr pra(h)ch-tiche(r) che(r)-sichte(r) ferkrey
I want some more films	ek wil nog 'n paar films hê	e(r)k vill noch i(h)n pahr filmss hai(r)

English.	Afrikaans.	Pronunciation.
do you sell photographic materials	verkoop jy afneem-(fotografiese) goed ?	ferkohp yey a(h)fneym (fohtohchra(h)feese(r)) choot ?
I want some mounts	ek wil 'n paar opplakkarte hê	e(r)k vill i(h)n pahr oppla(h)kkahrte(r) hai(r)
what do you require?	wat het jy nodig ?	va(h)t he(r)t yey nohdich ?
photographic chemicals	fotografiese gemikalieë	fohtohchra(h)feese(r) che(r)meeka(h)lee-e(r)
the shutter doesn't act properly	die luikie werk nie goed (mooi) nie	dee luikee ve(r)rk nee choot (moh'i) nee
were your snapshots successful ?	het jou kiekies (momente opname) goed gekom ? (goed uitgekom)	he(r)t yoh keekees (mohme(r)nte(r) opnahme(r)) choot che(r)ko(r)m ? (choot uitche(r)ko(r)m)
I am afraid they are all failures	ek vrees dat hulle almal 'n mislukking is	e(r)k freys da(h)t hulle(r) a(h)lma(h)l i(h)n misslukking iss
how disappointing!	hoe teleurstellend! wat vir 'n teleurstelling!	hoo te(r)lu(r)rste(r)lent! va(h)t fir i(h)n te(r)lu(r)rste(r)ling!
an amateur photographer	'n amateur afnemer	i(h)n a(h)ma(h)tu(r)t a(h)fneyme(r)r
sensitive to light	ligfyngevoeligheid	lichfeynche(r)foolichheyt

Religion (Godsdiens)

Is there an English Church here ?	is hier 'n Engelse Kerk ?	iss heeri (h)n e(r)nge(r)lse(r) ke(r)rk ?
what time is the service ?	hoe laat begin dit ?	hoo laht be(r)chin dit ?

English.	Afrikaans.	Pronunciation.
is it far from here?	is dit ver hiervan-daan?	iss dit fe(r)r heer-fa(h)ndahn?
who is the Clergy-man?	wie is die predikant?	vee iss dee prey-de(r)ka(h)nt?
the seats are free	die sitplekke is vry	dee sitple(r)kke(r) iss frey
the seats must be paid for	vir die sitplekke moet betaal word	fir dee sitple(r)k-ke(r) moot be(r)-tahl vort
where is the verger?	waar is die koster?	vahr iss dee kos-te(r)r?
can you find me a seat?	kan (u) jy vir my sitplek kry?	ka(h)n eû (yey) fir mey sitple(r)k krey?
prayers are being offered	daar word nou gebid	dahr vort no che(r)-bit
let us wait awhile	laat ons 'n bietjie wag	laht ons i(h)n beet-yee va(h)ch
let us go	kom ons loop maar	ko(r)m ons lohp mahr
lend me a hymn-book, please	leen vir my 'n gesangboek, asseblief	leyn fir mey i(h)n che(r)sa(h)ng book a(h)sse(r)-bleef
what other services are there?	watter ander dienste is daar nog?	va(h)te(r) a(h)n-de(r)r deenste(r) iss dahr noch?
there is a strong choir	dis 'n sterk Koor	dis i(h)n ste(r)rk kohr
have you a Bible?	het U (jy) 'n Bybel?	he(r)t eû (yey) i(h)n beybe(r)l?
is there a collection?	word 'n kollekte geneem?	vort i(h)n kolle(r)k-te(r) che(r)neym?
an offertory is taken	'n kollekte word geneem	i(h)n kolle(r)kte(r) vort che(r)neym

Legal and Judicial Terms (Wetlike en Regterlike terme)

Call the police	roep die poliesie	roop dee pohleesee
take this man in charge	arresteer hierdie man	a(h)rre(r)steyr heerdee ma(h)n

English.	Afrikaans.	Pronunciation.
he has stolen my purse	hy het my beursie gesteel	hey he(r)t mey bu(r)see che(r)-steyl
can you recommend me a solicitor?	kan jy vir my 'n prokureur aanbeveel?	ka(h)n yey fir mey i(h)n prokeûru(r)r ahnbe(r)feyl?
will you issue summons?	sal U (jy) 'n dagvering uitreik?	sa(h)l eû (yey) i(h)n da(h)chfahring uitreyk?
make a return within forty-eight hours	maak 'n relaas binne ag(t)-en-veertig-uur	mahk i(h)n re(r)lahs binne(r)a(h)ch(t)-e(r)n-feyrtich-eûr
the indictment is one of:	die aanklag is vir:	dee ahnchla(h)ch iss fir:
murder	moord	mohrt
manslaughter	manslag	ma(h)nsla(h)ch
theft	diefstal	deefsta(h)l
incendiarism	brandstigting	bra(h)ntstich-ing
embezzlement	verduistering	ferduiste(r)-ring
misappropriation	wederregtelike toeëining	veyde(r)r-re(r)ch-te(r)like(r) too-eye(r)ning
perjury	meineed	meyneyt
this indictment has been (is) withdrawn	die aanklag is teruggetrek	dee a(h)nkla(h)ch iss te(r)ruch-che(r)-tre(r)k
where is the court?	waar is die geregshof?	va(h)r iss dee che(r)-re(r)chsho(r)f?
what case is on?	watter saak dien nou?	va(h)tte(r)r sahk deen no?
who is the plaintiff?	wie is die eiser? (die aanklaer)?	vee iss dee eyse(r)r? (dee ahnklahe(r)r)
can we make an arrangement?	kan ons tot 'n verstandhouding kom?	ka(h)n ons tot i(h)n fersta(h)nthouding ko(r)m?
will you take charge of my case?	sal U my saak dryf?	sa(h)l eû mey sahk dreyf?

English.	Afrikaans.	Pronunciation.
the retaining fee is £...	die fooi wat moet vooruitbetaal word is £...	dee foh'i va(h)t moot fohr uit-be(r)tahl vort iss £...
what do you advise?	watter raad gee U vir my?	va(h)tte(r)r raht chey êü fir mey?
can we have an interpreter?	kan ons 'n tolk kry?	ka(h)n ons i(h)n tolk krey?
does the judge speak English?	kan die regter Engels praat?	ka(h)n dee re(r)ch-te(r)r e(r)nge(r)ls praht?
I apply for bail	ek vra vir borg	e(r)k frah fir borçh
send to my friends	stuur na my vriende toe	steur na(h) mey freende(r)-too
that is quite wrong	dit is heeltemal verkeerd	dit iss heylte(r)-ma(h)l ferkeyrt
it is not just	dit is nie reg nie	dit iss nee re(r)ch nee
I apologise	ek vra om verskoning	e(r)k frah o(r)m ferskohning
I accept your apology	ek neem jou apologie aan	e(r)k neym yoh a(h)po(r)lohyee ahn
I will pay	ek sal betaal	e(r)k sa(h)l be(r)tahl
it was all a mistake	die hele ding was 'n misverstand	dee heyle(r) ding va(h)s i(h)n misfersta(h)nt
he must be made to pay	hy moet betaal	hey moot be(r)tahl
I claim damages	ek eis skadever-goeding	e(r)k eyss skahde(r)-ferchooding
the case is long	die saak hou lank aan	dee sahk ho la(h)nk ahn
it is adjourned until ...	dis verdaag tot...	dis ferdahch tot ...
shall I have to come?	moet ek kom?	moot ek kom?
wait till you are subpœnaed	wag tot jy gedag-vaar word as getuie	va(h)ch tot yey che(r)da(h)chfahr vort a(h)sche(r)-tuie(r)

English.	Afrikaans.	Pronunciation.
I will be there	ek sal daar wees	e(r)k sa(h)l dahr veys
I shall appeal	ek sal appeleer	e(r)k sa(h)l a(h)p-pe(r)leyr

Commercial and Trading (Handelsterme)

English.	Afrikaans.	Pronunciation.
Where can I obtain a commercial traveller's permit?	waar kan ek 'n permit as ('n) handelsreisiger kry?	va(h)r ka(h)n e(r)k i(h)n pe(r)rmit a(h)s [i(h)n] ha(h)nde(r)ls rey-siche(r)r krey?
what is the fee for the permit?	wat kos so 'n permit	va(h)t koss soh i(h)n permit?
I represent the firm of...	ek verteenwoordig die firma...	e(r)k ferteynvohr-dich dee firmah...
may I show you my samples?	sal ek vir U my monsters wys?	sa(h)l e(r)k fir êû mey monste(r)rs veys?
send our account in monthly	stuur onse rekening maandeliks in	steur onse(r) rey-ke(r)ning mahn-de(r)liks in
give me a receipt	gee vir my 'n kwitansie	chey fir mey i(h)n kwita(h)nsee
Messrs....have failed	die here...is bankrot, insolvent	dee heyre(r)...iss ba(h)nkro(r)t, inso(r)lfe(r)nt
what assets (liabilities) are there?	hoe groot is die bate (laste)?	hoo chroht iss dee ba(h)te(r) [la(h)ste(r)]?
show me a balance-sheet	wys vir my 'n balans-rekening	veys fir mey i(h)n ba(h)la(h)ns reyke(r)ning
there is an error in your account	daar is 'n fout in U (jou) rekening	dahr iss i(h)n fo't in êû (yoh) reyke(r)ning
I shall send in a claim	ek sal 'n vordering in stuur	e(r)k sa(h)l i(h)n forde(r)ring insteûr

English.	Afrikaans.	Pronunciation.
will you accept a bill?	sal U 'n wissel aanneem?	sa(h)l êû i(h)n visse(r)l ahnneym?
... at three months	... op drie maande	...op dree mahnde(r)
what dividend is declared?	hoeveel diwident is verklaar?	hoofeyl deeveede(r)nt iss ferklahr?
your luggage is liable to duty	U (jou) bagasie is aan invoerregte onderhewig	êû (yoh) ba(h)cha(h)see iss ahn infoorre(r)chte(r) onderheyvich
this cheque needs endorsing	hierdie tjek moet geendosseer word	heerdee tye(r)k moot che(r)e(r)n-dosseyr vort
have you declared the value?	het U (jy) die waarde daarvan verklaar?	he(r)t êû (yey) dee vahrde(r) dahr-fa(h)n ferklahr?
I will prepay the carriage	ek sal die vrag vooruitbetaal	e(r)k sa(h)l dee fra(h)ch fohruitbe(r)tahl
quote me a price	kwoteer (sê of gee vir my) 'n prys	kvohteyr (sai(r) of chey fir mey) i(h)n preys
is there any duty on samples?	is daar 'n belasting op monsters?	iss dahr i(h)n be(r)la(h)sting op monsters?
please make me out a list of the samples I carry	maak asseblief vir my 'n lys op van die monsters wat ek saamneem	mahk a(h)sse(r)bleef fir mey i(h)n leys op fa(h)n dee monsters va(h)t e(r)k sahm neym
indicate the quality and quantity	duie die hoedanigheid en hoeveelheid (kwaliteit en kwantiteit) aan	duie(r) dee hoodahne(r)ch-heyt e(r)n hoofeylheyt [kva(h)leeteyt e(r)n kva(h)nteeteyt] ahn

English.	Afrikaans.	Pronunciation.
I shall indent your order	ek sal U (jou) order boek	e(r)k sahl eu (yoh) order book
it will take three months for the goods to arrive	dit sal drie maande neem vir die goed om hier aan te kom	dit sa(h)l dree mahnde(r) neem fir dee choot o(r)m heer ahn te(r) ko(r)m
our home-agent must buy first-hand	onse oorseese agent moet dit uit die eerstehand koop	onse(r) ohrseyse(r) a(h)che(r)nt moot dit uit eyrste(r)ha(h)nt kohp
we allow three, six, and nine months' credit	ons gee drie, ses en nege maande krediet	ons chey dree, se(r)s e(r)n neyge(r) mahnde(r) kre(r)deet
we will accept bills	ons sal bewyse neem	ons sa(h)l be(r)-veyse(r) neym

MONEY, WEIGHTS AND MEASURES

MONEY (Geld)

Union of South Africa

Afrikaans Money with approximate English and American equivalents.

Afrikaans Name.	English Name.	English Money.			American Money.	
Gold Coins (Goue geldstukke)		£	s.	d.	dols.	cents
20 sjielings ...	Sovereign ...	1	0	0	5	—
10 sjielings ...	Half-sovereign ...		10	0	2	50
Silver Coins (Silwere geldstukke)						
5 sjielings ...	Crown		5	0	1	25
Half-kroon : 2 sjielings, ses pennies	Half-crown ...		2	6	—	62
Floryn : 2 sjielings ...	Florin		2	0		50
Sjielings : 1 sjieling ...	Shilling		1	0		25
	Sixpence ...			6		12½
	Threepence ...			3		6
Bronze Coins (Kopere geldstukke						
pennie ...	Penny			1		2
half-pennie ...	Half-penny ...			½		1
stuiwer ...	Farthing ...			¼		

WEIGHTS AND MEASURES

(GEWIGTE EN MATE)

ENGLISH.		AFRIKAANS.	
Measures of Weights.		**Gewig maat.**	
16 ounces	1 pound (lb.)	16 onse	1 pond (lb.)
100 lbs.	1 Cape cwt.	100 lbs.	1 Kaapsehonderd gewig.
112 lbs.	1 Eng. cwt.	112 lbs.	1 Engelse honderdgewig
2,000 lbs.	1 Cape ton.	2,000 lbs	1 Kaapse ton.
2,240 lbs.	1 Eng. ton.	2,240 lbs.	1 Engelse ton.
Troy.		**Trooi.**	
4 grains	1 carat.	4 greintjies	1 karaat.
24 grains	1 pennyweight.	24 greintjies	1 penniegewig.
20 dwts.	1 ounce.	20 dwts.	1 ons.
12 ounces	1 pound.	12 onse	1 pond.

WEIGHTS AND MEASURES—(*continued.*)

Capacity.		**Inhoud.**	
1 pint	$\frac{1}{8}$ gallon, $\frac{3}{4}$ botl.	1 pint	$\frac{1}{8}$ gelling $\frac{3}{4}$ bottel.
2 pints	1 quart.	2 pinte	1 kwart.
4 quarts	1 gallon.	4 kwarte	1 gelling.
8 gallons	1 bushel.	8 gellings	1 bussel (skepel).
8 buckets	1 muid or sack (corn or mealies)	8 emmers	1 mudsak. (koring of mielies).

Length and Surface.		**Lengte and Oppervlakte.**	
12 inches	1 foot.	12 duim	1 voet.
3 feet	1 yard.	3 voet	1 jart.
1,760 yds.	1 mile.	1,760 jarts (treë)	1 myl.
12 Cape inches	1 Cape foot.	12 Kaapse duim	1 Kaapse.
12 Cape feet	1 Cape rood.	12 Kaapse voete	1 Kaapse roede.
144 sq. ins.	1 sq. foot.	1—4 vierkante duim	1 vierkant voet.
9 sq. feet	1 sq. yard.	9 vierk. voete	1 vierkant yd.
144 Cape sq. feet	1 Cape sq. rood.	144 Kaapse vierkante voete	1 Kaapse vierkante roede.
600 Cape sq. rds.	1 morgen.	600 Kaapse vierkante roede	1 morg.
1 morgen	$2\frac{1}{8}$ Eng. acre.	1 morg.	$2\frac{1}{8}$ Engelse akkers.
1,000 Cape feet	1,033 Eng. ft.	1,000 Kaapse voete	1,033 Eng. voete.
1 Eng. mile	426 Cape roods.	1 Engelse myl	426 Kaapse rds.
1 sq. mile	$302\frac{1}{2}$ morgen.	1 Vierkante myl	$302\frac{1}{2}$ morg.
4,840 sq. yards	1 acre.	4,840 vk. jaarts	1 akker.
640 acres	1 sq. mile.	640 akkers	1 vierk. myl.

Cubic Measure.		**Kubieke maat.**	
1,728 cubic ins.	1 cubic foot.	1,728 kubieke duime	1 kub. voet.
27 cubic feet	1 cubic yard.	27 kubieke voete	1 kub. jaart.

Time.		**Tyd.**	
60 seconds	1 minute.	60 sekonde	1 minuut.
60 minutes	1 hour.	60 minute	1 uur.
24 hours	1 day and night.	24 ure	1 dag en nag.
7 days	1 week.	7 dae	1 week.
365 days	1 year.	365 dae	1 jaar.
52 weeks	1 year.	52 week	1 jaar.

POSTAL RATES (Postariewe)

Class of Mail Matter.	Within the Union of South Africa, Bechuanaland and Proct. North and South Rhodesia, Prov. Mozambique.	For United Kingdom and all British Possessions (The entire Empire, Prov. Mozambique).	Foreign Countries.
Letters	1d. per oz.	2d. per oz.	3d. per oz.
Postcards ...	½d. each.	1½d. each.	1½d. each.
Letter cards ...	1d. each.	3d. each.	3d. each.
Newspapers ...	½d. each newspaper not exceeding 4 ozs.	½d. per 2 ozs.	½d. per 2 ozs.
Books and commercial papers	½d. per 2 ozs., or portion thereof.	½d. per oz.	½d. per oz.
Sample packets	½d. per 2 ozs., or portion thereof *For* Bechuanaland Protectorate, South West Africa, South and North Rhodesia and Mozambique, 1d. per 4 ozs., ½d. every additional 2 ozs.	½d. per 2 ozs., with a minimum charge of 1d.	½d. per 2 ozs., with a minimum charge of 1d.

Afrikaans Postariewe

Soort Van "Mail"	Binne die Unie van Suid-Afrika Betsjoeanaland, Noord en Suid Rhodesieë en Mosambiek.	Vir Verenigde Konin'ryk en Britse besettinge en Mosambiek	Vreemde Lande
Briewe ...	1d. per ons	2d. per ons.	3d. per ons.
Poskaarte ...	½d. elk	1½d. elk.	1½d. elk
Briefkaarte ...	1d. elk	3d. elk.	3d. elk
Koerante ...	½d. elk nie 4 onse te bo gaande nie	½d. per 2 onse	½d. per 2 onse
Boeke en Kommersieële papiere	½d. per 2 onse of gedeelte daarvan	½d. per 2 onse	½d. per 2 onse
Monster pakkies	VirBetsjoenelande. S. W. Afrika, Suid en N. Rhodesië en Mosambiek 1d. per 4 onse ½d. vir elke addisionele 2 onse.	½d. per 2 onse met 'n minimum van 1d.	½d. per 2 onse met 'n minimum van 1d.

Parcels (Pakkette)

Vir plekke binne die Unie; S. W. Afrika en Mosambiek: 4 onse nie te bo gaande nie 2d.; 1lb. nie te bo gaande nie 6d.; en 6d. vir elke ekstra 1lb of gedeelte daarvan

Vir Betsjoeanaland, 1/- per lb. of gedeelte daarvan.

Vir S. Rhodesië, 1/1 per lb. of gedeelte daarvan.

Vir N. Rhodesië, 1/3 per lb. of gedeelte daarvan.

Vir Groot Brittanje, 9d. per lb.

For places within the Union of South Africa, South West Africa, and Mozambique: Not exceeding 4 ozs. in weight, 2d.; nor exceeding 1 lb. in weight, 6d., and 6d. for every additional 1 lb. or fraction thereof.

For Bechuanaland Protectorate, 1s. per lb. or fraction thereof.

For South Rhodesia, 1s. 1d. per lb., or fraction thereof.

For North Rhodesia, 1s. 3d. per lb., or fraction thereof.

For Great Britain, 9d. per lb.

Telegrams (Telegramme)

Vir die Unie, S. W. Afrika en Lourenco Marques en Inhambane 1/3 vir die eerste 12 woorde of gedeelte daarvan; 1d. vir elk addisionele woord.

Nag telegramme word oorgesein van en tussen die vernaamste stede in die Unie teen 1/3d. vir 24 woorde, en 3d. vir elk addisionele 6 woorde, of gedeelte daarvan.

Vir S. Rhodesië en Betsjoeanaland, 2d. per woord, met 'n minimum van 2/3.

Vir N. Rhodesië, 3d. per woord, met 'n minimum vad 3/3d.

Vir Nyasaland Protektoraat, 5d. per woord, met 'n minimun van 5/3.

Vir die Verenigde Koninkryk (Kabelgramme), 1/8d. per woord.

Drukpers 3½d.

Vertraag 1/-.

Draadloos 8d.

For the Union, S.W. Africa and districts of Lourenco Marques and Inhambane, 1s. 3d. for the first twelve words or portion thereof; 1d. for each additional word.

Night telegrams are transmitted from and between the principal towns in the Union at the rate of 1s. for twenty-four words, and 3d. for every additional six or portion of six words.

For Southern Rhodesia and Bechuanaland, 2d. per word, with a minimum of 2s. 3d.

For Northern Rhodesia, 3d. per word, with a minimum of 3s. 3d.

For Nyasaland Protectorate, 5d. per word, with a minimum of 5s. 3d.

For the United Kingdom (Cablegrams), 1s. 8d. per word. Press 3½d. Deferred, 1s. Beam, 8d

P.O.8.120[M]